journey to one

Journey to one

a woman's story of emotional
healing and spiritual awakening

Kristi Bowman

iUniverse, Inc.
Bloomington

Journey to One
A Woman's Story of Emotional Healing and Spiritual Awakening

iUniverse books may be ordered through booksellers or by contacting:

iUniverse
1663 Liberty Drive
Bloomington, IN 47403
www.iuniverse.com
1-800-Authors (1-800-288-4677)

Because of the dynamic nature of the Internet, any Web addresses or links
contained in this book may have changed since publication and may no longer be
valid. The views expressed in this work are solely those of the author and do not
necessarily reflect the views of the publisher, and the publisher hereby disclaims
any responsibility for them.

ISBN: 978-1-4401-7911-2 (sc)
ISBN: 978-1-4401-7913-6 (dj)
ISBN: 978-1-4401-7912-9 (ebk)

Printed in the United States of America

iUniverse rev. date: 07/12/2012

Acknowledgments

I appreciate how the acknowledgments are written last. As the first 30 years of my life are laid out before me in these pages, I can clearly see just how many have helped me along the journey. No doubt, I will neglect to mention some of you, but know this is not intentional and you are loved and treasured the same.

It seems only appropriate that I begin with my mother, as it is from her that I began. Thank you for your love and for sharing with me your zeal for language, reading and learning. Without this sharing it would not have been possible for this story to be told.

I have so much gratitude to you, dear folks, who read the original manuscript and provided valuable feedback, as well as openly shared your emotional response – Karen, Terri, Nicole, Hector, Tamara, Claudia, Jill, Lori.

Deep gratitude and love to Jill Stevenson – friend, guide, mentor, and soul sister. You provided the nurturing environment for me to trust and remember.

Thank you for the forever-cherished laughter and love, Lizard Queen. You know who you are!

Thank you, Nicole, for providing a beautiful, loving container from which I was able to continue to unfold and expand.

To all my beautiful nieces and nephews (and great nieces and nephews!) – you are loved without limits!

My friends at the Y who are also my family, with a special recognition to Claudia, Kathy, Mona and Michelle, I am so thankful for your never-ending support. You are near and dear to my heart always.

A sincere thank you to Heather Ash Amara for your messages of Spirit and providing the safe space for me to finish exhaling, which allowed me to open to the most magical of journeys!

To my students from yoga classes, workshops and other adventures – I am humbled and grateful for the inspiration and teachings you continue to gift me.

Also deep gratitude and love to Shiva Rea. You are an incredible inspiration, river guide and mirror. ~ Riding the waves and lovin' it! ~

Finally, deepest gratitude to Spirit for providing such an ever-abundant supply of life experiences from which to learn and grow!

Dedicated to you

Author's Note

Life is beautiful. It continues to unfold in exciting and unexpected ways. This is my story, my unfolding, my journey. It is a journey that traverses quite a variety of terrain, which makes for an exciting adventure!

I am privileged to have crossed paths with so many on this journey. Some I continue to walk with, others not, having ventured in different directions. But each and every one, each and every connection I have shared, has been a huge gift, bringing the opportunity to experience more unfolding.

I have adopted fictitious names for some places and many of the individuals in my story, in order to protect anonymity. Some names are factual. You can play a guessing game to figure who's "real" and who isn't. No attempt has been made to create complete characterizations of the individuals, only to portray them as they relate to my story.

To assist with clarity, I have used italics to indicate direct excerpts from my personal journals, poems, quotes, thoughts and dreams. At the very least, may this story keep your interest to the not-so-bitter end. May it be a tool for further growth and healing. May it be yet another light shining on the path before us, should we be curious as to where our adventure-filled journey leads.

Stories are living things,
given to turns unpredictable.
From the movie *Neverwas*

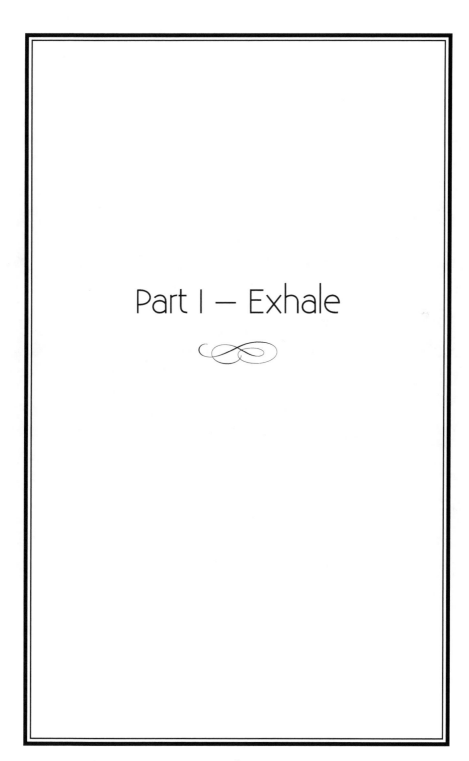

Part I – Exhale

Chapter 1

It is dusk. The lights remain off in the room. I hear the evening news muffled and distant. The anchorman is telling the story of the latest natural disaster, or perhaps the latest murder or serial rapist who is still on the loose. I hear him, but I am not really listening. I am concentrating, if you can call it that, only on the hundred different simultaneous thoughts swirling madly around in my head. I cannot pluck them apart and decipher them one by one, I can only feel the waste they emit piling higher and higher, burying me deeper and deeper.

My heart pounds so ferociously that my whole body is shaking with each pulsation. The sound of blood pushing through my arteries is beating in my ears, as if it's trying to tell me something.

The floor is cold. Cement, with a coat of smoke-gray paint and a coat of wax over it. I sit with just my underwear and a thin gown to cover me. My back is pressed firmly against the large oak door, and my legs are folded up in front of me, hugged by my arms. I stare straight ahead until I understand the message my blood pounding through my body is trying to convey. It is a yearning, a yearning for freedom.

With this newfound understanding I am forced to rise, though only a little. On my hands and knees I stay close to the floor while I crawl toward the window on the opposite side of the room. Through this window what little light the dying day releases creeps in. The light is dim through the thick, metal screen, enough by which to see, but not well.

Just under the window is an aging heating unit. It is heavy cast iron, painted the same color as the walls, a dreadful dark cream with a slight orange tint. The unit looks as if it is rarely used nowadays, if at all.

In my darkness I search every inch of the heating apparatus. My fingers are my eyes, peering around the edges and in the crevices in search of the key that will bring me release. Hovering above the floor a mere three inches, in that space where months, perhaps years, of dust has accumulated, is thin, semi-flexible metal, patterned in small, circular shapes. This pattern of metal is the frame that contains the heating filter.

My heart quickens its already accelerated pace. I reach the middle and ring fingers of my right hand into the circular spaces within the frame and will the metal to give and be weaker than I. If I will it hard enough it will happen, I just know it. So I pull with my two fingers, harder and harder. I feel the thin, dust-coated metal pressing deep into my soft skin. Harder, harder.

Finally, it breaks, and so does the skin. Warmth begins to cover my right hand. I pause for a moment, noticing the sensation, then quickly resume the search for a piece of destruction with my left hand. With the fingers of my left hand, I grip onto a small, half-broken piece of sharp metal and pull and twist until the piece snaps off. With torn right hand resting on my knee, my left hand takes the newly created weapon, and with it slashes the underside of my right wrist over and over again.

The tiny clang of the small metal weapon hitting the concrete floor is now heard. It is time to go. Through the dim, gray light of the room, I see a black puddle on the floor next to the heater. I slowly rise to my feet. My heart is now quiet; no longer is there a loud, pulsating message rushing through my ears. All frenetic thoughts have ceased, only peace. Breathing is slow and even. With left hand cupped under the right, attempting to catch at least some of the continuous flow of fluid, I walk through the doorway into the seemingly-glaring light of the hallway. Everything has slowed to half-speed. With calm, slow movements I approach the nurses' station. I simply glance at the women, who are laughing and talking behind the shield of Plexiglas, hold up my blood-covered hands, catching their attention, then turn around and slowly make my way back towards the room. Seconds later, I am whisked into the frenzy of a medical emergency, but inside, everything remains at half-speed and in a state of utter peace.

Chapter 2

Buttermilk pies would be in the oven, *All My Children* would be playing in the background, my grandpa would be snoozing in his chair, and the story would unfold, just as it had numerous times before.

As a young child and into my teenage years, I'd love spending time at my grandma's house. My grandparents had a farm where they raised cows, chickens, pigs and a steer from time to time for beef. They also had a large vegetable garden and lots of flowers.

My grandmother carried the traditions of the "old ways," making everything from scratch. Her days were spent milking cows, gathering eggs, working in the garden, cooking delicious meals and desserts, making quilts, and finally relaxing in the recliner.

She had the softest lap, where I would be found most days. She always had a smile on her face. She would sing tunes, using my back as the drum, and was always cracking jokes and making me laugh. She was a never-ending supply of comfort and love.

My grandmother always had a story to tell. This one is about me, my early beginnings, told not through my grandmother's voice. Rather, for the first time, my own.

My mom was standing at the ironing board doing her good, domestic duty, when "the fluid broke." I was ready to come out. But my mom wasn't ready yet; she had to finish the ironing. So she put a towel between her legs and continued with her chore.

I had often viewed this story that my grandmother so liked to tell as one of the first indications that my mother was emotionally neglectful and inconsiderate of my needs. After all, here I was ready to be born – the most amazing thing in this life! – and she just wanted to finish the ironing!

I had also figured that others hearing the story agreed with my point of view. I pictured them shaking their heads in disbelief thinking, "How could she just stand there and keep ironing like that? I can't believe she didn't immediately stop and go to the hospital!" They may well have been. I don't know if my assumption was correct. I had also assumed my grandmother was in disbelief over my mother's reaction, or lack thereof, to the water breaking, and she kept telling the story to try to make some sense of my mother being so oblivious and out of touch.

On the other hand, my grandmother may have liked telling this story for a different reason. Could I be the oblivious one? Perhaps through telling this story, she was conveying the strength of the women in this bloodline. She was giving my mom an indirect pat on the back. She was telling the world how proud she was of her daughter, proud of her strength, for my mother's strength mirrored her own. Likewise, my grandmother's strength mirrored my great-grandmother's, who raised 11 children in rural Missouri.

I was the last of five children. That alone demonstrates some strength of my mother. I see that now. My mom knew the drill, she was all too familiar with labor. Why not go ahead and finish the ironing? Now with the baby coming, she wouldn't be available around the house to finish anytime soon! So away she ironed.

At some point she realized she should probably call somebody. My mom called my dad, the logical choice. My dad refused to take her to the hospital, so the story goes. He was scared. He was afraid my mom would have me in the car on the way to the hospital. The hospital was close to an hour away. There is some logic in that... some.

So I felt this was an early indication of my father's emotional neglect and inconsideration of my needs, not to mention my mother's needs! As this story could portray the strength of the women, it could just as well tell about the weakness of the men in the family.

In fact, let me take it one step further, or one step back, rather. My conception had a rough start. My father had sex with my mother against her will, and then I came to be. (My older sister secretly told me this part of the story, which my mother later confirmed.) My dad wanted to have sex. My mom said, "No, this is not a good time," and he made her have sex anyway.

But getting back to my birth, so my mom then called my grandmother, who, of course, drove her to the hospital. Indeed, I almost *was* born in the car! By the time the three of us arrived at the hospital, my head was making its way out. Everything was happening so quickly. The nurses called the doctor, but there was no time for him to get there. So the nurses wheeled my mother into a room and snapped on rubber gloves.

After just a few more minutes I was born. I wasn't breathing, so the nurses scampered around and tried to suction out my nose and mouth. In the process, one of them dropped a tube on my nose. Later my nose swelled up and turned purple – broken.

I was also born with a cleft soft palate. In other words, there was a gaping hole in the roof of my mouth where the uvula usually is. There was direct access from my nose to mouth and vice-versa.

My mom was sent home later that day. After all, she was a seasoned mom and knew the drill. During the next several days and weeks, I was losing more and more weight. My mother just couldn't take anymore. She was raped by her alcoholic husband, she's the only one who did any work around the house, she had 4 other children to chase after, she was dealing with postpartum depression, and now little Kristi was getting down to skin and bones!

My grandmother offered to keep me for a while. In the story, she would tell how she would sleep with her hand on my chest while I slept in the bassinette next to the bed. While in this time period, where I teetered on the precipice between life and death, grandma wanted to make sure I kept breathing throughout the night.

During this time of keeping me, she discovered that if she squeezed a plastic bottle, making a stream of milk go down my throat, I was able to ingest enough milk to be satisfied. Due to my cleft palate, I simply could not create enough suction during breast-feeding or the regular method of bottle-feeding to get nourishment. Thus my life was saved.

The nurses did not give my mom any special feeding instructions upon discharge from the hospital, nor must it ever have occurred to my mother to call the doctor regarding my significant weight loss.

I used to reason this part of the story with the fact that my mother and grandmother came from the Ozarks. They were a hearty bunch. Doctors were not so readily available in those parts at that time. Families had to rely on themselves, their own doctoring. One of my grandmother's phrases was, "I'll doctor you up," when one of us kids got a cut or scrape.

Luckily it turned out okay. I went back to my mother and got enough sustenance by the bottle-squeeze technique.

If my grandmother told this story as a testament to the strength of the women in the bloodline, then she was also referring to me. From a very young age, I recall my grandmother making deliberate eye contact with me during key points during the story. She wanted me to listen. She communicated to me between the lines that, in addition to herself and my mother, *I* am strong.

When she told the story to all the different family members over the years, was she really just repeating it to me? Perhaps something deep down told my grandmother that I needed to hear it over and over, that I would need to remember my difficult beginnings, where I came from, that I would need to remember and know my strength.

※　※　※

My mother did not want me to have surgery on my cleft palate while I was a baby. She wanted me to be old enough to remember it, "so it wouldn't be traumatizing." She waited until I was 5 years old, a few months before starting kindergarten.

I spent the first 5 years of my life trying desperately to verbally communicate to others with no one being able to understand me very well. Around age 4, I remember standing in the kitchen, crying in frustration and disappointment to my mother. I was trying to ask or tell her something, something important. She couldn't make it out. She kept asking me to repeat it over and over, and I would, but she still couldn't understand. She apologized. Finally, I just turned and walked away, tears streaming down my cheeks.

It was as if I spoke a different language. I could not make certain sounds at all, such as hard G, K, and Q, basically anything that requires the use of the soft palate. I also could not make the sound of L, D and some others. I would substitute the sounds of Y and N for those of many other letters. For the word "lake", for example, I would say "yay". When I wanted a drink of water, I would say, "I wanna ning a wawa." It would also sound like I was running words together, not having clear separation between them, and my voice was very nasally. Yes, it was extremely difficult to be understood by others in my early years.

Following my mother's wishes, I remember my surgery experience. I remember being at the hospital and hearing that my mother could no longer accompany me to the next room. I was put in a metal cage and placed in the completely opposite end of a room as a woman sitting at a desk. She was doing paperwork. My mother later told me that it was a crib, not a cage. It had metal bars, and I was unable to get out – it was a cage. I wanted my mom to be with me so bad. I was so unbelievably scared to be separated from my mom and thrust in a metal cage in a strange environment with some woman who simply ignored me.

I pleaded for the woman's attention, telling her I wanted to see my mom. She looked up once, then resumed doing her paperwork. I pleaded until I remember no more.

The next thing I remember is waking up in a semi-clear plastic tent in a hospital room. I spent at least a couple days in this oxygen tent where no one could get in and I couldn't get out. My mom slept in the hospital at the foot of the bed curled up or in one of the uncomfortable chairs next to the bed. I felt so disconnected and trapped.

Finally the tent was removed and things seemed a little better. However, my tongue was still tied down to the floor of my mouth to keep me from touching the newly-built soft palate. I spent a couple days literally tongue-tied. It was *not* pleasant.

The first thing I did after being released from the tent was curl up in my mom's lap. I communicated with gestures and grunts to her. She finally understood that I was trying to say I wanted my tongue free. She had the doctor come in and cut the tie. Bit by bit I was being loosed from my torture chamber. Once my tongue was free and I could again be held in my mother's arms, things were good.

I was on liquids for a few days. My first solid food was a tray of hospital cafeteria food. The quality of it was equivalent to that of a cheap TV dinner. However, I recall eating the buttery peas and thinking they were the most fantastic things I'd ever eaten.

When I started kindergarten, my speech was clear and sounded no different from the rest of the students'. I recall the teacher's aide giving us a test, pulling us aside one student at a time. I was to draw a square then cut it out with scissors, tie a shoe, and a few other tasks. As she talked with me and I answered her questions, she was in disbelief that I had had a cleft palate. She asked if I had speech therapy after the surgery. I had not. She wondered aloud how my speech was so clear. The only thing I can surmise is that I always *knew* how the words were supposed to sound. My mouth simply could not make the correct noise. In my head, the words were always perfectly clear. That's why I'd get so frustrated when others couldn't understand me, I heard me just fine.

Chapter 3

"Why did you do this? *Why* did you do this?" Sarah asks, with a great amount of compassion, yet desperation, in her voice.

I've made it back to my bathroom and am sitting on the floor letting the blood run out of my finger and into the toilet. Sarah has two other nurses accompanying her for help. "Some women cut themselves to release emotional pain through physical pain. Is that the case with you?" she asks. I cannot answer, cannot speak, but in my dazed state I still consider her words.

Sarah and the other nurses raise me up and move me over to the sink. As they are rinsing my hand off to get a better look at the wound, I give in to the weakness in my knees and begin to go down. "Oh, no you don't!" Sarah protests, as she catches my weight and lifts me back to my feet.

Once she sees stitches are necessary, she grabs a towel, wraps it around my hand and instructs me to keep it above my head. I'll do anything Sarah asks. She is the most gorgeous nurse I've ever seen.

Arrangements are made for a trip to the emergency room for stitches. "How did she do it?" one of the nurses asks.

"She used her fingernails," another one answers. "The nails don't look very long, though," she thinks out loud.

I just shake my head.

I cannot be trusted, so a wheelchair is brought in that has leather wrist restraints. I sit down, get strapped in, and wheeled away.

The ER doctor asks the nurse how I did it. "Her fingernails," she replies.

I shake my head again. No, you stupid people, it was not my fingernails! "It was the heater filter," I say.

They look at me, blank-faced. It's the first words I've spoken all evening.

"These are recent," the doctor says to the nurse, pointing to cuts on the underside of my left wrist.

"That's what got her in the hospital," the nurse replies.

I watch as the doctor puts a needle in my finger in several places to numb it. As the suturing commences I am fascinated how the skin feels like rubber, unreal, detached, how it's pulled and sewn like a simple piece of cloth, how I'm in this body with this outer rubbery clothing layer, and so empty underneath.

%%%   %%%   %%%

To exit this place I must do this one thing: Agree that I will not hurt myself or attempt to kill myself by signing a contract. However, I don't want to. I want to be punished for all the evil that I have done. No one else will, so I must do it myself.

%%%   %%%   %%%

At about midnight, I return from the ER to the psychiatric unit, otherwise known as 3rd South. I am placed in a geriatric chair directly in front of the nurses' station to sleep. I finally fall asleep at 5:00am. I awake at 7:00am. At this time, I am moved from the "B" side over to the "A" side for closer monitoring.

The 3rd South wing is a long corridor with several rooms off each side of it. It is divided down the middle by a glass wall with a door that can only be opened by one bearing a key or by one of the nurses in the station buzzing you through.

The nurses' station sits smack in the middle, off to the west side. There is a Plexiglas barrier with only a hole to speak through just above the counter on the "A" side of the station. On the "B" side there is no barrier above the counter. From there you can speak freely, nothing separating the crazies from the sane. The "B" side has a half-door entering and exiting the nurses' station, while the "A" side has a fully-enclosed door. Patients are obviously more trustworthy on the "B" side.

So now I moved from being trustworthy to not. It's a double-edged sword, really. The less trust expected of you, the less reason to act in a trustworthy manner. At least, that is how I seem to exemplify that dynamic, not necessarily consciously but with some level of awareness. How is one to get out of that cycle, then? A behavior happens, trust is lost. Put you in a situation where now no one expects you to act responsibly, so you don't.

I am put in "open seclusion" in a room across from the nurses' station on the "A" side. The only furniture in the room is a twin bed on a wooden frame. No sheets, no blankets, just a covered mattress. The rest of the room is empty, just cold hard concrete. The door has a built-in window through which all eyes of the world, in this case the nurses and other patients of side "A", can gaze. There is a convex mirror in the upper left corner. If one looks at the mirror through the door window, she can see practically all areas of the room without having to step foot inside.

I can never get out from under those fucking eyes! Eyes, eyes everywhere.

There is a bathroom located off the seclusion room. Here I can get away from the eyes. I have a very limited time for my privacy. The nurses check the room every few minutes. They know if I'm in there too long and come in the room to check.

In the afternoon I seek comfort in the bathroom. My heart pounds and shakes my whole body. I examine the only possible source of a weapon there is – a metal toilet paper dispenser. There is a semi-flexible piece of metal bolted tightly to the outer frame, which allows a little give so that the toilet paper roll can be removed. I remove the roll and start to work on loosening the metal piece.

I must work fast, it's already been a couple minutes! My heart beats harder and faster. I cannot hear anything except the incessant beat. Shut up!

I grasp the metal piece and try to wriggle it back and forth, only moving it a fraction, but it seems like it may be starting to loosen. I wriggle it back and forth, back and forth for a couple more minutes.

It's useless. It won't come off. I put the paper roll back on. I inch my way under the sink and just sit and wait, treasuring each last moment of solitude.

The door to the main room opens. The nurse calls for me. The bathroom door opens. The nurse sees me, a thin, young woman in a fetal position hiding under the sink with one arm wrapped around the pipes. My eyes are closed.

"Come on, get up," the nurse instructs. I don't move.

The nurse grasps me around the one arm that is not wrapped around the plumbing and tugs. I resist. The nurse walks back out to the doorway of the room and tells one of the other nurses, "Call Code Strong."

Within a couple minutes I am being wrenched out from under the sink by two very large, and indeed strong, men and carried to the bed.

A nurse is holding leather straps with shiny chrome buckles. I start to cry. "No, no, no!" I am thrust face-down on the bed. I'm screaming and sobbing now, trying to get free. My wrists are forced down and strapped to the sides of the bed. My ankles are strapped to the foot of the bed. I cannot stop crying and wailing. I pull as hard as I can to free my hands. My wrists are turning raw after several minutes of my attempts to escape. I pull and I cry. I cannot get free, trapped.

I still struggle and try to raise myself up on my knees. A nurse comes in with another leather strap, pushes me down, places it over my lower back and fastens it to the sides of the bed.

Now I cannot move at all, just my head from side to side. The trapped feeling is overwhelming and all I can do is cry. I have no power. I feel like I am dying, like my life is being stripped away from me. I sob uncontrollably for an eternity, or maybe a couple hours, until I am weak, lifeless, no longer uttering any sound. Only then am I finally released from my hell.

Chapter 4

Memories of my childhood are crystal clear; I remember everything, and I remember everything well. I say this based on the fact that I can remember the names of all my childhood teachers. I can remember the names of my friends. I remember all the fun and goofy things we did. I remember field trips, the playground, everything.

I use my recollection of school as proof, a template of normal childhood. Here is a gauge with which to examine my life, no matter that it only includes the hours of 8:00am to 3:00pm, 9 months a year. I hold my life up to this template, see that it fits nice and snug, no overlays or snags, and conclude that my childhood was perfectly normal.

However, the time out of the classroom is not very clear. Sure, I remember things, many things, but the memories lack the crystal nature that my school memories possess. Polyester batting, like the kind my grandma used when making quilts. I see those other hours through this. Fuzzy, stuffy, overheated, scratchy recollections. Not only that, it's dense, condensed. From the ages of, say, 5 to 18 my childhood transpired within a year.

When I try to figure my age during a particular incident (if I cannot relate it to a specific grade in school), I have to just pick an age out of the air. I could have been 8, I could have been 15, so I'll say 11. Sounds good. My childhood at home is not divided so spaciously as it is at school. At school there are different teachers, different friends with which to gauge it.

At home it is the same parents, same family. So it all condenses. The year of my childhood. As it condenses, it restricts visibility, it becomes thicker, hazier, it restricts recall.

%%   %%   %%

There are small towns and then there are small towns. There are towns of 15-20,000, then there is Littleton, California, the place in which I grew up and lived 21 years, population 1,100. No one bothered to change the census sign in 30 years because not enough people moved in or out of town to warrant the effort of making a new sign. The same families resided, generation after generation, the children and grandchildren replacing the older family members who died off.

One main street traversed through town, one stoplight. On this main street were the usual small town businesses – Post Office, dirty, dilapidated hotel, bank, bar, antique store, barber shop, gas station, and family-owned combo hardware/grocery store. On the side streets there was a church on every corner.

I lived four miles north of town on a 5-acre parcel of land. This property was divided into two separate farms, one having a single-wide, aluminum-sided, canary yellow mobile home (with an add-on), housing my grandma and grandpa. The other half of the property had a single-wide, aluminum-sided, avocado green mobile home, with an add-on (there's always an add-on), housing me and my family. In my backyard, in a tiny travel trailer, lived my great grandma on my mother's side.

At one point in time, five generations of my family resided on that one area of land. I had the pleasure of sharing my mobile home with my parents, one sister and three brothers.

The elementary school, middle school, and high school in Littleton are all on the same grounds, three generations. Within this large, extended family I thrived and excelled. In elementary and middle school I was at the top of my class in practically all subjects. In 2nd grade my teacher recommended to my mom that I skip a grade.

"No," she said, "I don't want her to feel out of place socially."

In 3rd grade my teacher recommended I go into the Gifted and Talented Education (G.A.T.E.) program. My mother said no again. "I don't want her to be involved in any extracurricular activities outside the home. It would take away from more important things."

In 5th grade, "Can I be in the spelling bee?" I ask her. No. So I sat in the audience at the bee correctly spelling the words in my head, that I had not even practiced, as the students on stage were spelling the words incorrectly and being dismissed.

In 6th grade I had the fastest time for running a mile, so I wanted to try out for track. The track coach highly recommended it. My mom said no.

So I went to school, year after year, rarely studying for tests, doing my homework without much parental assistance and being in the top 5% academically.

I was 13 and just starting 8th grade. I remember the 8th grade well, though I attended only 2 months of it in public school. That was the year they were going to start requiring us to shower after P.E. That was the year I was sure I would start my period, and I was scared to death I would start it at school, completely unprepared.

I'm sure all young teenage girls have similar fears, but mine was absolute. I absolutely could not shower in front of others, and I absolutely could not start my period at school. I had to find a way out.

Luckily, there was one. I had a couple friends, a sister and brother, who had recently gone into independent study. Their mom had talked about the benefits of home schooling to my mom just a few weeks prior. She took the kids on "field trips" with other Jehovah's Witness children, she was able to provide them music lessons, and teach them more "real-life" skills. The kids seemed to enjoy it and they could finish up their day's work by noon oftentimes.

My mom was in the bathroom when I broached the subject. "Mom, can I go into home study?" I asked through the closed door as I stood in the hallway.

"No," she responds.

I could not take no for an answer, I had to find my way out! "But mom, pleeeease!" I pleaded.

"No. Why would you want to go into home study?"

"I don't know, I just do!" I replied. There was no way I could tell her the real reasons. I knew she would not understand my fears. "Jared and Melanie are in home study," I continued in true teenage fashion.

I could sense her now wavering. I continued to beg and plead with all my might. Then I went in for the kill: "I would have more time for 'spiritual matters'. And if I wasn't in school, I could be even less 'part of the world.'" Bible quotes could always carry a lot of weight.

"We can try it for the remainder of this school year and see how it goes," she said, finally giving in.

Home schooling was easy for me, and I flew through the assignments. At first I kept in contact with my good friends from school, but as time passed, we grew more and more apart. I went over to their homes less and less, we called each other less and less. It just sort of happened. Or, I just let it sort of happen. I did not feel isolated, however. I was too busy doing my school work. I finished all the 8th grade work and started on 9th grade work in the same school year.

I don't recall there ever being mention of me going back to public school. I'm sure if it had crossed my mother's mind, she would think about my siblings and their high school experiences. My sister had gotten pregnant when she was 16 years old, and married shortly thereafter. My oldest brother started drinking a lot and got involved with various forms of drugs. Some concoction that he ingested resulted in a severe and permanent alteration to his personality, perhaps even brain damage, according to my mother. My other two brothers also got involved with drinking and drugs. One got in trouble with the law, continually hanging out with the "wrong crowd." Not one of my siblings remained in the "Truth", much to my mother's dismay. One of my brothers, as soon as he turned 18, left home, never to return. He vowed to never be subjected to the religious beliefs again.

So my squeaky clean record kept any suspicions at bay. I spent my time doing school work, going to religious meetings, going out door to door "in service," taking piano lessons, climbing trees, riding my motorcycle and helping my mom around the house, nothing "bad" like my siblings. My mom was so proud of me, feeling she had finally "gotten it right" with me, the apple of her eye.

I completed high school when I was 16 years old. Now what?

Chapter 5

My mother is an extremely loving woman. In fact, she loves the world so much that she gave her only-begotten Son as a ransom sacrifice for humankind. Oh wait, that was God. Yes, my mother is very loving. She will tell you so herself. She will sit you down and recount for you the many hours she spends being loving, the many hours she spends out in the blazing sun and in the pouring rain with Bible in hand in an attempt to save sheep-like individuals from this depraved and wicked world that is doomed for destruction.

I was saved at one time, not saved in the sense of once saved, always saved, but in the sense that, if I continually slaved to do (what I was taught was) God's will, God would give me a grand reward. And did I slave away! I spent hours a day poring through the pages of the Bible and Bible-based literature and hours going out "in service" trying to teach poor souls about God's plan for the world. I even had a goal to become a missionary and go off to some foreign land with half-naked natives and oversized insects to reach those who otherwise might not have a chance. If anyone was saved, surely I was.

The problem is, I had God mixed up with my mother. Of course, I did not realize this as a teenager. I did not realize it until much later, until just now, in fact. God-Mother was an entity whom I always sought to please. If I just worked hard enough, I would please Him, Her, Them. If they were pleased, maybe, just maybe, they would love me.

Unconditional love is the most wonderful thing in the world, I'm told. It is complete, whole, without terms. There is no contract stating, "I will love you, but only if you…" Unconditional love states that I will love you whether you are a boy or a girl, whether you are black or white, whether you are a Jehovah's Witness or a Buddhist.

I understand where my mother comes from, I do. Unconditional love is out of the question because, according to her, God does not love unconditionally. After all, God destroyed humans in the great flood because he did not approve of what they were doing. Similarly, he destroyed people in Sodom and Gomorrah because of how they behaved. So mother must imitate God. One cannot give what she does not receive.

But I must digress. Even during the time before I could read or write, my mother would teach me about God, his Son, and his plan. She would read to me out of *My Book of Bible Stories*, put forth by the Watchtower Society (which are the Jehovah's Witnesses), about Adam and Eve, Noah and the ark, Jonah and the whale, the Israelites, David and Goliath, Daniel, Jesus, everything and everyone. The stories were all true, word for word, and I was to take them and use them as examples for how to act or not to act in order to please God.

From infancy I attended religious meetings three times a week. My family did not celebrate any holidays, including Christmas and Easter (due to their pagan origins), or even Thanksgiving (due to the fact that we had to be "no part of the world" and "the world" celebrated holidays). I did not have my birthdays celebrated, nor could I attend parties or eat cupcakes from my friends' birthdays. According to God-Mother, Jesus didn't celebrate his birthday, so why should I? Also, the Bible mentions birthdays only a couple times, and murderous acts happened at those times, so of course, birthdays should *not* be celebrated!

I did not salute the flag. I was to worship God, not our country. I was even forbidden from attending school dances and participating in any after-school activities, for I was to keep as "separate from the world" as possible. I was to take no chances of being "corrupted by the world's evil influence." After all, the world is now controlled by Satan, so one must be constantly on guard. Only by remaining separate can one be recognized as a true follower of God and be rewarded for all the hard work.

This particular belief attests that…well, it attests many things, but I will only include what I feel is most relevant to my story. It attests that this group of believers is the only group who is truly following Jesus' teachings and God's instructions, that that belief system as a whole is the Truth, with a capital "T".

They believe in 1914 that Satan was cast out of heaven and forced to reside here on earth. The worst war up to that time, the First World War, was an example of this evil presence. Satan knows he has a "short time," so he's doing the most he can in what time he has, exemplified by all the evils that befall us – murders, corrupt political leaders, rock-n-roll, you name it.

In the next few years, before the generation passes away that was around in 1914, a great many things will happen, including a political declaration of "peace and security," governments turning on all religions, a "Great Tribulation", much akin to Nazi Germany, concentration camps and all, and Armageddon. At this time, all people on the earth will have the choice to go with God's true followers, Jehovah's Witnesses, or follow the evil, Satan-controlled governmental system. After God's people have suffered at the hands of persecutors for a time, Armageddon occurs. This is where God crushes all the political systems and thus saves his people.

Once the governments are all destroyed, "God's people" will clean up the earth, and with His help, turn it back into a paradise like the original Garden of Eden, the original plan being fulfilled. This paradisiacal state is often referred to as the "New System." Oh yes, and Satan will have been cast into some pit and locked in irons and chains for 1000 years.

After the earth is back to a paradise, God will resurrect all the dead, so everyone can be reunited with their lost loved ones. Then, once the 1000 years have passed, Satan will be let loose one last time to test all those who didn't get tested earlier, namely, the ones who were resurrected back to life. Of course, some will follow Satan, some always do. Then Satan and his evil minions will once and for all be destroyed. The remaining people will live forever and ever, without disease, without fear, being restored to physical and mental perfection. The ultimate prize is this paradisiacal life on earth, for there is no belief in an immortal soul separate from the physical body.

Okay, that is it in a nutshell. Day in and day out since birth, these beliefs were fed to me. No, it goes beyond fed. It was the highly regulated air that I breathed. I knew no different. It was how I survived.

My mother was the primary dispenser of this air. She was, and still is, one of the "strong" ones in the faith, a shining example of how to serve God properly. She maintains such rigid control, I suspect so as not to go tumbling down some rabbit hole. If she were to loosen her grasp, even the slightest, her whole world may just unravel to reveal things she's not quite ready to see.

Even though I sought to please God-Mother more than anything, I was unknowingly starting to loosen my own grasp.

Chapter 6

When I was a very young girl, I would ask my mother, "If God created everything, who created God?"

"No one," she replied.

"Then where did he come from?" I continued.

"Jehovah has just always been," she tried to clarify.

"But that doesn't make sense!" I'd say with an agitated tone.

"It doesn't make sense, because our brains just can't comprehend something without a beginning and an end, because that's all we know," my mom would say.

Okay, I can understand that. "Why would God have always existed and then just recently create the earth and all of us? What did God do all the time before our creation, twiddle his thumbs?" still with an agitated tone. "Are there life forms on other planets?"

"No."

"How do you know?" I'd ask.

"Because they would be mentioned in the Bible if there were," she said. "He was busy creating the angels before the earth was created," she'd say.

"But what about before that?" I would persist.

"Everything will be answered in the New System," she'd say with a sigh. That was her fall-back line. "You can ask Jehovah anything you want in the New System and he'll answer it."

"You mean I can talk to God directly in the New System?" I questioned.

"Well, yes. You'll be perfect in the New System and so it'll be like it was in the Garden of Eden, when God would talk directly with Adam. Now we have to go through Jesus in prayer because we're so imperfect."

Hmmm. *But the New System could be a long way off,* I'd think. *I want the answers now.* I wanted them so bad it would hurt.

As I got a little older, I'd ask my mom, "Mom, how come there aren't any women Elders in the congregation?"

"Because the men are the head of the congregation like they are the head of the household," she'd reply.

But my dad wasn't the head of the household, I'd think to myself. My mom was. She took care of everything and made all the decisions. My dad just worked, then came home and slept on the couch. Just because he brought home the money didn't mean he was head of the household.

"But women would give good talks, too." I wasn't one for letting up.

"They do give talks when they do the 'presentations'."

"That's not the same! The presentations are only with another woman or child sitting at a table off to the side of the stage. They role-play some scenario for 10 minutes, only facing and talking to each other, and that's only on Thursday nights," I retorted. "The men get to stand up in the center, facing the audience on Sundays and give hour-long talks."

"Well, that's how it is," she'd conclude. I'd like to think she saw the inequity in it all, but she relied heavily on blind faith. If she let herself question even one tiny aspect of her religious beliefs, she would fear Satan would grab hold and lead her astray, and that road just leads to death. The vision and expectation of the New System was worth all the blind faith in the world. She taught that to me very well.

During my childhood and early teenage years, I was like a tender little plant, able to be shaped and directed how she saw fit. My mother, then, was the stake in the ground, ever strong and firm, and extremely effective in guiding my growth in one direction and one direction only.

///   ///   ///

With high school completed, I decided to now excel spiritually. I would be the "perfect" Jehovah's Witness.

My mother and I had always attended the meetings regularly and studied at home, but I felt I now needed to do more. I began to spend hours each day reading the Bible, minimum 3 chapters a day, in addition to reading the material in preparation for the meetings. I also went out in service 1-2 times per week for several hours at a time and prayed several times a day.

However, something felt amiss. *I must get baptized!* I thought. *That must be it! If I get baptized, I will feel a strong connection with this fatherly figure of a God and feel complete. As it is now, I pray and it feels like the words just go out into the ether…never falling on God's ears. Baptism will be like an electric line,* I reasoned. *It will focus these prayers and send them directly to God's heart. I will then feel the love for God that I'm supposed to, and I will feel God's love in return. I will feel the love of a true Father, not like the one I have.*

My plan to get baptized was much to my mother's encouragement. After several months of studying the necessary materials, I met with the Elders for my "test." All went well, and four days after my 18th birthday, I got baptized at an assembly of over 1,000 Witnesses. In my bathing suit, I walked down to the pool. As I arose out of the water, I half-expected to see a dove floating overhead, like Jesus saw upon his baptism. But there was no dove. I emerged, though, with the hope of stronger faith and the obliteration of the doubt that haunted me since childhood.

% % %

There seemed to be this unspoken hierarchy in the congregation, and organization as a whole. At the bottom were those who never came to meetings or came only once in a while. They were the "spiritually weak" ones, needing the most help. Next up were those who came to the meetings regularly, then those who also studied at home regularly, then those who also participated in the "Theocratic Ministry School" (those who participated in the aforementioned "presentations"). For men, continuing to move higher up the chart, there was the role of Ministerial Servant, then Elder. In the organization, you could move even further up by being a missionary in another country, a Circuit or District Overseer, or work at the headquarters in New York. For women in the congregation, you could be an Auxiliary Pioneer, which required 60 hours per month in service going door to door. At the top were the Regular Pioneers, committed to spending 90 hours per month in service, and missionaries. Men could also be "pioneers", for there wasn't anything a woman could do that a man could not, just vice-versa. Women could also work at the headquarters, but not in a leadership role.

Here I was now, a baptized Christian. I was still waiting for that electric line to fire up. *Perhaps it takes a while. I'll just keep studying,* I thought. However, it seemed the more I studied, the more unanswerable questions would crop up. So I tried harder. I'd write Bible and Bible-based literature (from the Watchtower Society) quotes on note cards and post them around my bedroom as reminders for strengthening my faith. "Use your energy to bring glory to God. Orient your life around the preaching and disciple-making activity, which will result in everlasting life for you and for those who listen to you," one note card read. Well, according to quotes like that, I needed to increase my door-to-door activity. I needed to orient my life around it. I signed up to be an Auxiliary Pioneer. Doubts kept arising. *My faith must not be strong enough!* So I signed up to be a Regular Pioneer. *I must study more, do more!* I spent practically every moment of my existence reading the Bible or the organization's literature, going to meetings and going out in service. Isn't this a "perfect" Jehovah's Witness? Am I not in the one True religion? Why was I still feeling my faith was failing? Jehovah's Witnesses are supposed to be the most "joyful people on earth," according to the Witnesses. Where is my joy!?

It was a spiraling feeling with the underlying darkness of fear at the center. The harder I worked, the more quickly the spiral circulated, sucking me deeper and deeper, a vortex to a never-ending abyss…

During this time, I asked Debbie, a friend of mine who was a beautiful woman in her early 30's, why I was feeling this way. I had just been crying in her arms for reasons unknown to me. She replied, "It's probably due to your recent baptism, and Satan is putting forth a lot of effort to turn you away from Jehovah." I listened to her. After all, she was the wife of an Elder in the congregation. She would know.

I was out in service with Debbie (who was also pioneering) one morning, and we were invited to sit down at one gentleman's patio area. The man was friendly and offered us some lemonade to drink. We were often invited to sit down when I was with Debbie, for many men found her to be gorgeous and wanted to spend time looking at her, feigning interest in our message. As we were sitting there, the man turned to me and asked, "Are you okay?"

"Yes," I replied. "I feel a little warm, but I'm okay." I actually felt awful.

"Because you look really sad," he said.

"She's feeling a little under the weather," Debbie chimed in. I just smiled, and concentrated on keeping the smile the rest of the time with him. *Joyful, look joyful!*

I truly did not know what was wrong with me, but there was something dark lurking under the surface, and now it was beginning to show itself to the outside world. I had a difficult time waking up in the morning. It took me an hour to get my shoes on. When I ate food, it had no taste. Everything seemed dreary and drab. My heart was aching and my mind was in turmoil.

One day I came across an article in one of the magazines I was reading in preparation for one of the meetings. It was on depression, and it had a checklist. It stated that if one was experiencing 10 or more of the symptoms, he (yes, "he") should look into getting checked out by a professional. I read over the checklist and checked off each and every one of the symptoms. *Well, that's it,* I thought to myself. *I'm depressed.*

A few weeks later, I was lying on my bed one afternoon contemplating life…and death. I could not stop thinking about all the horrible things transpiring in the world – war, starvation, homelessness, murder, rape, abuse. It's not like I was making it all up – it happens! Every day, every minute, every second, some devastating thing is happening. I thought about my life and how I just wanted to die. The world would not be affected by one more death. It is not the first time I thought about ending my life. I had thought about it hundreds of times before in the last couple months, and I had a plan to carry it out.

I decided to roll out of bed and walk into the living room, where my mother was sitting in the rocking chair reading a Watchtower magazine. I lay down on the floor. "Mom?"

"Hmmm?" she said.

"I think I'm depressed."

Chapter 7

As the nurses unbuckle my restraints, they tell me to go ahead and go into the kitchen, dinner is ready. I walk into the kitchen where all the other patients are beginning to eat their meal. My finger is bound up in gauze. I see some people make glances at it. I know they all know where I've been the last few hours, they've heard my screams. Yet no one says a word. They all pretend nothing happened, that everything is normal.

The following day, day 7, I feel a little better, but definitely not normal. I don't cry profusely like I have each day since admittance. I simply feel in a state of total physical and emotional exhaustion.

Two days later, due to good behavior, I get to go off the unit for a walk. It's a nice walk along a creek. There are lots of trees, a real nice setting. Except all I can do is think about how I want to jump off the side of the hill. I don't have any intention of doing so, but it is tempting. As I'm glazed-eyed staring at the creek below, the Recreation Aide interrupts my fantasy and comes in between me and the drop-off below. "Well, let's head back," he says to the group. Needless to say, I'm no longer allowed off the unit.

For the next couple days, I feel okay during the day. However, nighttime changes everything. As the sun sets and the room darkens, the demons come out. My breathing quickens, my heart races. I feel anxious and pace around the room. Or, I curl up in the fetal position. I want to be small. I want to hide. Since the beginning of my stay here, the nurses have found me hiding in closets and under beds. I feel like I have no choice, I *need* to hide.

I curl up in a fetal position on top of two chairs that are in my room. I am still across from the nurses' station under close watch. Sarah comes in and remarks, "Your behavior is that resembling someone who has been sexually abused. Have you been?" I don't answer.

Feeling too exposed, I move to the floor under the chairs, still in a fetal position. The nurses need to be able to see me from their station. At my present position, they cannot. Rose is an R.N. also on duty. She is a petite, older woman with graying hair and warm, caring eyes. She comes into the room with me. She tells me, "I've talked the other nurses into not putting you into restraints again." As she speaks, her voice is shaky and her eyes well up. In my non-caring, unfeeling state, I still manage to feel a hint of gratitude for her. She sits in one of the chairs and does paperwork, while I remain underneath. At one point she pauses in her paperwork and says, "You're living in hell right now…whoever it was sure did a job on you…but you're going to make it, you're going to be alright…."

Eventually Rose leaves. My behavior is not appropriate all night long, the nurses say, so "Code Strong" is called. Two burly men pick me up from the floor with ease and place me onto the bed. I stay put.

The next evening I have a visitor. Rod, my boyfriend, comes in about 8:00pm. He talks, but I cannot really hear what he is saying. My brain shuts off from listening. I feel very anxious. I really want him to leave. I keep telling him to go, but he's not leaving. He wants to see if I'm alright. Sarah comes in and asks if things are okay. "No," I reply.

"Visiting hours are up," she says to him. It's now 8:30pm and visiting hours ended at 8:00pm. I crawl to the floor and take up my familiar fetal position. Rod finally leaves.

I make my way back up to the bed even though the floor feels so much more comfortable. Sarah asks me if I will take a mild tranquilizer. I shake my head no. She says, "What if I tell you that it burns like acid as it goes down your throat, will you take it?" I crack a smile. This is perhaps my first genuine smile in weeks, maybe even months.

An hour or so later, I am in the bed with my hands "tied" behind my back. I cannot move them, will not move them. I can no longer stand being watched, so I roll off onto the floor. Sarah comes in a while later and "unties" my hands. She asks, "Were you tied up while you were being abused?" Where does she come off with all these crazy assumptions? She talks me into getting back in the bed. She tucks me in and puts the stuffed M&M guy that Rod had brought in bed with me.

The following day, I am faced with the choice of going home or going to a long-term facility in Sacramento. This psychiatric hospital is short-term only. I have stayed the maximum amount of 11 days. Reluctantly, and for my own good I suppose, I choose home.

Excerpts from the Discharge Summary

History: This 20-year-old woman was referred on an emergency basis from Blake County Mental Health Services. The patient was brought to the Blake Community Hospital Emergency Room after making a suicidal threat and cutting herself on the left arm in a suicidal gesture. She also broke a contract she had made the day previous with her therapist against self-harm and was unwilling to contract not to harm herself. She was felt to have a lethal suicidal plan of driving off of a cliff. She was determined to be a danger to herself and in need of emergency psychiatric hospitalization. The patient stated there were many things on her mind and that she did not want to live. She had lacerated her left antecubital fossa and made numerous superficial cuts on her left arm. A prior history of psychiatric treatment was noted.

Mental Status Examination: Revealed a medium-sized, brown-haired, neatly-dressed, 20-year-old woman whose thinking was consistent with depression related to conflicts in her life. She was somewhat vague and guarded about discussing these, however. She clearly stated that she did not want to live. She continued to be self-destructive and was not able to contract not to harm herself even in the hospital.

Hospital Course: The patient continued to feel intensely suicidal and self-destructive. She reported confusing thoughts. Her sleep was greatly impaired. On one occasion, the patient became very disturbed and lacerated her right forefinger on a heating unit which required suturing. Intense suicide observations were initiated. She continued to be very regressed, refusing most activities and stating she was not trustworthy off of the Mental Health Unit. She made specific references to jumping off of high places. She was limited to the inpatient unit. On her discharge date, she stated she would not kill herself, although she had continued thoughts of dying. Her participation was improved and she was no longer acutely suicidal.

Discharge Diagnosis:
Axis I.   Major Depression, recurrent. Obsessive compulsive disorder.
Axis II. None.
Axis III. Laceration of left antecubital fossa and right forefinger.
Axis IV. Psychosocial stressors: Severe

Discharge Condition: Improved   Prognosis: Very guarded.

Chapter 8

No Way Out?

It is a blanket of darkness
It has continually smothered until now,
I am rendered lifeless

No pleasure and no interest for so long,
for the misery and pain is just too strong

A black darker than the blackest night,
overwhelmingly so
Like being trapped in a hole that grabs hold
and doesn't let go
I would cry, "Let me out – please!"
A hurt that will bring even the strongest
man to his knees
Panic and fear become unbearable
Some want to help, but they are unable

Finally, a hand breaks through,
but I cannot take hold,
for I am tired and weak,
and caring has grown old
I've given up and given in
I desire help no longer, just let me end…

※　※　※

"Why do you think you're depressed?" my mom asked.

"Because I feel awful. I have no energy. I feel like I just want to die." I said. "Haven't you seen me moping around the house all sullen?" I continued.

"Yes, I've noticed," she replied.

"Well, didn't you think something might be wrong?" I questioned further.

"I thought it might be just a phase," she answered.

"A phase?!" I am in utter disbelief. Perhaps I could have gotten help sooner if my mother had asked just once if I was okay, if she just once reached out.

She then proceeded to tell me a story, which was news to me, about one of my brothers. She said how several months prior he tried to kill himself by overdosing on insulin. He's diabetic. I had heard how he was in the hospital, but I had thought it was an accident. That is how my mother had made it sound at the time. No big deal, he was fine. We didn't even go to visit him. "I don't know what is becoming of my children," she said, as she finished the story.

"I want to see someone," I tell her. This is foreign to my family, I realized. My mother did not ever go to the doctor. The only time I recall going to the doctor as a child was to get required immunizations. I went to the hospital emergency room when I broke my arm, but it took a couple hours for me to convince my mom my arm was truly broken. We were a family not accustomed to receiving outside help of any kind – medical, emotional, or otherwise. I told her about the article I read in the magazine on depression and how I met each thing on the checklist, and how it recommended to get help. I knew she couldn't argue that one. She couldn't argue with God.

My mom agreed to call a psychotherapist. I was too embarrassed to do so. I picked a name out of the insurance booklet, a name that

I liked, and she called. Unfortunately this therapist was not currently accepting new patients, but she referred us to another therapist to try. After my mother hung up the phone after scheduling an appointment with this therapist, I drilled her with questions. "What did her voice sound like? Did she sound nice? How old does she seem?" My mom said she couldn't tell much from her voice, how nice she was, how old she was, etc. I remember thinking, *If I had heard her voice, I would have been able to tell everything!*

One year and three days since my baptism, I walked into my first therapy session. Baptism symbolized a death to an old life and the beginning of a new, one now committed to God. As I walked through the door to this unknown therapist's office, I entered a whole new world. I was leaving behind something that was still very unclear, but it was old, and I was starting a new life, a life committed to myself. But that is not at all how it felt at the time.

Terri Hamilton-Gahart was her name. I liked the fact that her name was hyphenated. It meant she did not fully give up her identity for a man, but shared it. She had very short, red hair and was in her mid to late thirties. On our first meeting, she wore an ankle-length, navy blue skirt, a multi-colored sweater and black flats. She dressed and looked somewhat average, except for perhaps the short hair…and then I noticed her socks. She had funky, multicolored socks to go with her colorful sweater. I really liked the socks. They stood out. They expressed personality. This person was *interesting*.

Her office resided in an old, Victorian house. It had two chairs, a black leather couch with a couple of throw pillows, a large area rug with tasseled edges, a lamp, desk and bookcase filled with various types of psychology texts. There was a window off to one side, and through it one could see trees blowing in the wind. Some of the panes in the window were original. They were not crystal clear, but wavy. I sat on the couch and looked out the window. I immediately loved looking out that window. Perhaps I loved it so much because the distortion was familiar, it mimicked my internal, distorted world. Or perhaps it was because the panes softened the harsh edges of the world outside. In any case, I just wanted to stare out the window at the trees.

Interrupting my gaze, Terri asked me some questions. "How many brothers and sisters do you have?" "Are you going to school?" "Do you have a religious affiliation?" that sort of thing. Then she asked some more personal questions, "Are you sexually active?" No. "Do you have a boyfriend?" No. "A girlfriend?" No. I chuckle at this question. "Why do you laugh? It doesn't matter to me whether or not you're gay," she replied. "Have you ever been mugged or sexually assaulted?" No.

"Well, there was this thing with my cousin, but it wasn't traumatic," I replied. "I was about 10 years old, he was 12, and it went on for a few months, maybe over a couple summers. We were just messing around." She scribbles in her notepad.

A few minutes later she had me draw some pictures – a picture of a person, then a picture of a person of the opposite sex, then a house, then my family doing some sort of activity. She was most intrigued by my drawing of a house. She said that it showed I was depressed. I could have told her that. She explained the house and how it illustrated me being depressed. It was sort of interesting. *What am I doing here?* I thought to myself.

I saw Terri cross her legs, and I noticed she did not shave them. All of a sudden I started thinking, what if she is a lesbian? I looked at her ring finger and saw a wedding ring. *But that doesn't necessarily mean anything. She could just be wearing that and still be a lesbian. But what about the hyphenated name? Doesn't that mean she's married? She could have just taken on the other woman's name,* I continued to debate with myself. *Oh, I don't know if I can work with her if she's a lesbian. Remember Sodom and Gomorrah. I'll just assume she's not.*

I had pretty good health insurance through my dad at the time, so I was able to go to the therapy sessions on a weekly, sometimes twice-weekly, basis. I kept waiting each week to feel better, though. I kept waiting to learn about the *cause* of my feelings.

A couple months into therapy, I awoke one morning and went out in door-to-door service, like I continued to do several times a week. I don't know how much good I really could have been in saving people as I traipsed through the neighborhoods all depressed. When I got home, I wished I hadn't been out there. I just wanted to die.

I walked into my parents' bedroom. They were in Arkansas looking for property to buy so we could all move there. I opened the closet door and stared at the shiny revolver on the top shelf. A box of .22 bullets was right next to it. I took the gun down from the shelf. I had known it was up there for years, but never touched it. The gun was much heavier than it looked. I sat down on the floor and looked it over. I opened it up and figured out how to load it. I questioned for several minutes while sitting there whether or not I should put a bullet in it. I put one in, closed it, then took the bullet back out again. I put the revolver next to my right temple and mimicked the sound of a gunshot. I wiped off my prints from the gun and placed it back on the shelf in exactly the same place and position from which I had gotten it.

I called Terri to see if I could get an emergency appointment. I got one for 5 o'clock that evening. I drove the hour to her office, which was in the closest big city. Sessions usually are "50-minute hours". Occasionally they would be extended 55-60 minutes. It was now an hour and 45 minutes into our session. I was sitting on her floor with no reason to live. I was fantasizing about the revolver I was holding earlier, and how if I had it with me right that minute, I would use it. Terri was on the phone to the Emergency Psychiatric Hospital. She would like me to go there, she said. I told her in my depression-caused slow, soft speech that I didn't know the way. She offered me a police escort to get there safely. I decided I didn't want that. I'd rather just drive home.

She called my friend Debbie and told her how I was feeling. She asked her if I could spend the night at her house. Debbie said yes. So I agreed that I would do so. Terri also had me sign a contract: "I, Kristi Bowman, will not kill myself. If I feel suicidal, I will call Terri Hamilton-Gahart,

Ph.D. or Psychiatric Emergency Services. I will make an appointment with my physician for a medical evaluation for my depression and compulsive behaviors." Terri signed the contract stating she would check in with me daily until our next appointment. She seemed rather nervous during this whole process. I didn't feel anything.

Even though I had agreed to spend the night at Debbie's, I drove right by and went to my house. At 8:30pm Terri called to see how I was doing. I was feeling sick and death was tapping on my shoulder. She said she wanted me to go to the hospital, since that was the quickest way for me to get help and feel safer. I still didn't want to go.

Debbie then called me at around 9:30pm. She said she just got done talking with Terri and that I *really* should go to the hospital. She came over to my house, accompanied by her two daughters, who were really good friends of mine. I wished she hadn't brought them. I didn't like them to see me like that. Her husband was waiting in the car. After much pleading, I agreed to go to Blake Community, the local medical hospital. The doctor saw me in the emergency room at 10:30pm. He asked how I was feeling. He said, "I hear you want to kill yourself."

"Yes," I said.

"Do you have a plan?" he asked.

"Yes," I replied with a snicker.

"From what I hear you saying, and seeing how you seem to be inappropriately laughing, I'm going to have to admit you." My stomach dropped.

"I don't want to be admitted. I thought I was just coming in here to see a doctor and get some medication or something," I told him.

"No, that's not an option," he replied.

It was going to be a 3-4 hour wait to get a driver to transport me to St. Theresa, the nearest psychiatric hospital, about an hour away. Debbie and her family decided to drive me. I sat in the back with my two friends, flanked on each side. I knew that seating arrangement was intentional. It was sad that they felt the need to prevent me from leaping out of the car. I guess it was even more sad that I *did* actually need them to keep me from leaping out of the car. I tried to cover my illness as much as possible when I was around them. I sat quietly for the most part, making only a bit of small talk on the way to the hospital.

I arrived at the St. Theresa emergency room around midnight. St. Theresa, nestled in the mountains, the very hospital in which I had been born. It is as if I unconsciously needed to go back to this place of beginnings in search of truth. Go back to the source, where I first came out of the darkness of my mother and opened my eyes to the light. Perhaps here I would once again be able to come out of the darkness and experience life.

The nurses checked my vital signs. The doctor on duty asked me a number of questions, and he too felt I should be admitted on a 5150, a 72-hour hold. I was deemed a danger to myself. I got sent upstairs to the mental health unit. I was weighed and my vitals were checked again. My belongings got searched and taken away. I took an intake exam, and from that they could see that I knew who the President of the United States was, that I didn't have a glass eye, and that my skin wasn't green. I was trying to figure out how this knowledge would help me feel better.

I crawled into bed at 2:00am, still lying awake at 3:30am. The nurse gave me an Ativan, a mild tranquilizer, and I fell asleep around 4:00am. I was awakened at 7:00am, got my vitals checked once again, and my blood was drawn. Later that morning I saw the psychiatrist. He was an idiot. He asked the same questions I had been asked by the three other people just a few hours ago. Nobody shares notes? He started me on Luvox right away. Luvox was chosen because I had mentioned to him that I thought I had OCD as well as depression, and Luvox is supposed to help with obsessive thoughts as well as ease depression.

Like depression, I "diagnosed myself" with OCD. Beginning around age 13 or so, I went through a period when everything had to be "even." If I had an itch on my left arm and scratched it three times, I would have to scratch my right arm in the corresponding place three times, and so on. Otherwise, I would feel "lopsided." Little nick-knacks and stuffed animals in my room all had their place. If one was moved out of its place even half an inch, I would notice and go storming out demanding to know who was in my room. I was always correct in knowing someone had been in there. I was also a counter. I would count everything, from lines on the ceiling to buttons on a shirt, over and over. My writing also showed evidence of OCD. If I didn't like how my "s" looked in the word "constitution," I would erase it over and over, trying to "fix it." Eventually, I would end up erasing the entire word a few times so all the letters would "match."

As I grew older, my OCD took on other forms. One example is reliving a certain event or conversation that took place with another person. It would have to be considered an important event. I would feel that I needed to go over it many times in my head. If a dozen replays didn't kill the urge, I would have to physically act it out, like in a drama, playing each role, many, many times until I no longer felt compelled to do so. This was all because I was afraid I would forget.

%. %. %.

I toss and turn – synchronized with my thoughts.
I fear I'll forget.
I do: faces, events, feelings.
What is the purpose of so much effort? What good does it accomplish?
I cannot fully know those answers myself. I lose something.
They must be taken with me.
It goes beyond just the desire to remember.
It is an obsession that causes me great anxiety.
If I forget, a great void will envelop me, it seems.
A piece of me will break off. The more that break off, the less there is of me.
I can't really describe it. All I know is that I will lose something and lost things are gone forever…

% % %

Throughout the day at the hospital, I got phone calls from Terri, Debbie, my brother and my sister. In attempt to regain health through fresh air, I was forced by the nurses to go sit by the pool. Later I was made to go for a walk. I didn't want to do any of these things. I just wanted to curl up in a corner and die.

I got asked by different staff the same questions. Have I been eating? No. Have I been sleeping? No. Have I had thoughts of killing myself? Yes. Am I on any drugs? No, except the ones you give me. Can you come up with anything original? Apparently not. Do I find you annoying? Yes.

I had a medical examination in the late evening. Nothing interesting was found. I had slim hopes that I might perhaps have had a brain tumor, and it was the source of all the trouble. I had a group therapy session afterward. I hated it. At bedtime, I swallowed my Luvox, then opened my mouth and stuck out my tongue for the nurse as instructed. It was like the movie *Empire of the Ants*. There we all were, lined up just waiting to be shot with the pheromones from the Queen Ant. That would make us feel better, keep us under control. That would restore our purpose in life.

The next day I felt a little better. I actually kind of enjoyed the walk outdoors with the group. I was able to eat some lunch. The pool time was not as excruciating as it had been the day before. Then my parents showed up to take me home. My 72 hours were up, and I was no longer considered harmful to myself. "I thought you were in Arkansas." I said.

"We came back early", was my mom's reply.

"Oh." I was feeling okay all day, until I went home. As soon as I walked through the door to my house, I felt just as sick as I had the day before.

% % %

Outside the hospital, I continued on Luvox, 50mg per day. It seemed to start working a couple weeks later. I felt a little less miserable, but not by much. Two and a half months later, the Luvox ran out. I didn't get a new prescription right away, but I continued therapy with Terri. She referred me to a psychiatrist to get back on the medication. Another month and a half later, I was back on Luvox. I had medication, therapy sessions with a Ph.D., and therapy sessions with an M.D. Still there was not much improvement.

Soon, my dosage was raised to 100mg per day, then 150mg. It seemed like the medication would work for a short period of time, a few weeks, then stop working and I'd want to kill myself again. So, my psychiatrist just kept raising the dosage, hoping that would help.

I removed myself from being a Regular Pioneer. I got a part-time job and decided to start taking classes at the Junior College in the fall. Higher education is not regarded well in the Jehovah's Witness world. Despite this, my mom agreed that I could take a few courses. Perhaps she hoped that school would get my mind on something other than killing myself.

I started with general education courses, but had plans to major in psychology. From an early age, I had a passion for trying to figure out people. Starting at age 8, I would look through the outdated medical encyclopedia that my mom had. I was particularly interested in the "Mental Health" section. I would read through the pages time and time again, "diagnosing" various members of my family. I also tried to figure out what was wrong with me, since I felt so different from everyone else in my family. I guarantee those pages were worn more so than any other.

I did very well in college and enjoyed it, despite my continued depression. My first semester, I took 17 units, worked my job, and ended up making straight A's. I appreciated the enjoyment of once again getting an "A". I signed up to take classes for the spring semester. I just had to get through winter break.

Chapter 9

Flashes

Flash! Like a camera in a dark room
Flash! Uncomfortable, disturbing
So disturbing I want to scream, scare them away
Welling up feelings now that I didn't have then
Or did I?

Approximately 10 years have passed
Each day of that, forcing myself to forget
Thinking I will succeed in time – wrong!

Flash! In pieces, not whole
I want to get away from them, struggling
No matter how fast I run or how hard I fight
I'm unable to escape from what's forever with me

Flash! Pictures, unforgettable pictures
Keeping me awake at night
Filling my head with shameful, repugnant, drowning images
How will I get rid of them?
Release them through words?
Transferring these images to words is not an easy task
I know the time must come, but oh, how I dread it!

※　※　※

During winter break, one of my therapy sessions was "detail day." I was going to talk more about the "messing around" that happened between my cousin and me when I was 10 years old. I wasn't too worried about it. I had gotten over it.

As I sat on the couch I began to tell Terri what happened. "I don't remember exactly when it started, but I know my cousin initiated it, because I didn't know anything about sex…" I moved from the couch to the floor. "We would put a hand down each other's pants and fondle each other…We would be in my family's camper trailer and role-play kissing scenes like we'd seen in soap-operas. Except we'd take it further than just kissing and be naked and fondle each other…We did stuff like this all over. We had secret codes to each other, which were a signal that only we knew, telling each other we should go. There was never a name for it. We would go behind the carport, go in the barn… When I remember this, I see myself from an outside perspective, like I am a third person off to the side watching the two of us. We would pull our pants down, I'd bend over, and he'd try to stick his penis inside. It never went in, though. Mostly, he would just have it pressed against my anus…"

I thought I wasn't being that affected by telling Terri the story, but I felt extremely nervous during the telling, almost sick. About 5 minutes left in the session and I was in the fetal position, still on the floor. Time was up, and I had to go. Terri couldn't get me to stand and leave. I didn't know why I didn't/couldn't get up.

I closed my eyes. I felt like I was either *in* a little black spot, or I *was* the black spot, sinking into the floor, almost like the black spot was beneath the level of the floor. I opened my eyes. Terri gently pulled on my arm, and I was raised to a sitting fetal position. All the muscles in my body were flexed, so tense. Somebody was there to talk with Terri. I *had* to leave! She pulled on my tensed arm again. I relaxed it. I stood.

Everything seemed so fuzzy. She assisted me to the waiting room, to a chair. I chose the floor. She left. I cried. I wanted to cry. I wanted to cry harder than I had ever cried before. I didn't, though. I just cried a little.

Terri returned a few minutes later after speaking with the other person. I had moved myself to a corner in a tight fetal position. "Why aren't you helping me?!" I cried. Everything seemed so strange and unreal. I managed to pull myself together after a few more minutes and leave.

When I got home, I slept for a long time, and then lay around in my room the rest of the time. Later that night, I paced in a mechanical fashion for about half an hour. I wanted to stay awake all night.

%%   %%   %%

I remember it well. I was 10 or 11 years old. I was sitting in the Lazy Boy recliner watching TV. My mom had been sharing the seat with me as we were watching *Dallas.* The phone rang and she got up to answer it. The tone in her voice and the way she looked over at me made my stomach do flip-flops. I knew then and there it had come out what my cousin and I had done, even though it had already stopped several months earlier.

At some point there was a moment when my cousin said, "I don't think we should do this anymore," and so we didn't. All the guilt I had carried about sneaking around and lying to my mom about what the two of us kids were up to was going to end. It was a huge weight off my shoulders. It happened, it ended. We never got caught, and now nobody was ever going to find out. I could forget about it. Life could go back to "normal." Until the phone call.

My mom hung up the phone. She had been talking with my sister. I just kept thinking, *how could my sister know anything? How did she find out?*

I don't recall the exact words my mother then started speaking. My heart was pounding so hard and loud it was drowning out everything else. I recall, though, my mother being so angry. I had never before seen her that angry and upset with me. I told her it had already stopped. I just cried, for all the pent-up secrecy could now be released. She asked sternly what happened. I told her only some of what happened. She was already so angry. I told her about touching each other's genitals, but not anything else.

She asked me about my niece and nephew. I was bewildered. I didn't know anything about my cousin doing anything with my niece and nephew. My niece was 4 years old at the time and my nephew 2. She kept yelling at me. I was so confused.

Then this image came into my head. Several months ago I had seen my cousin looking into a storage trailer we owned. It had no top on it, only sides about 4 feet high. I walked up to him, stepped up the side of the trailer and asked, "What are you doing?" As I looked inside the trailer, I saw the scene. My niece and nephew both were inside the trailer with their pants down. My nephew had his penis pushed against the buttocks of my niece. I turned to my cousin and asked, "Where'd they learn to do that?" My cousin just chuckled. I knew for a fact they had not seen my cousin and me together.

"Okay, pull your pants back up," he tells them. I stepped down off the trailer and walked away. I did not equate at the time that my cousin was orchestrating the scene. I thought for some reason that my niece and nephew had just been messing around, and my cousin had been witness to the act and then told them to pull up their pants. I tried to forget it. I did not tell my mother of this either.

For discipline, she grounded me. I was to never be around my cousin again, and I was grounded to the inside of the house for a week. I had never been grounded in my entire life. I was a good kid. I always did as I was told.

My cousin was staying at my grandmother's house for the summer, and I did not see him again for about 8 or 9 years. I had missed hanging out with him during the summers. When I did see him years later, it was very awkward. I saw him only briefly, and we did not speak. I wanted so badly to simply talk with him for a couple minutes. I wanted to know if he also felt bad about what happened, if we could put it behind us. I wanted to know if he had later done it with other people, other children. But I did not speak with him. I was still too embarrassed and the opportunity did not present itself.

%% %% %%

In an attempt to try and figure out what happened at the previous therapy session, Terri had me go to the floor and position myself the same way I had been, in the fetal position. From there I talked about some more details of the things that transpired with my cousin.

It wasn't bothering me that much, but I felt myself start to drift a little, to fade. So Terri asked me if I could get back up on the couch. Even sitting on the couch, though, there was a problem. I just kept drifting further and further. I couldn't pull myself out of it.

Terri gave a theory that I dissociate. Dissociation is an alteration in consciousness. There is a continuum of dissociation – from the mild form that we all do, such as daydreaming, to more severe forms, such as Dissociative Identity Disorder (formerly Multiple Personality Disorder). Generally, the more severe the trauma, the more significant the dissociation. She said even though my childhood sexual experiences were not forced, they must have still been traumatic for me. I would dissociate to deal with it, and apparently I still dissociate. The objective, then, was to help me remember all the blank spots, the parts I don't remember, so I would no longer have to dissociate.

At the end of the session, I was very much in a faded-out state. Terri tried to physically remove me from the couch, since it was once again past time for the session to end. I cried and reached for the couch, struggling like a young child being separated from her parents. I could sense Terri's worry about how to deal with this situation. I managed to pull myself together somewhat, but I still felt very spaced out. Terri asked me if I would like a hug. "Yeah," I replied. It was nice. In that moment, I felt she really did care about me, that she wasn't just doing a job.

A couple months later, I asked Terri in one of our sessions, "Do you like me as a person?"

"Believe it or not, I do. I like you for your intelligence and your sense of humor. If you didn't have your sense of humor, I probably wouldn't like you as much," she replied with a wry smile.

I was feeling more and more comfortable with Terri. It took me a long time to build up any amount of trust with a person, so this was a big step. Our therapeutic relationship was feeling stronger and more secure, which would be pivotal for the issues we would soon be confronting.

Chapter 10

There was a family that had one daughter, just a year or so older than I, a son my age, and another son 2 years younger than I. Their mother was a friend of my mother. I was a friend mostly with the daughter and the younger son, Rod. Even though his brother was my age, Rod seemed more civilized somehow. I would spend time with Rod at the meetings, out in service, and also just hanging out. We had quite a bit of fun together. We would get a group of 3 or 4 friends together and go roller-blading or bowling or see a movie.

I started spending a lot of time with Rod. This didn't seem like anything out of the ordinary. Growing up, I actually preferred hanging out with the boys. They seemed to have much more fun than the girls, who just wanted to sit around talking about make-up or their hair. The boys played sports, rode bikes and motorcycles, climbed trees, played video games and did other fun activities that I loved doing. Rod was nice to me, and we had a similar background, interests and spiritual pursuits.

After all this time I had been spending with him, things started to shift. He started talking about how he had feelings for me. I liked him too.

As a Jehovah's Witness it was not allowed for people to date until one was "ready for marriage." People could not date until they were old enough and mature enough to do so. The dating would then take place in groups or with supervision. Two people of the opposite sex who were not married should not ever spend time alone together.

On my 20th birthday, Rod and I were at a meeting. We were holding hands for the first time. It felt pretty comfortable, pretty good. I passed him a note stating that we might as well start dating. We talked things over later that night. A couple days later, it was official. By Rod and I dating, we were saying we were mature enough for marriage. We had spent a couple days discussing it, so we felt like we were ready. He was not yet 18.

The spring semester at the Junior College had begun. I was excited to continue my courses and learn more about psychology. I had done so well the first semester, I had no reason to think I wouldn't do well the spring semester. I signed up for 13 units.

However, the depression remained…and then worsened. The psychiatrist increased my dosage of Luvox to 200mg per day. I felt very suicidal once again. I had to make an oral contract with the psychiatrist not to harm myself. I felt absolutely awful. I felt nauseous, shaky, weak, and sapped of all energy. Some days I couldn't go to school due to being so sick, and I had to call in sick to work. I could not function well. I could barely drag myself out of bed to take a shower.

One of the areas of focus in therapy was my family dynamics. I was given "homework" assignments, which I liked. Through these assignments, I was able to communicate more of myself to Terri. I told her how I hated my family. I told her how, when I first felt suicidal, the fact that I was trapped in the family contributed to my thoughts. Nobody in my family knew what was going on in my head and didn't seem to care. I was isolated in my room, yearning to die, and life carried on as usual just outside the door. In my family nobody communicates, or asks questions, and nobody feels anything. Feelings and emotions are *never* discussed or displayed. Being emotional and crying is considered weak, childish and immature. No questions or words were expressed pertaining to my hospital stay. I asked my mom why she never asks how I am doing. She replied that if I had something to say, I would tell her. Of course I wouldn't tell her! If she didn't show the interest to care, why should I!

I never felt like I belonged in my family. I felt different from everyone else somehow. I recall as a young child wanting so much to have been adopted, and one day I would find my true parents. I would find the exciting, young, fun-loving, affectionate, stimulating parents, complete opposites of the boring, aged, quiet-loving, stone-cold, deadening parents that I got who kill the spirit of life.

Therapy also had me think about what made me so scared about the present and future that I had to avoid it or deny it, wish to die rather than face it. I was still unclear about a lot of this, but I did come up with one thing. "Maybe it is because I don't think I am doing what I should be doing," I wrote in my homework assignment. "Jehovah God has given me a most privileged opportunity and responsibility to preach about his Kingdom and all the wonderful things it will bring, and what am I doing? Going to college to become a psychologist that can only provide short-term help at best. I can't solve all the world's ills! I am scared of the unknown. If I'm not doing what I should be right now, what will happen to me?"

Also, I felt like I was losing control. "My mind and body are betraying me. I feel naked and exposed to the world with all those dirty hands of life grabbing at me." I also wanted so badly to be able to voice my feelings during therapy and in life, to *feel* my feelings, but words would completely escape me at pivotal moments. Writing helped. "I fear that we are stuck and you (Terri) will have to give up on me. I'm so desperate for answers, so desperate for help. I am tired of living this way. My insides feel like a tornado, tearing up everything with devastating effects. My head is driving me crazy. My mind is always so busy. I can't go to sleep at night, because there are too many voices talking and it is just too loud. I want to scream, 'Shut up!', but it wouldn't work. I feel hopeless. Life is one big, cruel monster that has beaten me to a finish…"

%, %, %,

Commingle

Danger signs were flashing, yet I did not see them
I was screaming out in resistance, yet I could not hear myself
Silently, my mind was forced to create an escape route on its own
    – for survival
Sometimes I feel I haven't fully survived, though,
Only part of me living, while the other part died long ago,
Cleverly taking the feelings and thoughts along with it
If it is dead, then why are there signs of life creeping back into
    existence –
Actions that are not my own, voices I hear, but do not create…?
These make me afraid, afraid that I'm slowly going crazy
I don't remember, I don't remember, I just don't remember…
Oh, when will I recall? When will I be integrated once again?
Now, I ache and bawl as the painful process of gluing the shattered
pieces of my life back together again takes place

%, %, %,

Within two weeks of dating Rod, I wanted to break up with him, but we agreed to try a little longer. A week after that, Rod and I were talking about getting married, but we didn't yet pick out a date for the wedding. However, we did go pick out rings and put them on layaway. "I do love Rod. I know that now. I won't let us kiss until we're officially engaged. See how long that'll last," I wrote in my journal.

Not long. The next day Rod asked me to marry him in my parked car outside his house. I said, "yeah." It seemed stupid…and strange. We then kissed. I had not kissed a boy before.

Well, there was my cousin. Not the one mentioned earlier, but another one, his older brother. I also had not told my mom about that. He was about six years older than I. I think he just wanted to use me for practice, so he could have some experience kissing girls. It was slobbery, and I kept moving my tongue away from his in my mouth. I couldn't stand his breath and his taste and his tongue searching for mine. He would lie on top of me. All his weight practically suffocated me. I couldn't breathe. The kissing practice only took place a couple times. There were also a couple instances of him cornering me and sticking his hands down the back of my pants to grab my ass. I avoided him after that.

So I had not kissed a boy as an adult before. There seemed like a lot of concentration going into it. He kept sticking his tongue really far into my mouth, as if the deeper the better. Wrong. We kissed for almost two hours. Afterward, I went home and brushed my teeth for about 10 minutes.

I was able to get through the spring semester at the Junior College. With all the missed days, my grades weren't A's, but I skated by with B's and one C. That alone was devastating for me in one sense, since I was a perfectionist. But I also didn't care in another sense, because my life was continuing to unravel, and grades were not in the forefront of my mind.

My medication dosage kept being increased. It was raised to 300mg per day. Not any dosage seemed to be helping for very long periods of time.

Also at this time, my mom refused to pay for therapy any longer. From her viewpoint, it wasn't doing much good. I was only bringing in $500-$600 per month. I used this for gas to get to and from work and school, food, car insurance, textbooks, medication and therapy. But even the financial stress was not at the forefront of my mind.

For the next few months after our engagement, Rod and I "fooled around." Numerous times we had sex, but with our clothes on, so it didn't really count as sex in my mind. This was mostly in my parked car somewhere, late at night. There's always a way to get around not being alone together. We would hang out with a friend, then go drop off the friend. Before we would make it to Rod's house to drop him off, we'd park the car somewhere. We eventually got to where we would expose our genitals to each other and then use our hands to give each other pleasure. He would put one or two fingers inside me, and I would rub his penis. I cannot say whether I enjoyed any of this or not. My dissociation frequently caused me to experience no feelings. And still, I did not consider even this to be actual sex.

After a session with Terri I wrote the following: "I FEEL A MIXTURE OF ANGER AND LONELINESS RIGHT NOW. I WANT TO SCREAM AND CRY ALL AT ONCE. I WANT TO DISSOLVE. I WANT TO BE HURT. I WANT SOMEBODY TO HURT ME, IF NOT, I'LL DO IT MYSELF. I FEEL SO MUCH ANGER THAT I CAN TASTE SOMETHING DISGUSTING INSIDE, BUBBLING AND VOMITING ALL OVER MY EMOTIONS. I'M OBSESSED WITH PICTURES OF BIG, UGLY PENISES INVADING MY MIND. SEX IS DISGUSTING AND PAINFUL AND MAKES YOU FEEL SICK AND POLLUTED INSIDE. MY BODY BETRAYS ME TO PUNISH AND DO HORRIBLE THINGS TO MY HEAD AND FEELINGS."

Later that day, I don't know if I went to the religious meeting or not, probably not. In the evening I called and left a message for Terri to call me. I did not feel well. Rod came over to my house after the meeting. I was in my room. My mom and my brother and sister-in-law were in the kitchen. My brother and his family were living with us at the time.

Rod and I were behind my locked door on my bed with our clothes off. We were going further than we had previously. Rod could get two fingers inside me, but not his penis. I don't think he fully knew what he was doing, and I wasn't there. We changed positions – me sitting on top. He placed his penis, or I did, in the right place and then he pressed my body down over his. I kept myself up as best I could, while he kept pressing down with more force. If his penis went inside me, *that* would be sex. I was hovering, literally, at this point of reckoning. I finally gave in and gave up and let my body be lowered down, taking his penis inside me.

I immediately said, "Stop! Stop!" as I lay on top of him. "What are we doing?!!" I ran into the bathroom adjoining my room and started crying. The phone rang. My heart sank. It was Terri returning my call. My brother answered the phone, then called out my name. I got dressed and, sobbing uncontrollably, went out to the living room and picked up the phone. Terri asked what was wrong, and then I started sobbing even more. I could not speak. I slumped down to the floor. All I could do was lie there and cry. Terri made an appointment for the following day.

My family thought it was Rod's mom on the phone making me cry. They didn't realize that I was crying before I picked up the phone. After I hung up, I ran to the other bathroom in the house and sat on the floor, continuing to sob. My sister-in-law was there on the floor with me, comforting me, but not knowing what was happening. My brother came and stood in the doorway and asked what was wrong. Then Rod came into the bathroom, looking to be in complete and utter shock, asking what was wrong and saying over and over again, "I'm sorry." I told Rod to leave, that I just wanted him to go home. He didn't want to leave, but eventually he did. I didn't want any male around, including my brother. I was in the arms of my sister-in-law crumbling into a million pieces.

%%   %%   %%

Over the previous two years or so, I had spent a great deal of time with Debbie and her family. I felt I was very good friends with her two daughters, though they were a few years younger than I. Even in the darkest days of my depression, the two girls could make me laugh. Things would seem a bit lighter around them. I also spent considerable time with Debbie, since we were Regular Pioneering at the same time. She seemed to take me under her wing, and I used her many times as a confidant and shoulder to cry on. She was like an older sister. Perhaps she also thought she could help me get better. If she provided a supportive, loving and fun environment, I would get past this darkness. I loved just being in the presence of her family. They would eat meals together, talk and share their day, and especially joke and laugh together. I valued each moment I had with them. They were like the family I always wanted.

However, the family was not as perfect as it seemed on the outside, as is the case with most families. They were having considerable financial difficulties, which were putting strains in a lot of other areas of their lives, such as having a house in which to live, a car to drive and food on the table. But they continued to go about their day-to-day lives with a smile on their faces.

There would also be times when Debbie just wouldn't "feel well." She normally would dress up, have her hair done and make-up on her face. On the days she didn't feel well, she would wear her baggy, gray sweats, not wear any make-up and spend considerable time lying in bed. I did not think much of it. We all have days when we don't feel well. I was all too familiar with that feeling.

One evening, I was over at their house. It was dark and Debbie and I were outside. Somehow the conversation topic got around to me and my current state and how Satan was the primary cause of it.

"But what if it's not Satan?" I asked.

"Of course it is. That's just what he wants you to think, that it's something else, to keep the focus off of him," she replied.

"But I can't help it! I don't know why this is happening to me! I wish I could just snap my fingers and feel better, but I can't!" I started crying at this point.

"Then you're letting Satan win!" she said, raising her voice.

"No!" I screamed. "I don't want Satan to win!"

"Then fight it!" she continued, most likely an attempt to exercise "tough love."

"I am!" I started bawling at this point and headed quickly into the house. Debbie was right on my heels.

I went into one of the bedrooms and crumbled to the floor. Debbie came up behind me and held me and rocked me. She too was crying. It was as if I had a major breakthrough. I made the statement that I didn't want Satan to win. But I felt no different. I didn't *feel* like I had any kind of breakthrough. I just felt hopeless that I would ever get out of the miserable state I was in. But Debbie was there holding me, and that was enough.

At one time Debbie had stated that if I ever needed anything, *anything*, to call her and she would be there for me. The following day was one of those days that I felt I needed to talk with her and figure out what happened the night before. I picked up the phone and dialed her number. Her husband answered the phone. I said hi and asked for Debbie. There was something in his voice that I was trying to pinpoint. He had me hold for a moment, then he came back on the line. "She can't come to the phone right now. She's not feeling well," he said.

I hung up wondering if I had been the cause of her not feeling well. *Did I make her sick? I shouldn't jump to conclusions*, I told myself. *It's not like I'm the center of the universe. She's probably just not feeling well for whatever reason. But it seems too coincidental that she's not feeling well the day after the big melt-down incident at her house. Don't jump to conclusions!*

The next day, I saw Debbie. She was wearing her baggy, gray sweats and didn't have any make-up on – not a good sign. "How are you feeling?" I asked.

"Not very well," she replied in a tired, soft-spoken voice.

"Did I cause you to get sick?" I asked, needing absolute clarity.

"Yes. The other night just wiped me out...I need some space for a while." She made it very clear.

I could not stop thinking about how she told me that if I needed anything, I could go to her. I was thinking now how it was a lie. People shouldn't make statements like that if they cannot hold true to them. But most of all, I felt absolutely awful for having pushed her away from me.

Not too long after that, they moved. I was out of town when they moved and did not know they were even thinking of doing so. My first reaction was sadness over the loss, but I quickly covered it over with not caring. It didn't matter. Nothing mattered.

% % %

As scheduled, I had a session with Terri the day after having sex with Rod. I don't recall what happened at the session. I had been in a dissociated state on her office floor throughout the hour. Time was once again up, and I wouldn't leave her office. Terri seemed upset and frustrated. With the threat of referral to a new therapist, I gathered myself up enough to leave.

The next day, I wrote a letter to Terri:

"I finally found the line in you that can be dangerously crossed. The line found in many other friends that I have used to prove my prediction that no one could possibly love or like me. The line that I seek in everyone getting close to me, yet I fear the most. I can use it in you to prove you wrong that you will always be there and won't give up on me; to force you to send me to another therapist. Those self-fulfilled prophesies that I am so good at. It's different now, though, because it has been brought to my conscious awareness that I do it. I don't want to cross those lines anymore. Quite frankly, despite my distorted thoughts and hopes, people *do* care! I'm sick and tired of hurting other people just to fulfill my selfish desire to hurt myself!

"Life is extremely difficult at times, but I *have* to take responsibility and face it! It's *so* hard… I know I can't change overnight, but I can continue to fight my way up that hill, through the sludge, and against the wind. At least I will be moving forward, though slowly. Difficulties in life sometimes seem so much stronger than I. I feel powerless to change them, feeling that any attempt would be futile, so why bother? I don't want to give up…I want to feel that great sense of accomplishment of conquering this agonizing struggle and not letting it conquer me. I want a happy ending."

The following session, Terri said she got the message I left for her in the bathroom. "What message? What are you talking about?" I asked.

"The blood on the wall," she replied.

"I didn't leave any message on the wall," I said. Just then I recalled going into the bathroom in her office complex after our previous session to use the facilities. I remembered standing and looking at the inside of one of the bathroom stalls. I thought in my head, like they do in the movies, to write, "Help Me" with blood pricked from my finger. But that was it, I only *thought* about it. I didn't actually *do* it. At least, I didn't remember doing it.

But Terri said it was there. I argued with her. "It had to be someone else!" I exclaimed. "Where would I get the blood? I didn't have anything with which to prick my finger. I wouldn't deface someone's property." It was the most unnerving feeling – to do something completely out of control and without recollection of doing so. It was the most severe example of my dissociation.

I signed a contract stating that I would "leave each session on my own or with minimal physical assistance without exceeding 60 minutes." Also, I agreed to no longer sit or lie on the floor. "If either of these agreements is not kept, I understand that Terri will refer me to another therapist."

Yes, I had pushed Terri to her limit. I found her boundary. She genuinely wanted to help me, yet I acted in ways that pushed her away. She was in quite a predicament. It was in my capacity to act in such a way as to "prove" my belief that no one would stick by me through all the hard times, and that no one could truly love or like me. If she ended up referring me to another therapist, my belief would be reinforced. However, Terri could not work with a patient who would not leave her office on time. Finding her limit satisfied me…for a while.

I was actually impressed with how Terri handled difficult situations. Her actions were very different from Debbie's. Debbie's actions seemed to, in the long run, actually stunt my emotional growth. She didn't mean to, of course. Mostly from my own personal experience, I knew that I could control my actions more than I actually did. I sometimes *allowed* myself to spiral downward. After all, sick people get more attention than well ones do. Terri's reactions, in contrast to Debbie's, did not encourage the episodes or spiraling. Debbie, by her sympathy being expressed in overly-dramatic ways, only encouraged me to allow myself to melt away rather than fight it and keep myself together.

%   %   %

My conscience was bothering me about "the incident" (as I called it) with Rod. A couple of the Elders in the congregation had called the two of us into a private room to talk about how we seemed to be sitting just a bit too close to each other during the meetings. Indeed, we had been sitting practically on each other's laps. I asked if I could speak with them privately. My heart pounded so fiercely. Rod was dismissed from the room.

I started crying and told them that Rod and I had had sex. I tried to explain to them how it was a self-destructive act, not an uncontrollable act of passion. Gag!

The discipline to be doled out to the two of us was being "publicly reproved." This, in effect, is an announcement to the entire congregation of just that. It is also the taking away of certain "privileges," such as going out in service and commenting at the meetings.

I went to the meeting when it was to be announced. I walked through the door to the Kingdom Hall, just as I had done thousands of times before in my life. I looked around at the beige world created in the room. This Kingdom Hall was fairly new, having been built only a few years prior. It had brown carpeting, light beige metal-frame benches with a slightly darker beige upholstery on the padded seating area. There was beige paint on the walls with a darker beige trim. Everywhere I looked there was beige. There was no color anywhere, and it wasn't just my eyes.

I recalled the original Kingdom Hall that used to be in its place. It must have been built in the '70s, because it had mustard-yellow carpeting, green seat upholstery, and the women's bathroom had orange and pink walls. There was color.

There was also, behind the podium, a 9' x 12' print on the wall. It was in strips, because I could see the paper peeling a bit around the edges. The picture was a wooded nature scene. There were trees and a clear stream that meandered its way through the land. I remembered when I was very young, as young as 4 or 5, having to sit still and pay attention during the hour or two hour talks, I would stare into the picture, giving the impression that I was listening. The speaker's voice would fade out, and I would find myself walking along the stream with a deer or raccoon by my side. I would listen to the flow of the water over the rocks and smell the sweet pines all around me.

But now back in the beige world, there was nothing to bring comfort. Rod did not show up to this meeting. I felt he was a wimp for not being there. "Kristi Bowman and Rod Burton are publicly reproved," one of the Elders announced. That was it. Everyone knew what it meant, what was taken away. I gather everyone also knew we had sex. What else would two young people who had been sitting on each others laps do? "Public embarrassment" is what they should have called it.

As soon as the announcement was made, I went into the beige women's restroom and started crying. My sister-in-law came in, put her arm around me and comforted me. My mother also came into the restroom. She stood a couple feet away. She said she was proud of me, that it was difficult to do. It felt like I blanked her out.

Coming from such a strong-in-the-faith mother, and not having any prior instances of imperfection, the Elders granted me to have partial privileges restored the following month. Partial in the sense that I couldn't just jump right back into Pioneering if I had wanted to, I suppose. The problem was, I didn't want the "privileges" back. I wasn't ready. I heard the Elders did it so I could take advantage of going out in service with a visiting Circuit Overseer. However, I did not take advantage of this man's visit. Over the next few weeks, I had also ceased attending the meetings. Such a thing is called "disassociated" by Jehovah's Witnesses, where one of the flock leaves of his or her own accord. Disassociated and dissociated. Go figure.

Chapter 11

After you have suffered a little while,
the God of all undeserved kindness... will
himself finish your training, he will make you
firm, he will make you strong. 1Peter 5:10

How long is a "little while"?

%%   %%   %%

I signed up at the Junior College for the fall semester, but I had to withdraw from all my classes. Frankly, I could not drag myself out of bed a lot of the time to get to class. I didn't have the energy to do the homework. I didn't have the strength to push myself anymore. So I got big "W"s on my transcript that semester.

My parents moved to Arkansas. The original plan was for me to move with them. I had visited Arkansas a few times already, to visit my dad's family – his parents and sister. I went to visit my grandfather when he was dying of cancer. He died during our stay. Then I went for another visit to go to the funeral of my grandmother. Perhaps this aided to me not liking Arkansas – sickness and death all around. I also disliked the backward, ignorant people (that is, my family), the heat and the humidity. It was very stifling in more ways than one. I was already in internal hell, there was no way I could bear to move to what I surmised was physical hell.

I convinced my mom that I needed to stay in California. She ended up conceding, much to my surprise, only because my sister, Melissa, and her family were going to move into our house to rent it, and I would stay with them. They could "watch over me."

Rod proposed again, this time with ring in hand and on bended knee. It was in my bedroom at 1:30 in the morning. I said yes again. The plan was to have the wedding in the spring.

In therapy, we attempted to do hypnotherapy to uncover the source of my current hopeless state. We stopped trying after only a couple attempts, though. I felt I could not go "under," that it just wasn't working. So we resumed our usual therapy.

After returning home from one such regular therapy session, I was very quiet. I laid in bed the remainder of the day. I was seething with anger, though I did not know the source. Terri called me later in the day and said I should force myself to lead a functional life. I was not sure how that was going to be accomplished.

I didn't want to go to the meeting that night. I had a plan. The rest of the family was getting dressed to go to the meeting and were doing their hair and such. I figured in a few minutes they would come to my room and ask me if I was going to go with them.

I was changing with a different purpose in mind. I dressed very warmly, for at 6:20pm during the first week of January it is quite cold and already dark. I quietly slipped out the back door of the house. My bicycle had a flat tire, I discovered, so I found my nephew's and began to ride up the dirt road. I rode past the neighbor, fearing that he had seen me as he glanced out the window. Even if he did see me, he would have mistaken my identity. It was dark, I was dressed all in black, and I was wearing a baseball cap with my hair tucked under it. From a distance, I was a boy.

After riding a couple miles, I was almost to my destination – the cliff. I climbed off the bike upon reaching the overgrown trailhead that led to the cliff. Suddenly a car came! I quickly threw the bike down and ran behind a tree. I panted out of fear as I watched the car slow for a few seconds then continue on. *It must be my brother-in-law out searching for me,* I thought.

I trekked around in the heavily-wooded area. After a few minutes I lost the trail, for it was not well marked, and it was too dark to follow. It did not occur to me that I should have brought a flashlight, because I found the darkness strangely comforting. I wasn't worried. I knew those parts well from hiking around with a friend when I was younger. I continued to walk in the general direction of the cliff, tripping and bashing against branches in the process. *No one will find me out here!*

The property that I was on was owned by a cattle rancher. I had hopes that the cattle were going to be grazing at the north end of the large ranch, but no such luck. There were several cows nearby. They didn't seem to know what I was, so they just ran away. Sometimes the bulls could be dangerous, so just in case I came across one charging towards me, I checked for trees that were easy to climb in a hurry.

I was a little relieved when I realized that the cliff was just ahead, past a stand of trees. No bulls would be grazing on the rocky precipice. I found my favorite rock, sat on the edge and waited.

I envisioned what was going on back home: They discover I'm nowhere to be found. The cops are being called. Flashlights are being gathered. Everyone, with his or her worried face on, is dressing warmly in preparation to look for me…or what's left of me.

The stars were so amazing. The sky was just beautiful. The darkness. The tiny twinkling lights. One would think the vast blackness would simply envelop any sign of light, swallowing it up, making it insignificant, even invisible. Yet, when looking into the great expanse, one sees, not the enormous black space, but the tiny balls of fire glowing weak, then strong, weak, then strong.

After being carefully positioned on the edge for a considerable amount of time, I decided to go back home. I figured the family had had enough worry for one night. As I rode the bike closer, I noticed how the house was eerily quiet. I knew then that no one was out looking for me. They had all gone about their business, attending their religious meeting just like they did every Thursday night.

I put my nephew's bike in the exact spot I found it. I checked my watch: 9:25pm. They would all come home soon. *If I was still not home when they arrived, they would surely be worried! I must extend my plan, give them one last chance. It's all a dream anyway. Kristi would never do something this childish and stupid. It's just a game. Life is a game.*

I left a note the second time, marked the time I first left, 6:20pm. "I've gone for a looooong walk," it read. I slipped it under my pillow with just a corner sticking out. If anyone made even the *slightest* effort, it would be found. Not too much to ask.

I walked towards the old barn not too far from the house. This barn was built over 80 years ago by a man who died before he could complete it. It had just been sitting there slowly rotting ever since. It sat at the front of a 20-acre field that lay just to the south of our property line.

This field, over the years, became a pet cemetery of sorts. Whenever a cow or goat died giving birth, or a cat died from leukemia, or a rabbit died from chewing poisonous wood varnish, this is where its carcass ended up. Never buried, simply thrown out onto the land for the turkey vultures to pick apart. I could point out each spot of ground surrounding the old barn where each animal was tossed. As a child I either watched or helped transport the lifeless bodies to the field of death.

It was to this very place that I decided to travel. I crouched behind one of the stall doors in the old barn and watched and waited. *I still should be close enough to the house to hear what will be said.*

My fiancée, Rod, had said earlier that he would stop by my house after the meeting to see how I was doing if I had not made it to the meeting, so I wasn't surprised to now see his car coming down the road, followed by my sister and her family. I watched Rod as he briskly walked into the house, heading straight to my room. The light flicks on, he looks around, finds the note possibly, and the light flicks off.

I continued to wait, for an eternity it seemed. I was so cold. I hopped up and down and flailed my arms in an attempt to keep the blood flowing. I brought my scarf, but I could not wear it over my face. Every time I put it over my frozen nose and lips, my glasses fogged up, clouding my vision. It reminded me of how the world looked previous to starting my anti-depressant medication.

Virginia Woolf likened it to seeing the world from the inside of a grape. There is no longer clarity. There is a barrier, though not solid, between you and the world. For me, this barrier caused colors to fade to the point that everything around me looked like an old black and white movie. In addition, there was a thicker border of gray fog outlining each frame of my life movie. There were no longer edges to anything. Everything simply gradually disappeared into the clouds. And the clouds tumbled over into the other senses as well, with noise sounding muffled and food tasting gray. We think of the mind as this beautiful thing, when all it is really is a mass of gray matter. Perhaps, in reality, that's all the world is too.

Finally some life emerged. Rod trotted out of the house, jumped in his car, and sped down the road. He stopped at a gas station a couple miles away and asked if anyone has seen a young woman fitting my description. No one had. He heard the water of the river rushing under the bridge nearby, swollen from the onslaught of recent rains. Pictures of police helicopters with their searchlights illuminating the water in search of my lifeless body invade his mind. With tears streaming down his face, he drove off again. With sight blurred, he continued searching, driving at dangerous speeds. Bearing no news of finding me he returned to my house.

As he pulled into the driveway, Rod saw someone slip in the back door. He was unsure of the person's identity. Perhaps it was just

Melissa returning from feeding the horses. He rushed out of his car and followed the mystery woman through the back door. He opened the door to my bedroom and there I stood. He grabbed hold of me, crying. "You scared me! I love you. Don't ever do that again," he said through his sobs. I simply stood there looking at him. No expression. I just went for a walk is all. Meanwhile, my family was in the living room watching television.

%% %% %%

Even after both Rod and I had partial privileges restored in the Jehovah's Witness realm, we had sex, once. It was in my parked car. Maybe it was twice. We had penetration a total of three times. The first time was mentioned earlier. The second time was so painful. I was in tears and holding myself after I told him to stop. The third time, I experienced no feeling at all. While he was thrusting, I was watching the twinkling light of an airplane slowly float its way across the sky. I remember thinking, "When is he going to finish?" I was bored and tired and surprised that I felt absolutely nothing.

In January, during the cold, dark winter, I experienced the depth of my own cold darkness. One Friday afternoon I sat at home alone. I walked into the kitchen and opened the drawer that contained the knives. I pulled out a serrated steak knife. I walked slowly down the hall to the bathroom and closed the door. I kneeled down next to the bathtub, my left arm outstretched, my right hand with knife blade poised over left wrist. I took a breath in and on an out-breath, pressed down and quickly sliced my wrist.

I experienced the sensation for a moment. It was as if time stopped. Within a few seconds, time resumed and I returned to my task. I sliced again and again and again, horizontally, vertically, searching for the arteries. Small amounts of blood were draining out of my flesh and spilling over my arm, but not enough. I paused and moved the knife further up my arm to the inside of my elbow, where the nurses draw blood, to the large, clearly-visible artery there.

I positioned the knife and sliced. I looked at it, then positioned the knife in the exact place and cut again. The cut was fairly deep. My heart started pounding. I knew one more slice in that same place would open up the artery and allow it to freely spill its contents. It would mean my death. It would mean the end to this suffering. I moved the blade to the artery once again. I paused with knife at the ready......I couldn't do it.

My aunt then showed up to my house, calling my name. I do not recall how she knew to get me. I think Terri called her. I must have called Terri at some point. She wrapped my arm in a towel and we headed to the emergency room.

At the hospital I got my wounds cleaned, received a tetanus shot and waited for the driver to take me to St. Theresa. During the 4-hour wait, my aunt and I had a good discussion about having sex and dealing with the guilt. I love my aunt. She was very calm about the whole thing. She was in the medical profession. She actually worked in the ER at that hospital, so she had seen a lot.

The driver came and put me in the backseat of the car. There was a metal barrier between the front and back seats, like in police cars. The driver seemed very nice and tried to make conversation, but I didn't say a word. I pretended to sleep in the backseat the whole trip.

Once I got through the familiar intake procedures, I was shown to my room. It had two twin beds with peach-colored bedspreads. I had the room to myself. During the night I hid under the bed and hid in the closet. I felt I needed to hide from the staff. And I cried.

The next day my roommate arrived. She was young, around 17 or 18, with long, dark hair and a small, gold cross around her neck. Cecilia was her name. In my great wisdom I diagnosed her with Paranoid Schizophrenia. I didn't speak with her all day, but when night came and it was time to go to bed, she told me to leave the light on.

"It has to be left on all night," she said. "Otherwise the devil will suck your soul out." She would not stop talking about how the devil sucks people's souls out. She was scaring me, but I tried not to let on that she was scaring me.

I casually took my blanket and walked out to the hallway to the nurses' station. Cecilia followed me like a shadow. "I need to sleep in a different room," I whispered to the nurses.

"Okay," the nurse says, loud and clear, "let's see if there is another room available." *Great, now Cecilia knows I'm trying to avoid her. I hope she doesn't start stalking me.* I got my own room, and the rest of the night was quiet.

The next couple of days were filled with scouring the rooms in search of items with which to cause myself harm. I felt obsessed with my surroundings. I analyzed everything in sight, from the non-glass mirrors to the bed frame to the plastic forks. There wasn't a moment that went by that I wasn't thinking about a possible means to harm or kill myself.

I had talked with Terri on the phone. I was so angry with her by the time I hung up. It felt like she could see right through me. She spoke to me as if she knew I was capable of more, or, in other words, capable of less drama. I couldn't see it, didn't want to see it. My mind was on one track and one track only – ending this existence.

I was placed in open seclusion. This means I wasn't locked in, but I was on close watch. "Patient continues to be restless and unable to contract not to harm herself. Inability and lack of response to direction by staff. Patient seeking continued means to harm self. Patient isolative and depressed in affect," wrote those observing me.

Something happened that day that changed my attitude. The tool that did it – communication. I wanted so desperately to hurt myself, maybe even kill myself. It's more punishment, though, to *live* with the pain. I was amazed and angered that I could not find a single instrument with which to accomplish this. Everything was locked, plastic, or bolted down. I was angry at the room, angry at myself for wanting to hurt myself, and very worn out by dealing with this tug-of-war situation. I cried. I wanted to die and I begged for life. COMMUNICATE!!!

I pressed the nurses' button in the room. A male nurse arrived. I felt very resistant at first, being that the nurse was a man. However, I decided to go for it. I talked about sex, religion, guilt, being a drama actress, a whole set of issues. I realized then what a huge, huge issue my religion had been in the past and still was at present.

Religion was a touchy subject for me. I was always ashamed to talk about my religion, then I was ashamed I was ashamed. As I spoke with the nurse, I took a chance. It seems like such a small thing, but it was a tremendous step for me. *He* wasn't ashamed to talk about God. He was understanding and reasonable. What a relief! My first reaction, though, was to ignore his words, to fight to not be "corrupted by Satan's tactics." I heard the voice of my mother in my head. But I let go.

I talked about feeling so trapped. I felt so awful I simply wanted to die. God is supposed to be Love. Here I am suffering. Where is the love? How much longer must I suffer?! I cannot even escape the suffering through death at my own hands, for suicide is a grave disrespect for life. So I wouldn't be resurrected to Paradise? But wouldn't God have pity on me and understand my state and want my suffering to end? Maybe I didn't even want to be resurrected! Maybe I didn't want to live in a place with a God who allowed the world to be in the state it is and couldn't understand my current desperation and have mercy. I didn't know anymore…

I listened and pondered what the nurse said. For the first time, I came to see things differently. Perhaps there is a bigger picture than the one Jehovah's Witnesses see. An indescribable feeling! I didn't totally abandon my faith, but I did come to the conclusion that God is perfect, humans are not, their interpretation of God is not. Each person is unique and I should not expect a given set of rules to apply to all. Only God knows our deepest thoughts.

The nurse and I also spoke about finding different ways to "punish" myself. Of course the goal was to eventually not have to feel I needed to punish myself, but for now, one step at a time. He spoke of exercising, "feeling the burn." "But I want to *see* the pain, *see* the suffering," I said.

"Then video your arm and hit rewind," he replied. I had to laugh at that one.

My next step was to reexamine where I stood on the religion issue. I figured religion or faith/beliefs could be used as a life-saving tool, but it could also be used as a very lethal weapon. It must be used properly. I needed to find solid ground.

Another goal was to believe not all men are pigs. I needed to find men who are not pigs, like the nurse, and talk with them, get to know them. I still wrestled with a feeling, though, that underneath that kind exterior, they could be abusing their own children. Another goal: deal with sex.

The next day I was moved back into the room with Cecilia. By this time, she had been medicated. She talked to me, stating how when she first got to the hospital she heard herself talking about the devil and couldn't figure out why she was talking that way. She couldn't control it. I guess the medication was helping.

Nighttime came. Cecilia was out in the "day room" watching television with some of the other patients. I was alone in the room with the lights off. I felt extremely anxious, like I needed to hurt myself once again. There I sat…on the cold, cement floor in just my underwear and thin hospital gown, with my back pressed firmly against the oak door, listening to the blood pounding in my ears…

Chapter 12

Red and Black

In the frigid darkness and the warmth of my bed,
I lie alone
The sounds of those with me are obtrusive, deafening
With futile hands I clutch my ears,
Attempting to drown out the noise –
Only in vain
I have to acknowledge defeat in order for them to cease
Merciless pummeling of my intestines,
Brutal stabbings to the head
To murder the blackness and silence the uproar,
Life gushes forth from my outer wrapping
(Defeating its primary purpose)
Enveloped in a rich, crimson flow,
Freeing drops of past, present, and future
Death, crouching below with eager hands, awaits each one

※   ※   ※

I agree, upon leaving the hospital for the second time, to join group therapy for depression. So I meet with the therapist for a screening at the county health agency, then a week later, I attend the session. Let me tell you, there is nothing more depressing than to be in a room full of depressed people! I decide to not go back to any more group sessions. Individual therapy suits me fine.

Two months later I have a session with Terri that seems to go very poorly. I tell her how I intend to hurt myself. "I don't think I can leave. You don't think I'm serious," I say.

"I do too," she replies. I expect her to call my family, friends, the police…somebody, but she doesn't, and the session ends. I am so angry! I still intend to hurt myself and the anger only fuels it.

My plan begins. Once I begin my plan, I feel I *must* finish it or else I am not taken seriously, and I feel I lose. I decide to go to a nearby hospital. I go to this particular hospital for two reasons: 1. I hear it's a good place for psychiatric conditions, and 2. Terri is on staff there.

I don't know where it is located exactly, so I stop at a phone booth to find the address. After looking at the address, I still don't know where it is, so I go to a gas station and look at a map. By now I feel less angry and less determined, but I have already begun and I must carry it out to the finish.

I find the hospital. I park my car in the parking lot. I am sure there is a razorblade in my car, so I begin searching every inch for it. It is a rusty, old razorblade that I have had in my car for several months, but for some reason I cannot locate it now. During my search, I notice an ambulance parked near the doors, not too far from my car. I give up on the razorblade search, figuring I must have taken it out at some point, and begin to look for something else.

I have a tiny, dull pocketknife. I try to sharpen it against a piece of metal under my seat. I start cutting myself on my left wrist. The ambulance drives by. It's not bleeding much, so I have to cut until I have enough blood to make it look serious. Finally, it's bleeding fairly well. I grab a dirty napkin, which is all there is, to hold on it so blood doesn't get on my good clothes. Some blood has spattered on my shirt, sad to say.

I climb out of the car and walk into the hospital with the dirty napkin on my wrist. I am shaking from nerves. I say nothing. I simply show the woman at the desk. She calls somebody to come down. A woman arrives and escorts me to a tiny room with nothing but a small table, two chairs and a garbage can. The woman starts asking me questions. I, still with knife in hand, proceed to cut on myself more. Now I feel that it is no longer I that is acting this way. It is as if someone has taken over my body while I've checked out.

After several slices, the woman observes what I am doing and takes the knife away. 911 is called. An ambulance arrives that will transport me to the county hospital. I enter the ambulance and sit down where I am told to sit. I hesitate to fasten the seatbelt myself because of the blood on my hands. One of the paramedics does it for me. She says the blood doesn't matter. I think to myself, "*How could it not matter that I would get blood on the seat? That means someone would have to clean and sanitize it. Better to not have to do that, right?*"

The paramedic asks me why I cut myself. "I wanted to," I say.

"My partner saw you in the parking lot sawing away at your arm," she continues. I was hoping no one actually saw that. I didn't reply.

Once at the hospital, it is the usual routine. The cuts are examined and disinfected, then I wait forever. I am then taken by ambulance just across the street to the psychiatric unit of the hospital. I wait there forever as well. At first I could have left. The cuts were superficial. However, by the time I say, "Can I change my mind and just go home now?" it is too late. Around 11:00pm the driver arrives to transport me to St. Theresa.

I enter St. Theresa with the plan of leaving within a day or two. "Don't worry, I won't be here long," I tell the nurses as I get buzzed through the door that opens onto 3rd South.

The following day the nurses say to me, "Tell us when you want to cut on yourself." Yeah, right. I'm in my room, overwhelmed with anxiety, pacing, heart racing. "Tell us when you want to cut on yourself." If I tell, I can't cut, thus finding no relief. It's a quandary. I don't want to exit the room, so I press the nurses' button. I crawl into the bathroom adjoining my room, with sharp object in hand, fighting back the urge, and wait for the nurse to arrive.

A woman I haven't seen before comes. I'm crying. She asks, "What's going on?"

I slide the sharp object over to her and say, "Do you know how hard it was not to cut myself?!"

"No, I guess I don't," she replies. *At least she told the truth,* I thought. She says she will be back in a minute and leaves.

An hour, maybe two hours, later I still feel like cutting on myself. *I didn't get any relief the last time by that woman, so I will have to cut myself first, then press the nurses' button*, I reason. I am getting these sharp objects from the heater filter, same as last time. I find it terribly interesting that I am put in the exact same room where I cut my finger two months ago. I can still see the dried blood on part of the heater filter.

With the piece of metal I proceed to cut my mid-arm, trying to open the large artery. It isn't working, so I try to bore a hole, hoping to puncture the artery. Frustrated that this isn't doing the trick either, I throw a couple meaningless slashes elsewhere on my arm, then resume working on the artery.

A nurse arrives. "Why didn't you tell us you were having these urges?" she asks.

"I did."

The nurse says that the woman I called earlier was from a different department and "not used to these sort of things." Well, that is fine, but no help to me!

Time passes, day after day. During the daytime I am okay. After nightfall, something happens. I grab the sharp pieces of metal and cut away. I cut on my left wrist, horizontally, vertically, every which way. Then I go to work on my right ring finger again, like two months ago, hoping I will lose a lot of blood, maybe even need stitches. Sarah comes in. "She's done it again!"

One evening I am in my room with the light off. It is dark. I feel very anxious and scared. I don't want anyone to see me, and I don't want to speak to anyone. I know "rounds" will be in a few minutes, so I position myself as a barricade against the door. A nurse comes to the door, calls my name, then uses her key, perhaps thinking it got locked by accident. She calls for a second nurse to help. "She's barricaded the door!" I hear. They both push, I push back, and the door doesn't budge. "She's strong!" the second nurse says. They call for a third nurse.

After some struggling, the three nurses get the door open. I fall to the floor in tears. I still feel so scared. I must go to seclusion for my actions. I don't want to go, of course. "Code Strong" is called because the three nurses are unable to move me, and they don't want to get hurt in the process.

Before "Code Strong" arrives, Sarah says to me, "This behavior is ridiculous. Be a big girl and walk in there."

"I don't want to be a 'big girl'," I retort.

"She's just doing it for the attention. She wants to have to be carried in there kicking and screaming so all the other patients can see her," she continues.

"I am not!" I reply, in pure childlike manner.

"Then prove it, and stand up and walk in there on your own two feet!" So I do, angrily.

In seclusion, I hate being watched. I discover there is one small area, about 3' x 2', in a corner of the room that is not visible from the viewpoint of standing at the door, looking at the room through the convex mirror. I am not seen if I lie down in this very spot. So this is where I sleep. The cement floor is very hard and cold, but it is worth it. The nurses have to open the door, take a few steps into the room and turn to check on me.

I also like staying in the bathroom as much as possible. It is here that I try to tear apart the zipper to my pants to create an object with which to cut on myself, since there is no heating unit in the seclusion room. A nurse comes in and asks what I am doing. "Nothing," as I throw the pants away. It wasn't working anyway. Later I tear apart the toilet paper dispenser, finding a perfect tool to do slicing and have at it. I keep trying to tear away at that inviting artery.

One morning, at breakfast, I find a familiar face, a fellow patient I had seen on my first hospital visit. Gracie is an African-American woman in her late twenties/early thirties, I'd say, with wild, bushy hair in need of taming. She may be older, for there are a few gray hairs casually dispersed throughout the do. Whatever her true age, I get the sense that she is very young. Though Gracie is a tall and large woman, she reminds me of a little person, even a toddler. She has a child-like gait and has an air about her of needing constant attention. She talks with the nurses often, asking for things and trying to be special. She *is* special. Gracie is known by the nurses, known because she is a regular here at the hospital. I didn't realize this on my first visit, but I did see that she has had a long career as a mental patient upon first glace of the many stories carved out upon her arms.

Gracie's arms are what catch my attention first. They are what I will remember forever and most clearly. Ten years from now I may not be able to recognize her face or even her frizzed-out hairdo, but I would be able to pick her arms out of a line-up any day. To put it simply, they are shocking.

The stories carved out on Gracie's arms are stories of great pain and suffering. The marks on my own arms, though plentiful (one for each year of my life), look like chicken scratches compared to hers. My God, is that what will become of me? Is that what I have to look forward to?

Gracie's scars are pale in color, creating a contrast that draws my attention even more. The raised ridges snake around both the underside and the topside of her forearms. The slashes criss-cross this way and that, forming a morbidly beautiful lattice-work of abused flesh. Some scars have faded with age, some are fresh. How many years has this woman succumbed to this dreadful impulse? How many years will I...?

I can't believe it, she's back again! I think. I am back, too. What a coincidence that she and I are at St. Theresa again at the same time. Perhaps the odds aren't that high.

We say hi to each other, and ask how each other is doing. She doesn't say it in so many words, but I can tell by the sound of her voice, which is partly sad, partly relieved, partly happy, that she will be staying for a while here at St. Theresa. St. Theresa, where Gracie can receive attention, where Gracie can be known, where Gracie can be special.

I imagine Gracie every few months walking through the doors of 3rd South with a security guard on one arm and blood-soaked gauze bandages on the other. She heaves a great sigh of relief in this parallel world that tries so hard to resemble the real thing but never quite makes it, thank goodness! She sighs, for now she can recoup and for a few days forget about the pain in the world and the pain within that prompted her to carve the latest story using a knife as her chisel and her flesh as the stone.

I think of Gracie, and I wonder how I will manage to get past the cutting and learn healthier ways to deal with the pain. Gracie keeps coming back, and here I am again, too. How can I move on? What will enable me to do that? The pain is there, stirring under the surface. What will enable me, no, what will *prevent* me from slashing through that top layer, digging and chiseling into my own flesh to let out the demons? What will prevent me from showing the world my own carved-out stories of great pain and suffering?

One afternoon I am assigned to a male nurse who is the most boring person one could ever meet. I ask to switch to a new nurse, not because of his boring personality, though that would be enough, but because he is a he. I get Trisha, the female nurse who accompanied me to the ER to get my finger sewed up during my previous stay.

I communicate to Trisha the stages I go through. I decide to do this prior to it getting dark. The stages are: 1. I become nervous and agitated. 2. I become isolative. 3. I tend to hide. 4. I become totally or almost completely quiet or mute. 5. I hurt myself.

Later that evening, feeling anxious, I alert her. I agree to sit in the day room for 15 minutes with some other patients to see if I still feel anxious afterwards. While I am in the day room, I gather whatever sharp objects I can find, already planning stage 5. After my 15 minutes are up, I go to my room. I tell Trisha I have 5 objects in my pockets. She doesn't take them away, like I expect her to do. Instead, she talks about taking responsibility and control.

My stages continue to progress through the evening. I find my chance and sneak into the shower, leaving the light off. The anxiety is just too great. While in the shower, I cry and I ask a lot of questions, and I make resolutions. Even though I only know Trisha as my nurse, I do not want to let her down. She put the control in my hands. She trusts me. "I am going to quit allowing myself to lose control," I tell myself. It is past due to take responsibility for my actions. "I'm not going to make *this* my life!"

Trisha opens the door. "I didn't do it…I didn't…cut myself!" I force out between the sobs.

"She didn't do it," she tells the other nurses, who act as if they fully expected me to. But who can blame them considering the last several days.

Something seems different now. The shower incident feels like a major accomplishment!

The following evening I switch nurses to Sarah. I had wanted to talk with her since I first arrived, but she was never my nurse. It is nighttime again, and I'm feeling scared. I feel like I need someone around me, so I press the nurses' button.

I am curled in a fetal position completely under the covers. Sarah comes. She thinks I need to feel secure right now (which I do), so she tucks me in tightly. After a moment she says, "No, we need to get you out of this bed." I suppose she realizes this after recalling my previous behavior that occurred after nightfall. Sarah then assists me out of the covers. She sits alongside the bed. I have my head resting on her lap, still in a fetal position.

I am making subtle sounds that indicate I am in pain, and my body is trying its best to protect itself by being curled up as tight as possible. In my head I hear a sound of flesh and wetness. "I hate this sound!" I say out loud.

"Stay right here," she says and gets up to leave. Sarah comes back a few minutes later with Haldol. I refuse to take it. The last time I took a major tranquilizer, I was knocked out for 2 full days. Besides, I knew what I was hearing was in my head.

Sarah leaves again and brings back a rolling office chair. She asks me to sit in it. Despite my efforts to remain in the fetal position and wanting to just go to the floor, she talks me into sitting in the chair.

I'm sitting in the chair, hunched over. Sarah says, "Repeat this out loud, 'I am not going to be a victim any longer.'" I say it, even though it doesn't mean much to me. "You've probably never said that to yourself before in your life, have you?" she asks. No. "You are not going to remain in this victim's position," she continues.

I'm bent over in the chair, practically in a sitting fetal position, and Sarah tells me to sit up. I can't do it, it's too hard. She then says, "You wanted me as your nurse, so you are just going to have to trust in my judgment." Sarah gives a gentle push on my shoulders so that I am sitting up straight in the chair. At this, I let out a scream-wail and start sobbing, as I bend back over towards the floor. "Good, let's do it again!" Sarah says, getting emotional herself. I sit up again and continue to sob. I can't take it anymore, so I crawl back onto the bed, crying. "You can either stay in here, isolate yourself, and remain a victim, or you can come out and sit by the nurses' station and change this," she tells me.

After a few minutes of crying on the bed, I wrap a blanket around myself and venture out of my room and sit by the nurses' station. Sarah comes out from behind the station with a caring, understanding smile and says, "I'm proud of you." Exhausted, I force a smile in return. Another breakthrough. I need not be a victim the rest of my life. Also, I have to exert effort, though it is very difficult and intense, to change things.

These two realizations bring about improvement rather quickly. A couple days later, I talk one of the nurses into giving me a rubber glove so I can make a balloon. I couldn't have a pencil prior to this, let alone a dangerous weapon like a rubber glove! Trust is restored.

The driver comes, picks me up, and I begin my journey home.

Excerpts from the Discharge Summary

<u>Present Illness</u>: The patient is a 21-year-old female admitted for her third St. Theresa psychiatric hospitalization. The patient apparently went to a local hospital seeking help and while there superficially cut her wrists and stated that she wanted to die. She complained of persistent suicidal thoughts and that her thoughts were racing as well as significantly confused. She was struggling with significant self esteem issues in the sense that she felt like a failure in life and had no further motivation to try to succeed. She stated that she had been living "a self fulfilling prophecy" in that she was so convinced in her own mind that she could not succeed at anything that that is how her life was in fact turning out. She recently had to drop out of school because of poor focus, and she also lost her job at the time of her last psychiatric hospitalization earlier this year. She reports that she is preoccupied with dying and suicidal thoughts. She has been living with her sister and brother-in-law who are having problems with the patient because of her mood disorder. The patient was admitted to the acute adult locked psychiatric unit for her safety and for further treatment.

<u>Hospital Course</u>: The patient tended to be labile and isolative during the early phase of hospitalization. She would have periods of time where she was virtually catatonic and mute. She would frequently engage in bizarre behavior such as sleeping on the floor or crawling around on the floor and under furniture. She reported that this behavior was an attempt to "find some peace and privacy." She was not judged to be psychotic. She was felt to be depressed. On several occasions during this hospitalization she further superficially scratched herself with sharp objects. Toward the end of her hospitalization her mood brightened and her bizarre behaviors as well as self-destructive behaviors diminished. At this point in time it is felt reasonable and safe for the patient to continue treatment on an outpatient basis.

<u>Discharge Diagnosis</u>:

Axis I.   Major depression, recurrent, with self-destructive behavior.

Axis II. Borderline personality disorder.

Axis III. Superficial self-inflicted lacerations. No other acute somatic pathology.

Axis IV. Moderate.

<u>Discharge Condition</u>: Improved   <u>Prognosis</u>: Good.

Chapter 13

Two days before being discharged from the hospital, I was taken off of Luvox and put on a low dosage of Prozac, 20mg per day. I guess the doctor felt I needed a change, since Luvox did not appear to be doing its job. He had written upon my discharge that I tolerated this medication well and hinted that because of it I showed marked improvement. I do not know how he could have come to that conclusion since I had only been on the medication two days. There was no mention by the doctor of the work of the nurses or my realizations having anything to do with my improved condition.

The two doses I took in the hospital are the last two doses, I decide. I am un-medicating myself. Yes, it is time for a change.

%   %   %

I feel unwhole. If I were a puzzle, there would be many pieces missing. I am confused about my behavior. I used to be such a "good girl." I feel it is related to childhood abuse, but it is only a vague notion. I feel I remember the majority of the events that transpired with my cousin, but perhaps I am wrong, and more happened there that I have blocked out. Or perhaps there was someone else. *There's more than one,* I hear a voice speak. I don't know the source of the voice, probably just my imagination.

I feel pain in my vaginal area each night as I try to sleep. I feel suffocated by a weight on my chest, making it impossible to breathe. I must sit up or stand up to make the suffocating feeling go away. I do not sleep. I know from therapy that these are "bodily memories." But memories of what?! At 3:04am I lie awake, trying to recollect, trying to dig down into the darkness to shed some light on my life, my past. I feel when people look at me, they see only a handful of pieces thrown together, mismatched this way and that, with gaping holes of blackness in between. How am I ever going to find the rest of the pieces and then know how to put them back together?

%% %% %%

A Sleepless Night

In company with only the fish
Of those who are left awake
I lie here
Obsessing over the most bizarre of things –
Of dreams past,
Nightmares unclear,
Reciting poems I have never read,
Simply words swirling around and penned
On the tablet of my mind:

"A black box with no beginning, simply an end
Exploding forth through its tiny holes
Is the liquid of the past
Unable to retreat at its own speed, for the force behind it
Merely able to catch just one stream
While the remaining six gush to the floor

The splashings of those lost still longer
Coupled with my own impatience
Produces a sound that is intense and deafening."

At present, locked in a time not my own,
Rather of one just read about
Using a language that moves inside,
Yet halts at the opening of my mouth,
Coming out the common one
Not a suspicion aroused
No symbols, no illusions;
A poem of literal words this proves to be

Resentfully, I rise and give life to these feelings
Preventing self-maim and being left for dead

※　　※　　※

I have a therapy session with my sister and brother-in-law. Much to my dismay I must sign yet another contract. In it, I agree that when I need to talk with someone, I will:

1. Stay with people.
2. Stay out of my room.
3. Write a note to my sister.
4. Talk with my sister.
5. Call the emergency psychiatric services number.
6. Call Terri.
7. Paint/draw/write.

I will only do numbers 6 and 7. My family does not understand me. I feel they are merely putting up with me at this point. No one visited me in the hospital during the last stay. I guess they are getting used to me being "crazy." I have found that writing is the thing that keeps me going. I'll even go so far as say writing keeps me alive much of the time. In this contract, I also agree to start changing my style of life. No hiding.

During the next few months, I read every book under the sun on sexual abuse – autobiographical, self-help and clinical textbook. As I read through the pages, I see that I fit 99% of the criteria that would describe one who was abused. Yet, I still have doubts. I don't remember! I also read to understand the therapeutic and treatment process that I am going through, as a way to analyze myself and have a more knowledgeable role in my treatment.

I go back and forth numerous times trying to figure out if I should continue therapy. Sometimes I feel like it is working, other times not. I have family members telling me that I need to quit, that I just need to start going back to the religious meetings. I feel pulled in two directions.

I blame Terri for when I feel bad. During the week, things start looking up, my mood feels better. Then I have a therapy session, and I feel like death warmed over. I get so angry at her for ruining a perfectly good week.

After a while I realize that I am the one responsible for how I'm feeling. Where previously I would simply feel sorry for myself, I now start to take control of my life and feelings. It seems ridiculous that I didn't see this earlier, but I had myself caught in a web.

The work in therapy becomes a delicate balance of trying to keep me functioning in daily life while also exploring the root of my symptoms. I feel like the actual therapy sessions don't get anywhere at times, a lot of times, because I just become quiet and dissociative. However, I write about it afterward. From these writings there is slightly more clarity, or at the very least, a voice. I then bring these writings into the therapy sessions and share. Movement happens, though slowly.

I am feeling alone, alone in the sense of different and separated from everyone near me. I feel thrown back into toddler-hood. I know nothing; I have nothing. I have very poor social skills. I do not know how to communicate effectively. I request people to speak the truth but I deny, ignore, or simply close my ears when they comply. I ask for suggestions, I don't take them. I think that I am always right while everyone else is wrong. I keep everything inside and though I yearn to speak out, I just cower in the corner in fear. I yearn to know *how* to speak out. I cannot speak my feelings! Half the time I cannot even *feel* my feelings. I am stone – cold and heartless. I feel as though I am yet again four years old, and I am trying so desperately to speak. I know what I am trying to say, but it won't come out right and no one understands, leaving me frustrated and in tears.

It is now springtime, the flowers are blooming, the sun is shining, the air is fresh and fragrant with new life. I am still in the cold darkness of winter, sitting in Terri's office at the end of a session, and I'm not leaving. I am "deliberately" breaking the contract I had signed earlier. I am suicidal, yes, but I'm not to the point of actually killing myself. Or am I?

Because of my not leaving the office on time, the poor patient who is scheduled after me has to reschedule his appointment. Terri calls the cops. I figure I'll leave before they arrive. I just want Terri to know how much pain I am in.

I go to the floor and curl up in a ball when Terri leaves the room to see if the cops have arrived yet. This is breaking the second part of the contract. I know Terri will not refer me, but she is giving the impression that she will. Somehow I know she won't, because that is not what will be best for me.

I figure the cops will be arriving any moment now, so I begin to get up. It is very difficult. My body feels dead and now I'm crying. It's too late, they are here. Terri and the two men step through the office doorway. Terri says, "I know what you're doing!" That's great, because I sure don't. She asks the cops to step out for a minute, then comes up close to me and says again, "I know what you're doing. You're breaking the contract so you can go kill yourself!" So that's it. Interesting. I think about it, then I say through my tears, "It isn't me! It isn't me!!!" I would never dream of such a thing as getting in trouble with the law. I feel like it's all just a dream.

The cops come back in and try to reason with me. I am trespassing and the doctor wants me out, they explain. "If you don't move, we will be forcibly removing you." I start to stand up, and one of the cops grabs me by the arm. I want to do it myself! "Don't fight!" the cops say.

"Just don't touch me and I'll go. Don't touch me!" I tell them. They don't listen. I'm crying still, and being partially dragged, partially walking. "Just don't touch me!" I say again. I cannot stand to have their hands on me. I'm perfectly willing to walk out on my own. I hate that they are man-handling me. Surely Terri will step in, knowing my history and say it would be better if they just let me leave on my own, without forcing or touching, but no. She just stands back in the corner, away, not helping. How can she disappoint me and not care?! Perhaps because I am doing the same to her.

We go into the conference room next door. I sit on the floor. The cops threaten to arrest me. They say I cannot stay in the room, that I have to go out and get in my car, go completely out of the building. They tell me that Terri told them that I am going to kill myself. I deny it. Sure, I feel really really bad, but this is common. I'm not going to kill myself. I get up, reluctantly, walk out of the building and drive away. They let me go! Ha ha ha ha! I can't believe they let me go!

At our next scheduled session, Terri tells me how she realizes that referral would not be the best. Abandoning me would be just that. She tells how she feels I would not take the time to get to know another therapist, and I probably would kill myself if she calls it quits. I've been with Terri a little over two years by this point. So Terri goes back on her word, but it is therapeutically for the best, ironically. She will not be like everyone else and be chased away by my attempts to make people abandon me! She will hang in there and try a different route.

Again I put her in an extremely difficult situation. She is probably right. In fact, I know she is right. There is no way I would find another therapist. With no one to listen and try to understand me, I would have nothing to hold me back from ending my life, except, perhaps, writing. The amount of gratitude I feel for this woman is indescribable.

Terri's plan is to hold my sessions in the conference room across the hall. So that is where we meet. For the next few months, the sessions go pretty well, except for the time I throw a screaming fit, and the other time where I bang my head against the wall. But other than that, therapy continues as usual, and Terri remains despite me trying to push her to her very limits.

I decide to sign up for a few classes at the Junior College for the summer session. It is difficult to get back in the swing of things, but I plug forward. I have to withdraw from one course, but I manage to complete two courses.

I also get a job, after 6 months of being on disability, at a watch and jewelry repair service located in a department store. The pace of work is very slow, not what I am used to. It feels too slow, almost achingly so, and I quit after only three weeks. I get hired on at Safeway, but I immediately start having problems with my back and cannot work. I quit after only a week, and I beg for my other job back. The woman who supervises the watch and jewelry repair department, Karen, comes to my defense when speaking with her boss, enabling me to get re-hired. "I don't think this is a pattern for her," Karen explains. "I think she was just confused and deserves a second chance."

❧   ❧   ❧

The following is a self-examination report, a homework assignment given to me by myself. The subject is signs and symptoms that point to a childhood traumatic experience, particularly incest. There are 10 main areas, or symptoms, discussed in this report. Each has a brief explanation, an example or two, then a chance to ponder whether it would stem from early childhood sexual abuse or not. The following list is generally in the order of occurrence, except where some symptoms appeared simultaneously.

1. ANXIETY (from before age 10 to present):
    As a child, I remember constantly being sick to my stomach. Mother said that I was anemic and gave me vitamins with iron to take. I don't know if it helped or not. I know now that I am not anemic. Maybe all of my nervous episodes were from genuine physical problems. However, it seems that there were many days where there was no physical explanation for my sick stomach other than, "Are you taking your vitamins?"
    The many days that I feel nauseous now, I know are from anxiety. I have a very "nervous stomach." Occasionally I find myself driving down the street and suddenly being struck with an extreme case of anxiety and feeling so ill that I believe I might throw up. I can usually find the trigger to it, but I cannot figure out *why* it made me so anxious. I am always dreading something, but I'm not sure what that something is.

2. CHILDHOOD SEXUAL ACTING OUT (from 8-10 years):
    Somewhere between the ages of eight and ten, many sexual activities transpired between my cousin and me. I believe I was talked into, but not forced or coerced into these acts. This is something that I remember vividly and would very much like to forget.
    At around the same time, another cousin took advantage of my inability to protest. I recall only two incidents with the second cousin. A few years later there was an incident with an older teenager in a swimming pool, in which he tried to put his hands up under my bathing suit bottom, and wanted me to go into his hotel room with him. I was so scared that I was frozen and shaking profusely, barely able to speak. I got out of that situation, however.

I figure one of two things "caused" these incidents. One, I was a shy, gullible kid who could be taken advantage of too easily. Or two, there was some form of sexual abuse in my early childhood that led me to be more "uninhibited" sexually to later occurrences, or led me to be identified as "easy prey" by abusers.

3. LACK OF EMOTION (from about age 10 to present):

This is hard to explain because it's not a lack of all emotion, just certain ones, like sadness and anger. There seems to be a great many years when I rarely, if ever, shed a tear, and was ashamed if I did. I remember two crying episodes between the ages of ten and eighteen. The first episode was when one of the goats on our farm died. It seemed to suffer tremendously before it died, and we never could figure out what was wrong with it. I couldn't stand to watch it anymore, so I escaped into the house just minutes before it expired. I bawled and bawled, punched my fists into the pillow and bed and kept asking, "Why?" That would be the final time I ever truly expressed my anger.

The second episode was when I heard of my grandfather's death. It was kind of an odd experience. My dad was the one who notified me as I was standing at the kitchen counter writing something. His voice broke in mid-sentence. With my back still to him, I froze, not knowing what to think. A tear hit the paper I was writing on, and I was surprised, because I didn't feel it fall, though I knew it had to have come from me. I then walked quickly into the bathroom, closed the door and wept silently for about 5 minutes, hoping no one heard. I mourned much more intensely for my goat than my own grandfather.

I remained dry-eyed the remainder of the 8-year span. Just because I shed few tears didn't mean I was happy. It was a very distant and recessed period in my life. I will even go so far as saying regressed.

4. VIEW OF MEN (from about age 11 to present, gaining strength as time passed):

I hate men. Too bad those words don't do my feelings justice. I don't think any words could accurately describe my feelings about the male of the species. Words don't go deep enough. I don't think my view of men has ever changed, as in from good to bad. I have never felt positively about them. Rather, it has been from bad to worse. Why am I so vehement? Give me one, just one, thing that men are good for. Nothing comes to my mind.

5. INTERPERSONAL PROBLEMS – TRUST, AFFECTION, AND THE "WALL" (from age 12 to present):

A person just doesn't start having problems relating to others, it begins probably minutes after birth. I chose to put 12 years old as the beginning, because that is when I noticed marked changes in my relationship with others. At this age I made a vow to my mother and myself that I was going to be the "perfect" child. I was going to make up for all the "bad" things that my siblings had done and that I had done in the past.

As the years passed, I was living up to these unreasonable expectations. One problem, though, as mentioned earlier, was a regressed state of self. I stuck to my mother like glue. With the incidences involving my cousin, I had lost her trust in me, and now I was going to earn it back. I must have been afraid that I was going to lose her somehow. I craved affection, more than the average teenager, more than the average infant, mainly at nighttime, just before bed. I didn't want to go to sleep and be left all alone. I would hang on my mother, begging her not to go to bed. This irritated her, but I couldn't help it.

I eventually "out grew" that embarrassing period of my life. I then did just the opposite and distanced myself from all adults, especially my mom, harboring deep resentment toward her for being such a "horrible" mother. She would reach to give me a kiss, and I would shrink away and run.

Debbie was the first to notice the ugly wall I had built for myself. She attempted to help tear it down, to no avail. The wall was worn a little thinner in spots, though, allowing a keen eye to catch small glimpses of what lie on the other side. Our close friendship ended with her frustrated and my wall left very much intact – trust no one.

6. VIEW OF SEX (from about age 13 to present):

Sexual Aversion Disorder. I like the sound of that. It is in the category of sexual desire disorders. It involves an extreme distaste for sexual contact with another person. The mere thought of having sex is repugnant and often causes phobic anxiety. Engaging in sex causes extreme disgust. I would have to say that about sums it up.

The penis is an ugly thing, but it can be wielded, much like a sword, and great power and control can be experienced over the male by doing such. Afterwards, the guilt can be so intense that taking your own life is a welcomed idea.

7. DEPRESSION (beginning about age 17):

Seeing the future as hopeless and oneself as helpless leads to a very black hole. That hole is depression. In the darkest times, I can't sleep, eat, get out of bed, shower, or even move, much less work or go to school. I figure I will die soon, even if I don't kill myself. I feel like I am dying, more like already dead. Nonexistence, zeroness, is constantly on the mind. I don't ever want to be in that darkest place again.

8. NIGHTMARES (from ages 19 ½ to 21):

Sex, often accompanied by violence, permeated my dream life. Whether violent or not, it was always welling up anxious and frightening feelings in me that lasted up to days afterward. Some dreams were bloody and violent without the sexual aspect. Each night would contain two or three nightmares. All this together led to a fear and dislike for sleep.

9. DISSOCIATION AND DEPERSONALIZATION (from 19 ½ to present):

A thing like dissociation does not all of a sudden begin at age 19 when nothing "significant" happened at that age. However, that is when my "fading spells" were named. Unlike many problems of mine, I did not "diagnose myself" on this one. That may be one of the reasons I still doubt the diagnosis from time to time. The condition is believed to be caused by severe trauma, particularly extreme physical and/or sexual abuse.

Dissociation involves an alteration of consciousness that results in a severe disturbance of personality functioning and a disruption of the usual mental organization. Depersonalization is a feeling of being unreal, as if in a dream. One might feel that one can see himself or herself from a distance. This is a very common feeling for me. My dissociating goes further than just feeling unreal at times. I am not able to describe it all at this point, but with continued self-examination I feel I'm getting closer.

10. SELF-DESTRUCTIVE BEHAVIOR (beginning at age 20):

There were many, many occurrences, one of which was destroying a heater filter (the sharpest object I could get my hands on), bleeding like a stuck pig, and requiring stitches. Also considered self-destructive was setting myself up to have sex, even though I didn't really want to, so I could feel so guilty later on that I would want to kill myself.

It all goes back to the anxiety. There exists an entangled mass formed out of an extremely intricate substance in my mind. It is what gives fuel to the obsessive thoughts. This mass is also behind other occurrences that manifest themselves in ways hard to describe. It is a busy sensation, never at rest. It apparently orbits the core of my existence because there are certain times that it is closer to consciousness, more intensely felt. The majority of the time, it remains far into the dark recesses.

All of these descriptions bring images to one's mind to aid in understanding, but don't keep it superficial by allowing them to remain mere images. It's not the images I want you to absorb, but feelings. It is this *feeling*, which lies *behind* the anxiety, the obsessive thoughts, the strange sensation of hearing something that produces no noise, that also lies behind the self-destructive behavior. This feeling has no name.

CONCLUSION:

What has resulted from this self-study is not what was originally expected. I thought I would be able to make a decision, one way or the other, whether or not there was incest involved in my early childhood. That remains unanswered. I will take a guess and say there probably was not. Some people consider what happened with my cousin to be abuse, or incest. If that is the case, then I am an abuse victim and all these "symptoms" can be explained away by those occurrences. I feel, however, that the situation with him was not traumatic. Argue if you will.

A question arises: How well do we know ourselves? Are gut feelings and intuitions to be relied upon? If I say that there is "something" very confusing and powerful exerting tremendous pressure on my sanity, am I to brush it off as an active imagination and over-dramatization, or do I take it seriously…?

Chapter 14

Unholy Copulation

I fear the colored world that invades my neutral body. I raise my pale face to the sun. Arms outstretched and mouth wide open, yellow pours in, filling me. Blood-filled red takes in the light, savors it, then swallows it down into the darkness. A song is heard.

I fear the colored world that invades my neutral body. I raise my hips to the sun. "Open wide." Yellow and blood-filled red pours in, filling my darkness, my hole. My whole. I drown in the warmth. A scream is heard?

I stand motionless. Naked. Eyes gray, skin pallor. A fight between life and death. Needle colors fly toward me. Prick. Prick. Needle colors piercing my skin. Azure becomes crimson. Forest green becomes crimson. Burnt umber becomes crimson... Time shows no feeling, shows no concern, no remorse, despite my attempts to hold back the hands. I simply swing in circles. It continues on. Life meets death. Death meets life. Things come. People cum. Things pass. People...become invisible.

A drowning requires a purging and a resuscitation if survival is to be had. Saliva drips off my tongue like dew off a leaf. Gathering more weight, more weight until it can no longer hang on. Becomes too fat and lazy. Drip.

To breathe. Take shallow breaths. Never let him hear. Never let anyone hear. Never even let yourself hear.

We are gathered together today in the presence of God to join this dick and this cunt in unholy copulation… Let us bow our heads:

Dear Heavenly Father,
May the two standing before us live a long life in secrecy. May the one exercise his God-given headship over the other. May he dominate her and shame her and use her flesh as he sees fit. May he view her as merely a body at his constant disposal with which he may carry out his sick and twisted impulses. And may Kristi now fulfill her God-assigned role as the submissive female. May she allow herself to be shamed and abused. May she value the truth conveyed to us through your Word that her body does not belong to her. Her body is a gift to any and all males who wish to make use of it. May the two before us remember that you, dear Father, are our redeemer and protector. And, of course, may this dick and this cunt always remember that you are the God of Love. In Jesus' name, Amen.

⁂　⁂　⁂

My boss at the watch and jewelry repair center, Karen, mentions that she is thinking of renting out a room in her house. She has two teenage children. Her husband passed away a year or so ago from cancer. I ask her if she would be interested in renting her room out to me. She says yes.

I move out of my sister's place and in with Karen and her family. She is very nice. At work, she and I talk about family, philosophy, religion, you name it. She is very open in her religious beliefs. She believes in the Bible, but not in the sense that every single word and letter is written by God. We differ on that. She was raised Catholic, but now she studies eastern religions and a number of other belief systems. Whenever we talk about religion, she listens intently on what I have to say. She then talks about her beliefs. She does it in the most gentle, caring way I've ever experienced. She does not try to convince me that her beliefs are correct (like I try to do with her). Instead, she simply shares about other beliefs that are out there in the world. She shares with her heart. Over time, I begin to open up…very, very slowly.

※　　※　　※

I lie in bed, close to sleep, but not fully so. Images come to mind. Inanimate objects associated with work – clocks, tools, stapler – are alive. They move on their own free will and are attempting to breathe freely. The objects are me. It feels like a bad dream but I am awake. I see a diamond with many facets. My face and my life are reflected in each of these facets. I feel dizzy from it, literally. These are not thoughts, they are image/feeling invasions that I have no control over.

I feel like I can't breathe and sit up, gasping for air on the edge of tears. I am not allowed to shed tears, though. My mind is having a hundred different things going at once. I need to cut myself, but I can't. I'm past that. I need to close my eyes to go to sleep, but I can't. Once I close my eyes, I feel ill. I cannot pinpoint any pain, but my insides seem to physically hurt so bad it's making me crazy. It's the pain that is making me feel ill, I think, but what pain?

I can't close my eyes because it is so intense and scary. I can't sit still either. I don't know what's happening and I'm scared!!! Death is invading these images. Death of the inanimate objects, though. This is impossible to describe. I feel I must cut on myself again, so I get up and search around. I feel like I must die like my mind is telling me. I've never experienced anything quite like this before.

It won't let me go to sleep! As soon as I get close, that suffocating feeling and the illness overwhelms me again, forcing me to open my eyes so I can better bear it. There are not as many images when my eyes are open.

Death, death, death. Die, die, die…

Why is it torturing me like this!!?

I think I am going to vomit.

Where are these images coming from? I don't understand. There are no words to really describe what is going on. I feel like I'm approaching that line that separates sanity and insanity, the break with reality. It's very close.

I try closing my eyes once again, telling myself to have "normal" thoughts. I find myself writhingly moving in an attempt to get away from the pain that isn't there. I must physically remove myself from the bed once again. I rock myself. I want so desperately to be able to cry, to release some of this pressure. I can't do that either.

I'm so desperate that I seek relief in a way that has been neglected for several months -- prayer. Never mind. I'm not going to be selfish and go to God only when I'm in need of relief.

I've successfully killed all close friendships to enable me to kill myself. I have intricately planned all possible methods. I only wish I had access to more methods, a gun, for example, to be sure the attempt is a success. My method of first choice allows me to punish my body for betraying me before I put it to rest, something I've wanted to do for a long time.

I have begun a rough draft of my final note. It's difficult to write, for I don't know what to say. What really *can* I say that would make anyone feel better? Nothing.

I had a dream last night about saying goodbye. Some people that I haven't seen in a while were in it.

I look at school and see that it has been totally pointless all along. I don't have what it takes to be a therapist (a good one, anyway). I wish I did. School is just a source of stress.

My mother says that she is so disappointed with me. She's disappointed because of my turning away from the religious faith that she instilled in me. There was only one other time in my life that she was disappointed in me. That resulted in a sort of death also. Part of me died long ago.

There is one concern of mine pertaining to my death. Religious beliefs pervade this concern, a fear of being resurrected. Wouldn't it be cruel to bring to life someone who doesn't want to live? Since I suppose no time passes when one is unconscious, it would appear that I never died at all, defeating my very purpose. However, I feel God is not cruel and he knows what is best for everyone, whatever that means.

This dissociation that I've developed has been nothing but a hindrance to experiencing life fully. Fully, being with all my senses. It has caused nothing but problems in interpersonal relationships. Dissociation is supposed to be a defense, a protection, a wall to separate the pain from the consciousness. It has accomplished the wall, but the pain still seeps through. There are holes that pain can seep through, but total separation remains in being able to get close to others who could help me deal with the pain. It has been a protection from all of the good, but not all of the bad. What benefit is that?!!

Life is no longer a challenge, which can be a good thing, but a hellish existence, begging for relief…

All of the "yanking", as Terri says, that I have done with her over the past couple of years has taken its toll. She at times distances herself. It is very subtle, but I feel it. Who can blame her? She has to be constantly on guard to see if I am going to lie, break contracts or manipulate her.

The changes in her voice mean more to me than any words being said. It is these times, when her voice switches from a therapist to a filled person (filled = containing substance, not merely consisting of outer layers), that I truly listen and understand that she really does care. I feel I have to keep reminding myself of that; it doesn't sink in with ease. The pathway is jagged and twisted, and that realization makes great effort to reach its destination – my heart, that part of me that is capable of feeling, of grasping something foreign.

She says I don't have to act out my pain in order for her to feel it. She says she understands. She's right, she's not my family. She is capable of feeling, of understanding. I feel bad that I transfer everything onto Terri. She doesn't deserve it.

Communication is one of the strongest, if not *the* strongest, means of "healing" from wounds inflicted on us by experiences, past and present. Yet, this powerful tool evades me, it escapes my mind, thus escaping my lips (or *not* escaping my lips, as seems to be the case). I don't understand how I can keep forgetting the importance of it. This is the dividing line between my living and dying. The fallacy that prevents me from communicating is, "It's too complex, you wouldn't understand it (because I don't understand it)." Also, "What's the use, we can't change it anyway." And even, "What will he/she think of me?"

One fall morning I stop into a former teacher's office. She teaches child development courses at the Junior College. Even though I am not currently taking any of her classes, I decide to keep in touch. She is one of the few teachers I felt connected to and even shared some of my life.

She first notices my naked ring finger. I fill her in on much of what happened over the previous year since I last saw her. She is stunned as I tell her of the recent events: my wedding being called off, my job loss and change, going back to school, moving in with Karen. I even tell her about how I was hospitalized. I am impressed by how much she remembers about me. Up to this point, I thought she considered me just another student.

I'm very cautious about whom I speak to about my depression. It tends to make people draw away. Perhaps they fear it's contagious. She asks questions, though, being unafraid. We talk about coping strategies. She is understanding and attentive. She then says, "You're a survivor."

She also says there is a "lightness" about me, one that she had not seen too often during the time she has known me. There are good days and bad days, and I purposely chose one of the former for the visit.

I ask her if she wouldn't mind providing a recommendation letter for my college application. I am in my last semester now at the Junior College, getting all "A"s, I might add. I want to transfer to a 4-year college, still majoring in psychology. She answers, not by saying, "Sure", like I expect. No, she says, "I would be honored to do that for you." Honored.

I thank her, and after our visit, I get to thinking about the interaction as I walk to class. I can't include myself into that *strong* group of people who are considered survivors, because sometimes, a lot of times, that *all* I do – survive. Oftentimes, I don't even want to do that. When you get right down to it, though, I *am* here, I *am* surviving. I know each and every day that simply surviving is really not simple at all. It can involve a mountain of an obstacle that takes tremendous strength to climb, reach the top, and come out victorious. It takes even more strength to come to grips with the possibility that it will be just as difficult tomorrow, but decide to go ahead and face the mountain anyway, rather than turn and run, or worse, sit motionless and waste away.

To hear someone call me a survivor infuses me with even more determination to live up to that name; to not only live, physically, but also emotionally, for one *can* be truly dead and still be walking…I should know.

I know immediately that this day is one to be remembered, for even through the muck of self-resistance, this day is powerful enough to push me a little further along this road to health.

I remain ambivalent about therapy. I feel I need to go to therapy, but I always feel ill when I go and even worse afterward. Why do I keep going, then? Doesn't it seem self-destructive to keep subjecting myself to this week after week?

It isn't going to therapy that is causing such ill feelings – it is not the parking lot, the building, the therapist, or even the miserable little conference room I'm finding myself in nowadays that is directly causing such discomfort. It is I. Parts of myself that have been smothered too long are telling me something. They are climbing upward. They want freedom. They are screaming to tell their story. They want to show me life, that thing I want to squash so often. They want to help me broaden my experiences. They want to show me that life *can* be *so* wonderful. Call me selfish, but I want, I *need*, all those parts of me to surface, good or bad. How could I possibly live unwhole? I cannot be satisfied while there are parts missing. *That* is why I keep going to therapy. *That* is why I put up with the nausea, the headaches, the physical pain, the fear. The ambivalence is me! I want freedom. I want to be whole, one, yet I'm too scared to accept it. It's very similar to self-mutilation, exchanging one form of pain for one that's easier to bear. The depression, anxiety, and fear must be much easier to handle than what lies in store.

※　※　※

I want to murder her. I want to abort her. I want to reach into my uterus and pull her out with my bare hands. The blood would be everywhere, saturating the bathroom rugs and the clothing on the floor. She deserves to die. A long knife would reach her if inserted far enough. It would splice her limbs and spill her intestines. She would cry. She would scream a scream so shrill it would hurt my ears, like a young pig being butchered alive. I would hold the tiny, mutilated body in my blood-stained hands and wash it with my tears. Then, I would flush it down the toilet. Good riddance.

※　※　※

I've been trying to prepare myself: I tell myself that I will feel bad because of digging this "stuff" up, whatever this "stuff" is. I try to prepare myself for the intensity of the memories, but no memories come. I cannot prepare myself for dealing with the fact that I'm getting nowhere, and that I'm just another abuse statistic. I'm just another sexual abuse victim who dissociates and refuses to remember and accept what happened.

Here's my problem: My "mission/purpose" in life is to serve God. In order to properly do so, I must preach from door to door in an attempt to shove the Truth down people's throats. After all, if they don't listen they will be destroyed. Those who listen may live forever on earth in perfect health, happiness, blah, blah, blah. I know a lot of wonderful people – Karen, Terri, my teacher, the nurses at St. Theresa, amazing people I've read about – dead, all dead. Why? They didn't serve Jehovah, not in the way that they "should" anyway.

I want my religion to be wrong; I want to have the belief that all religions lead to the same destination. That way, no one gets destroyed by a vindictive God.

%% %% %%

Bubbling Tar Pit

Deep into the recesses of my skull lies a bubbling tar pit. I stand within myself on its edge, mesmerized by the low tones of the bursting bubbles (which are strangely soothing), gazing somberly into the viscous ebony, searching for answers.

The atmosphere around the pit is only slightly less dismal than the pit itself: crimson fog, mildly diluted by a hard, stiff gray. The air is so rank it takes all I have to stand my ground. I take shallow breaths.

There are answers written on a slate lying at the bottom of those murky depths. They are hidden, held captive for an indeterminate amount of time by one who does not want to ease up on her grasp. Occasionally, a piece breaks off (or, perhaps, a piece is purposely broken off when the time is right) and finds its way up to the surface, through the dark sludge. The bubble bursts and spills its contents – a picture, a thought, a feeling – all from times past. I blink and it's gone, sinking back down to be caught once more.

Something glittery catches my eye. Not concerned with being burned, I bend down and pick it up. It is a fragment of the fragment left floating on the surface. I place it on the pile with the others.

I continue to stand here, not knowing how or when I will be able to know all that lies below. My legs grow weary from standing, and my eyes begin to blur from the constant strain of watching for little glimmers of hope. Obviously, I cannot dive in, but I cannot continue to stand here forever, either. The answers are down there. If I turn away I may miss a vital piece. What do I do? Where can I go?

Someone beckons me from behind, startling me: "Come, Kristi. Look what I have made for you." The voice is neither separately male, nor separately female, but both, woven together in harmony and synchronicity. It is warm, gentle, and caring. Compelled so strongly to know the source of such a wonderful voice, I turn. The beauty is so striking I must catch my breath. I begin to weep.

There is an arm extended toward me, the other, toward a beautiful garden. The garden is full of everything one could possibly yearn for: clear water, clean skies, animals to play with, plant life of every kind. There is plenty to eat for everyone. No one is sick or in pain, physically or emotionally. No one is prejudiced towards others. No one is being raped or battered. All the children are happy and well cared for. There are friends and family there you love and who love you in return.

The vision has rendered me speechless. The tears streaming down my cheeks speak for me. They are not tears of joy, however.

"Picture yourself there, Kristi," the voice says, breaking me free from my trance.

"I cannot," I say. "I never could, even when I was a child."

"Sure you can. Just try. You will know this place if you just put effort into it."

"I don't want to be there," I clarify. "How can you expect me to know this place when I don't even know myself?"

I don't care if this place is "Paradise," it's not for me.

I am left to stand alone with my decision.

Another voice enters from my left. It is all too familiar. A woman's voice. "Kristi, look," as she points to Paradise. "Look." I see it. She begins to cry. I've never seen her shed even a single tear before.

"I'm going to be there. Do you know how disappointed and sad I would be if you weren't there with me?" she cries.

"I can't help it if I don't want to be there," I say.

"You're grasping at straws, Kristi! You're stuck in the past. You need to be thinking about the future. You pine away over that black pit of yours looking for something that isn't there!"

Bitch.

I look at Paradise then back to the woman on my left. People are not so perfectly dull, and she doesn't show emotion. This isn't real. I am not wasting my time. After all, look at what I have found so far.

I am left alone with my decision.

A third person stands off to my right. This one does not say a word. I look at her for an eternity, it seems, wondering why she has not spoken. I finally realize it is because this is not her place. She is not here to speak. She is here to listen.

She comes near and joins me at the edge of the pit. She begins sorting through my pieces, grouping, organizing, and laying them all out for us to view. I resume my "pining away," keeping watch over the pit, waiting for the next little shiny fragment of a fragment to catch my eye.

I am not alone in my decision.

Chapter 15

It is not the suicide attempt itself that galvanizes the spirit to return to life, but a willingness – perhaps for the first time – to allow the pain to surface without turning toward suicide, and to feel the grief, despite the fear of being overwhelmed by it.

– Richard Heckler, Ph.D., *Waking up Alive*

% % %

Okay, I'm quitting therapy for real. I feel awful. I've been extremely suicidal for 2 ½ weeks straight. I don't think Terri can help me anymore. She doesn't understand, no longer attempts to understand. I will tell her at our next session, two days from now. Maybe I can find someone else who can better help me. I will also need to find someone who will be lenient with the money situation. Terri has been charging me only half the amount of the cost of sessions, since I'm paying for it out of pocket.

Also, without Terri, I will have no one left who really knows me. I can kill myself with less guilt. If Terri is no longer my therapist, maybe she won't feel so bad when I'm gone. She will think, "Well, I did everything I possibly could, and then some." She still may shed a tear, though.

Dream:

It is the day I'm going to tell Terri that this is the end of therapy. I'm in her office. I keep saying, "I want to tell you something. I want to tell you something," but she keeps talking over me and interrupting. I am so nervous and upset that I put myself in some sort of self-induced trance state (part of me does not want to stop therapy, also).

My eyes are closed while I'm fading away. I am lying on my stomach and she puts her hands up my skirt. She is massaging my inner thighs and genital area. I am so scared! I don't know what she is doing. I am still in a trance so I can't tell if it is Terri or someone else. I keep flashing back and forth between past and present. Part of the time, though, it is Terri, with the intent of inducing an abreactive episode.

I can't help but think she is enjoying it. I am screaming, crying, and trying to squirm away while she is massaging and touching me. The whole time she is reassuring/seducing me saying, "It's alright, just let it come. Just relax and let it come."

I say, "No. Mommy!" Then I start talking about toys and other things. I'm not making any sense in my altered state. My speech is slurred, so she isn't able to understand me.

There are times when I see the situation from her point of view. It's as if I'm looking over her shoulder.

I'm on my back now (my eyes are still closed). There is a penis placed between my legs. I grab it in my hand. I don't know where it came from or whom it belongs to. I can picture how it looks, more like "see" it with my eyes closed. I can feel it. It cannot penetrate me, though, because I have nylons on. I feel powerless. It is an extremely INTENSE episode!

Once it's over, I get up and run to the bathroom. It is down 7 or 8 flights of stairs, but I take a short-cut and arrive in just a few seconds. I open the door to the bathroom and there is really no room at all, just a toilet sitting right inside the door. I put my finger down my throat and vomit (I've never self-induced vomiting before, but it seems like second-nature here).

There is a blob of hard stuff stuck in my throat and mouth. I grab it with my fingers and pull it out. It almost seems like it is part of me, attached. After a couple of minutes, Terri comes up behind me. We head back up to her office. She is supposedly interpreting what I had said in my abreactive state.

The stairs are out of reach or blocked, so we head to the elevator. It is padlocked. Someone is paged to come open the elevator. Terri and I are waiting for the person with the key to come open the door as my dream comes to an end.

I go to the actual therapy session two days later. I am embarrassed to go over the dream with Terri, embarrassed that she is portrayed in the role of abuser. But we go through the dream, piece by piece and try to figure it out.

I also talk with her and speak of her therapeutic wall. Therapy is an interesting thing, providing a wonderful, yet at times difficult, relationship. The wall is there for the good of the situation, but it is still a wall. Walls equal distance and lack of trust with me.

I don't mention quitting therapy. At the end of the session I say, "This was a really good session, don't you think?" She agrees, then asks me what made it so good. I say that I think it is because she thinned her wall some. Terri looks startled. "You don't know when you do it?" I ask her.

"No, I can feel when it's gone," she replies. Gone.

I go on. "Also, I spoke about my thoughts and feelings more than usual."

Terri breaks in, "I was going to say, *your* wall was thinner too." We both smile, and I leave.

Maybe I will stop trying to destroy our relationship so I can destroy myself. Maybe. I later tell Terri, "You know, I was serious about quitting therapy, it wasn't just a dream."

"I know," she says. "I'm glad you stayed."

Shortly after, Terri leaves for a 2-week vacation. Prior to this, each time she took a vacation I would have a major meltdown and engage in a great deal of manipulative behavior. Major separation anxiety and abandonment issues. This time, though, I don't leave urgent messages on her voicemail about how I'm planning on killing myself or how I want to find some anonymous, sleazy guy to have sex with so I can punish myself about it later. I leave no messages. Instead, I make a self-resolution, a contract:

I will quit deflecting the pain and will allow it to surface.
I will face my pain head on.
I will not give up…

I will respect my own system's defense mechanisms;
I will not pressure myself to remember, but, rather,
allow my protective inner guide to tell me when it's okay,
when it's safe to experience the memories.

I will try to keep things in proper perspective;
I will fight to step back when necessary in order to view the bigger picture.

I will remind myself again and again and again,
"Suicide is no longer an option."
I will turn around, see the pain, respect why it's there,
and then take the necessary steps to lessen it, i.e., by recognizing the *feelings* involved and expressing them in healthy ways.

Only healing, learning, and the continual quest to grow are options, and all that they entail (or do not entail).
One thing that they entail is patience. Be patient.

I will face my pain head on;
I will not turn away;
I will not give up!

My first meeting with Terri after her vacation is very busy! I talk more in that session than 10 sessions combined! I say everything I want to say, and I am proud of my commitment.

Unfortunately, though, it is not like a magic wand that makes all the pain go away. For weeks and months afterward, I still have times where I feel suicidal. The suicidal feeling has a different texture, though. As much as I want to, I cannot crawl any deeper into that familiar hole of depression. Something is blocking me. It is as if the hole got filled in with some dirt, so it isn't so deep anymore, the bottom isn't so far down. At times, I want to kill myself, but even more than that, I want a *stronger* desire to end my life. Too much of me now wants to live. I know that things will get better, and yes, they will get bad again, but then, once again, they will get better.

The different texture in my depression and suicidal feelings started to show itself just before the contract, which instigated the creation of the contract. At first, I didn't want to tell Terri, because then I would be held more responsible for my actions, and I wouldn't be taken as seriously or with such urgency. I told her, though, for this is growth.

※　　※　　※

I still feel fragmented. I will give voice to some of these fragments.

K #1: ANGER PERSONIFIED. I see her. She looks like me, but is not. She has a frown, no, scowl, on her face. The edges of her form sneak out every once in a while, displayed in facial expressions, tone of voice, and body language. She hates men with a passion. She hates Terri, too. I'm not sure why yet. Maybe it's because Terri doesn't pay enough attention to us. Maybe it's because Terri knows too much – more than we know. Terri's not the same person she was when therapy began. We *all* miss that. She is more distant because of our actions. K #1 wanted to act out her anger rather than deal with it. She would make Terri suffer with worry, like she herself suffers. Her anger is a ploy to keep her distracted from her hurt, her real issues.

K #2: PAIN PERSONIFIED. She used to reside inside K#1, but now she is out, as her own being, separate. She is a little girl, cowering on the floor usually. Her voice is tiny. Everything about her is tiny. She likes pillows and finds comfort in being held, though this rarely happens. She peeks out every now and then, choosing her times to emerge very carefully, making sure it's safe. I hear her, quite often lately. I hear her crying. Her crying is *always* very intense. She experiences *raw pain* and not much else. Sometimes her presence comes close to the surface, throwing me off balance psychically. They are brief near-contacts, but they still are very disturbing.

If it makes any sense, for a few short seconds, I can feel the rawness of her pain, her deep sadness. It's too overwhelming for me, so she quickly retreats. But I can still hear her crying...

She avoids Terri because Terri is able to pull her closer to the surface. The surface is frightening. She doesn't trust Terri or feel completely safe yet. K #1 doesn't trust her either, but she usually verbalizes that through a lot of four-letter words.

K #3: RATIONALITY PERSONIFIED. Just call me Ms. Rational. That's not my real name, of course. I go by Kristi, but that name does not really belong to me, it belongs to the little one. I figure she doesn't mind that I borrow it, for the time being, anyway. I'm the one who thinks things through, tries to see both sides of the coin, goes to school, etc. I'm the one who writes most of the time, though occasionally someone else butts in. I think, I don't feel. I leave the feeling to the others. The only times I partially feel is when one of the others comes near the surface. Actually, I just don't feel emotions like sadness and anger; I feel emotions like happiness at times. We all in a way watch and wait, hoping to learn more in time.

%% %% %%

In the therapy session, Terri remarks that if she stays a little distant, I feel hurt and angry, because I feel neglected. However, if she gets too close, I feel hurt because it pulls the pain, or that little girl part of me, closer to the surface. It is a difficult place to be in either way. Because *all* of me still wonders at times if Terri truly cares, she says she will bring me something concrete, substantive, as a token of proof.

We will also do a split-room session next time, half in the conference room and half in her office. I didn't realize Terri ever planned on having me back in her office, to tell the truth. I tend to "fade" the second half of the session, so the second half will be in the conference room. If I do get "stuck" in her office, she has ½ hour to remove me. It's kind of funny.

It has been 8 months since I was last in her office. I can't believe that much time has gone by. The first split-room session feels odd. She's changed her office around, which is a little unnerving. I feel very nervous, and I'm not sure why.

I start "fading" a lot in the first half of the session, while in her office. I am lying on her couch, and I feel myself passing through different levels of consciousness. I try to describe the feeling to Terri, but I am not too successful. Half way through, we move across the hall. I now realize how much I am dissociating with the change in venue. It is like walking into a different universe.

I am more comfortable in her office the next time around. After that session, I call my aunt with whom I was close when I was younger, and proceed to tell her that I feel I was sexually molested when I was young. She accepts what I say without question. She is very supportive and loving. Letting someone else know about the abuse is so relieving, almost refreshing. I still don't know who the perpetrator is from when I was very young, but by now I'm 99% sure it happened. Putting all the clues together – the hundreds of dreams, drawings, writings, bodily memories, dissociation, self-destructive behavior, and acting out – leads me to that conclusion.

The following session, Terri gives me a small, hand-carved turquoise cat as the token of her genuine caring. It is fantastic! And, we don't switch rooms. Also during this session, we speak of homosexuality. I tell her about my "attraction" to some women with short hair, but not sexual attraction. This too, has been coming out in my dreams. "However, sex is disgusting any way you look at it," I quickly add. Terri asks where my broadened perspective all of a sudden comes from, that I would even mention or entertain the idea of homosexuality. I'm not afraid to let myself consider the possibility.

"I don't know," I answer. "I'm just resurrecting, coming alive."

In a later session, we discussed "popping." The analogy is of a piñata with all the "goodies" inside. "You're very close to popping," Terri says.

"I feel like it, physically and emotionally. What happens after I pop?" I ask.

"Then we get to view the candy and pick which ones are good and discard the rest. You get to keep all the good ones," she continues.

"What good would that do?" I reply. "It's time to share."

I have wanted Terri to try to work with me again using hypnosis. She has been refusing, though, because "trust has to be present, and you haven't displayed enough trust in me." I bring up the topic again. Terri responds, "We can do the hypnosis by remote control. I can be in another room, and you can take your recorded words home with you," Terri says with a smirk on her face.

"That's awful," I say.

"Why is that awful?"

I want you to hear them, too," I say.

"When did you start trusting me?" she asks with a grin. It must have been the turquoise cat, we both feel. Terri agrees to try hypnosis with me again.

I can't believe it! I trust Terri!!! I feel so happy right now!

We later try the hypnosis, but I have too many rules and too many barriers of my own to allow myself to relax enough. It's funny, because

I put myself in a self-hypnotic state all the time, but when someone else is involved, I get nowhere. The main gift from it all is I feel trust for another person. I'm just not ready to relinquish control at this point.

I walk into a session with Terri and sit down on the couch. "You're in a weird place right now, I feel it," she says. Yes, I'm in a weird place. I've been very stressed out with registering for classes. I got accepted at a really good, 4-year, Catholic college. My mother's going to love that. I have scholarships to pay my way. Being stressed out throws me back into suicidal thinking.

Again I rant to Terri about how I don't think it is right that therapy leaves me feeling worse 95% of the time. I feel angry at her, but mostly just sad and sick. "We've been through a lot together," Terri says, "I'm sure we can get through this, too."

I have been obsessing over who my abuser could possibly be, the abuser from when I was very young. I ask Terri who she thinks it could be. "It's too hard to narrow down. It could be any family member with a penis," she replies. She gives me a rundown on some of what she feels happened: 1. There was penetration. 2. I was on my back, at least some of the time, which is where the suffocating weight on my chest comes from. 3. It must have taken quite a long time because of the feelings I get in my legs of weight and numbness. 4. I focused on his breathing changes. The changes in his breathing meant his climax and also nearing the end. I controlled my breathing at all cost.

I feel sick when she is finished with the list. I want to throw up. It all feels so true. It is all based on information that has come out in our work together, as well as in my dreams and bodily memories. But *who* is it?

That information does not seem to want to come, so my therapy focuses in on the therapeutic relationship. That relationship is a reflection of what I did not receive growing up. It is as if I am growing up a second time, going through each developmental process, finally receiving emotionally what I did not receive the first time. In growing up, there is the early stage of acting without awareness, then acting with awareness. This leads to choosing to act or not to act. There is a progression of nonverbal communication, acting, then picture (drawing, painting), then words and verbal communication. In my own life, there was OCD, then depression, then memories through dreams and body. At this point of development, I am moving from withholding information to interacting and fully sharing with others. There are many layers to development and I see the progression through my behavior the last few years. I learn to be an adult for the first time with Terri. It's a very unique, powerful and healing process all in the environment of talking on a couch.

"I want to know how I affect you, how I touch your life," I tell Terri during one session. "I don't want all of this to be nothing. I don't want it to be that I am simply paying someone to sit with me an hour each week. I want it to mean more, that there is some deeper purpose to it all. I want to feel Terri as human, pure and true, not professional and clinical.

"As I walk out of the therapy session when my 'time is up', and the next client walks in, I overhear the first few words. There is light-heartedness and laughing. It is a strange sensation. It makes me feel totally forgotten, like I don't exist as soon as I step through the doorway," I tell Terri. "It's not that I don't exist, I rationalize with myself. I'm not forgotten. It's simply that the next client *does* exist and must be remembered. It must be difficult to switch gears at times. It can be from one extreme to another."

"You have never been forgotten," Terri assures me. "You are too special to be forgotten!" Terri then steps out of her role as therapist and shares with me some portions of her personal life – her family, her husband, her decision to become a therapist, and her choice to not have children. She goes beyond what the therapeutic relationship calls for. She shows her humanity and herself, a beautiful gift.

I'm changing. I've cut my hair short and highlighted it. I'm getting contacts. I'm a new woman on the outside to reflect the new woman emerging on the inside.

I'm communicating with Terri, even about the really hard abuse topic, as opposed to acting it out. I'm even communicating about my own sexuality. I've tried masturbating. It's a good way to explore my body. The first few times were difficult. I felt like I was dying, and I wanted to throw up afterwards. But I pressed onward in order to grow. In this growing, things start to come a little closer to the surface.

Chapter 16

Dream:

I am very small. I am between 4 and 6 years old. I'm in the dining room of my childhood home, before the addition was built. There is a man standing and holding me. He is wearing a white t-shirt. He's not just holding me, though. He is sexually aroused. I can feel his penis hard in his pants. He positions me so that my genital area is directly on top of his erect penis. I don't make a sound and I don't struggle. It feels nice. Our pants are apparently quite thin because I can feel his penis easily against me. I may be having an orgasm. I think he may be, too.

The man is supposed to be my dad or my uncle. It isn't my uncle, though – no beard. It is also not my dad because the build of his body is not at all like my dad's. As I am writing down the dream, I start feeling genital pain. I focus in on it and it intensifies. It stays pretty intense for about a minute, enough to make me squirm. It is the same painful feeling I felt when Rod tried to penetrate me, but was having difficulty.

I woke up early this morning, right when the dream ended. I immediately thought, "This is one of those dreams that is an actual event." It feels very different from my other dreams.

I am preparing to leave for a session with Terri. I'm sitting in the bathroom and a scene unfolds in my mind: I walk into Terri's office crying. I take off some of my clothes – shoes, shirt, socks – and I plop down on her couch face down, still crying. I can do nothing but cry because I am reliving something.

I go to the session in actuality and tell Terri of the earlier scene. "What is it that you are 'reliving'?" she asks.

"Some guy lying on top of me," I reply. "I am a little kid going through a well-known ritual. When the sign is given, I take off my clothes, lie on my stomach and wait for him to lie on top of me and have intercourse."

"Maybe that is remembering," Terri says. Just as she says that, a wave comes and floods over me, but only for a second. It has to be a wave of memories, for nothing else can feel so intense. Perhaps not a wave of memories, but a wave of the memories catching up to this time period, a wave of acceptance.

"I want to let this go," I tell Terri. It feels like stronger, clearer memories are just under my skin's surface, aching to burst through the pores. Part of me is still hanging on to it, though.

"It must be getting close, because you're getting grumpy," she says.

"Of course I'm getting grumpy. This is uncomfortable! I hate this!" I respond. When the memories feel on the verge of emerging, I feel that I will completely lose control.

*%   *%   *%*

From birth to age 3, I slept in a crib in my parents' room. When I was 3 years and 2 months old, my family moved to the property with the mobile home. At this point, I slept on the couch in the living room, which was the only place for me to be. My 3 older brothers were in the room adjoining the living room. My sister had a room of her own, and my parents had a room.

When I was age 5, my sister, Melissa, who was then 17, married Marty, age 19, and they both lived at my home. It was kind of a forced marriage. My sister got pregnant at age 16. She thought she loved Marty. My mom gave her the ultimatum of never seeing Marty again or marrying him to regain her respectability. Being the impetuous teenage girl who was utterly "in love", she chose the latter.

An addition to the home was being built, and people were shifted around. But for a while Melissa and Marty were in the bedroom adjoining the living room, with me still on the couch.

I really liked Marty. He was just like a brother. He would play and swing me around. He was fun. He could be really nice, or he could be kind of cruel.

I remember one time when I was around age 5, Marty and I rode our bikes to the end of the paved street where it intersected with the highway. My mom told me to not ever go across the highway, that it was dangerous. I was already pretty far from home. When I was by myself on my bike, I just stayed on the dirt road near our property.

Marty wanted to go across the highway, saying it would be fine. So I followed him across the highway. There was another street directly on the other side of the intersection that curved around to the left and headed up a short hill. It was a short street, and I never saw any cars driving on it. At the top of the hill, at the end of the street, was an auto wrecker junkyard. Before the junkyard, as you rounded the bend in the road, there was a target-shooting place on the left. It had a simple frame structure to provide a bit of shade. People would stand at this structure with their guns and shoot at clay disks in the direction of the junkyard.

We rode our bikes up the hill towards the junkyard. I felt very nervous, worried that my mom would find out I was over there. I wanted to just turn around and go back home, but I didn't want to cross the highway alone.

Marty rode all the way to the top of the hill and disappeared. I said I didn't want to go to the junkyard, so I stopped my little, yellow bike on the hill portion of the road and waited. Part of me was curious to know what it looked like at the top, but I decided to just wait, anxious to get home. He showed back up after just a couple minutes, and said, "Okay, let's go now." I was relieved. Then he took off really fast down the hill and he was gone.

I crawled off my bike and started crying. I couldn't believe he left me by myself! I was scared and angry. I took my bike and pushed it away from me. I remember watching it in fascination how it didn't fall down right away, but instead stayed upright, traveled several feet down the hill, then ran into the ditch and crashed into the side of the hill next to the street. I decided to just start walking home.

After I got down the hill a ways, Marty showed up, coming from the direction of the target shooting area. I was still crying, tears running down my face. I was happy, though, to see that he had not gone home like he said. "Where's your bike?" he asked.

"Up the hill," I replied.

"Let's go get it. I have to show you this really cool place I found." So we *still* weren't going home yet. Well, at least I wasn't alone.

Marty took me over near the target-shooting place and showed me a bunker. It was from here that someone would stand, pull a lever, and release the clay disk targets. Marty crawled inside and wanted me to crawl in after him. It was dark inside and the temperature was much cooler than outside. I could feel the cool air from the opening. I had the curiosity to experience what it was like inside. After all, I really liked forts. But something pulled on me to not go. Something made me want to turn away and not even look inside.

My sister divorced Marty after only a couple years. She says he raped her after they were separated, living in separate bedrooms. This rape resulted in her getting pregnant with her second child. Melissa says she also found out he was cheating on her with other women.

Marty seems a likely candidate for being my first abuser. There is a photo of Melissa and Marty's wedding day. I am in it, holding Marty's hand. I liked him, may have even loved him, God forbid. Could he have betrayed my love and trust?

Dream

There is stuff in my mouth. It is liquid at times, chunky at other times. I keep thinking that the chunks are pieces of my lungs breaking off and coming up. I keep spitting them out, but they keep coming. I keep gagging over and over.

Dream

I think this is a dream, but it seems too blatant. There doesn't seem to be the symbolism typical of my dreams. *It is a question-and-answer session with my mom. Mom says that Marty was 19 when he and Melissa married. She says, "Yes, I did leave you alone with him at times. I knew he may have been hurting you, but I chose to leave you with him anyway."*

This doesn't seem like a dream, more like a vision.

% % %

You fucking little bitch. Open your eyes. Open your fucking eyes! No, I'm asleep. Now go away. Just go away. (Pretend you're asleep.)

% % %

In a session with Terri I feel very agitated. I feel hateful feelings towards her. I'm sitting on her couch hugging her throw pillows, and my legs are curled up to my side. "I hate you right now," I tell her.

"You're avoiding things, trying to push them away, focusing on the hatred, instead. Look at your toes." I look down at my feet and toes, which are flexed and pushing against the couch.

"I want to do something to make you hate me," I say. "That way I can end it all." We both know there is not much behind the suicidal words anymore.

"Your mom does that for you already," she responds.

"No, she doesn't hate me. She just disapproves of my life. I've abandoned my religious upbringing. I'm going to a Catholic college. I'm pursuing a career in psychology."

It has been a long time since I went to a meeting. I no longer claim to be a Jehovah's Witness. This is the most devastating thing for my mom. Also, getting a higher education is looked down upon by Jehovah's Witnesses. They don't want you to start thinking critically and questioning, or exploring other belief systems.

"I want you to hate me, Terri," I say again.

"You can leave all the hate here in the room, or you can take it along with you," Terri continues. I decide to take it along with me.

Later that night, my anger and hatred begin to dissipate. I try to focus it on where it belongs, with what happened to me. It's so hard to focus it in the correct place when I have no clear, image recollections of the things that happened, the things my body feels and remembers. I just want to see a face.

I'm sitting in my closet. I have a very strong urge to insert a knife into my vagina. I want to do damage. I decide to get up and brush my teeth instead. The urge is a little less strong afterward, but it is still there.

I call Terri. I let her know what I refrained from doing. I feel like I want to force myself to cry, but I cannot. "There is a phrase that I keep hearing. It's in a man's voice. It keeps repeating in my head and won't shut up," I say. I cannot bring myself to tell her what it is, though.

At the end of the phone call, Terri says she will call to check on me the next evening. "Would you like that?" she asks.

In a drawn-out, tentative voice and manner, I say, "Yeeess."

"Is that a 'yes' or a 'no'?" she questions.

"It's a yes. I just can't concentrate because of that voice in my head," I clarify for her. The next thing I know, the words come pouring out of me uncontrollably, along with sobs and wailing: "YOU FUCKIN' LITTLE BITCH! YOU FUCKIN' LITTLE BITCH!" I cannot stop crying now. The same kind of wave that I felt before in Terri's office is felt again. I feel myself go into a different state of consciousness. The wave crashes and knocks down all my defenses – my wall, my denial, my fear, my numbness. The pain emerges. My body feels like it is purging itself. I rock back and forth, and I pound my fists against the floor, then I rock some more. I want to thrash my body and let the demon be released.

I can hear Terri's sadness on the other end of the line. "No wonder you've been angry," she says, "your little girl body was violated, then he was saying those awful things to you."

"I don't hate you, I hate *him*!" I tell her.

"I know," she says.

A personal observation: When I feel like I must force myself to cry and/or hurt myself, I used to think it was a mere ploy for attention, drama. But now I realize that it is not a ploy, not a mere means to deceive or manipulate. My body is speaking to me. It is saying, "Get this shit out of here! I don't want it anymore!" The dramatic feeling is a prelude. It is the opening act for much more painful feelings, if I should choose to let the body of the drama unfold. A release is what is needed, what is screaming for attention.

%   %   %

I hear Little Kristi. She is crying again as usual. She is wandering, lost in the darkness. She holds all the memories. I am grieving/mourning the loss of this child. It is like a death. I don't know what to do but mourn.

%   %   %

Dream

I am being hunted by a man. I am constantly running to stay away from him. He has a gun with which he continues to shoot at me. I am not sure where I am exactly. It looks like a junkyard, for there are quite a few cars around. There are a lot of people around, also, and I am afraid that he will hit one.

At one point I am about 20 feet in front of the man. He is shooting bullets straight at me, but I am able to dodge them. They are rather large bullets, and shiny, almost like bubbles, so I am able to see them in order to dodge. They fall around me and fly over me. I know, though, that if one hits me I will die. I am hiding behind a car for protection.

I have a gun in my hands now. It shoots bolts instead of bullets. I shoot the man and hit him the first try. He isn't hurt. My gun is useless, so I dispose of it.

An Asian woman inside of the car I am hiding behind is hit by one of the bullets. I grab her and drag her to a nearby place, risking getting shot myself. I decide to do CPR. The woman turns into a white t-shirt. She is lying flat on a table in front of me. I put my mouth on a certain part of a design on the shirt and blow. The shirt fills with air, then goes back down. I realize, then, that all that remains of her is a shirt – she is dead. Not just dead, disintegrated, dissolved!

I am on the run again. He catches me. He has no pants on, so I grab his penis with both hands (because it is so large) and pull and twist as hard as I possibly can. It doesn't hurt him one bit. He just smiles.

I'm flying, still trying to get away, flying like I am swimming. I'm paddling as fast as I can, with the least amount of wind resistance possible, but I can see he is still gaining on me. He is coming up on my right. He is stronger, so he can paddle-fly faster. He comes right up next to me with that grin on his face. I desperately try to maneuver around him, but he grabs my arm. I start screaming, "Help! Help!" to the people around. My voice is so tiny.

I wake up from the dream lying on my belly, gasping for breath. My throat feels sore as if I were actually screaming. It takes a while before my breathing and heart rate return to normal.

Dream

I'm at work. Karen has just left for a lunch break and a swarm of customers come. There are all sorts of new merchandise that I don't know about. A man is asking me for a particular watchband. As I search to see if we have it, I feel something in my mouth, stuck in my upper front teeth. It is meaty. It just forms out of nowhere as I am trying to help him. It's embarrassing and is affecting my speech. I try to talk with only a slight opening in my lips.

I run into the back room. "What is this stuff?" I grab it, yank it out, choking and gagging, and throw it in the trash. It is now all over in my teeth. It is a pale yellow color. I have to go back to help more customers, so I decide to remove the rest later. At least the front of my teeth look okay now.

When I go back out, it forms again. I keep trying to figure out what I ate that is now stuck in my mouth.

I feel a lot of energy bubbling inside of me right now. I do not know the source, but I'm attempting to channel this energy through my arm and out the tip of my writing instrument.

My back and neck have been bothering me more than usual lately. If bodies speak, what is mine trying to tell me…?

It never appeared odd to me that I do not know the source of my back and neck problems. I thought things just go out of alignment on their own. When people find out that I see a chiropractor from time to time, they ask, "What happened?"

"I don't know," I tell them.

"You don't know?" they ask, as if there is something out of alignment with my response. What *did* happen? Perhaps it is a genetic defect.

Or…maybe…being put in an awkward position as a young child and having the weight of a grown man bearing down on me is the source of my problems, my neck and back problems, that is. My head shoved into the pillow, turned toward the side (so that I could breathe), hips hiked up in the air, him putting pressure on me, surely could push things out of place.

My pelvic bone also tilts, going out of alignment. Why is this the case? I suppose when one aspect of the young, impressionable, tiny skeleton is pushed out of alignment, other areas and bones have the same fate, for they are all connected.

Each memory fragment is connected. A long chain. I have to feel my way along this chain, for I cannot see the path before me. There is a blizzard. The snow and ice is hurled at me by my many family members who would rather not have me find my way to the end of the chain. If I find what is at the end of my chain, they will be forced to acknowledge that each member has a chain of her own, and then, pain of all pains, follow the chain to her own horrid memories…or responsibilities.

I have a session with Terri. I've been feeling sick and suicidal once again. I have an intrusive line running through my head. After much difficulty, I reveal the words to Terri: "There's blood in the bathwater." The words are spoken in a woman's monotone voice.

%% %% %%

I look into the bathroom mirror at my reflection. I decide to cut myself. I know I don't have to, but nothing is holding me back. It's an odd feeling to give into something that isn't even overwhelming. It isn't weakness, it is apathy.

I go into my walk-in closet. I take an old razorblade and cut a few lines on my leg. They aren't deep cuts. They hardly bleed.

I call Terri and leave her a voicemail message (mistake #1). I leave the message in the best "help-me" voice I can muster. I know she won't call back, but I would like it if she did.

The cutting doesn't make me feel anything like I had hoped. I'm not going to beat myself up for doing it, no harm done. I have no intention of ever doing it again.

I go back to working on my homework. I can't concentrate, so I decide to go into the kitchen to fix something to eat. I hear a pounding on the door. I feel nauseous all of a sudden. I can't hear the person at the door, but Karen's end of the conversation sounds peculiar… "we're all adults here…" The man at the door asks to see the roommate. Karen calls out to me by my first name.

I step into the living room as the man walks in the door. "Kristi, Kristi Bowman. You know how I know your name is Bowman?" *Let me guess, you're psychic?* I think to myself, already irked by his attitude.

"I'm the fire chief, and the police are on their way, and so is the ambulance." He calls off the ambulance, seeing there is no medical emergency. "Have you been making crank calls?" he asks. I wish he would just get to the point.

"No."

"Are you seeing a doctor for anything?" I tell him I am seeing a psychologist. "Hamilton?" he asks. Close enough.

"Yes," I reply, as I sit down on the couch.

"Why would you want to be making crank calls? I know you left a message saying you had a razorblade and was going to cut yourself." At this, Karen goes into the kitchen to try to give me some privacy.

"Can we go somewhere else to talk about this?" I ask him. So we head to my bedroom. I gather up my homework, which is scattered across the bed and sit down. He stands just inside the doorway, closing the door partially.

"What's going on?" he asks. "You've got the whole police force out here. You better have a good explanation. You just did it for the attention, didn't you? Well, you got it. Didn't expect *this* kind of attention, though, huh? Why would you call him and say that?"

"Her."

"He must have been worried about you…"

"Her."

"Sorry, *her.*" This guy seems like a jerk, and I just want him to leave.

A young police officer comes in, then, taking his place. The fireman goes to the kitchen to talk with Karen, who also thinks he is a jerk. The policeman is nice, but sneaky. "I can't let myself leave without feeling that you will be safe," he says to me in a gentle voice. "So you have to give me a good explanation why you would tell your doctor that you cut yourself, why you lied like that."

"I didn't lie. I did cut myself," I tell him (mistake #2). He asks where, and I tell him on my thigh, but they are nothing, just scratches.

"Since I'm a guy, I can't just have you drop your pants to see if they are indeed superficial, as you claim. You'll need to get checked out at the hospital." Great…here we go again. "It'll only take a few minutes," he assures me. I know better. He asks for the razorblade, and I give it to him. "I really appreciate your cooperation," he continues in his kind and sneaky manner.

He leads me out to the patrol car. All the neighbors are standing on their front lawns, trying to get a glimpse of the action. Karen will have some explaining to do, I'm sure.

I get to the local county hospital emergency room. I wait in an exam room with the police officer. He has to wait also, because now I am on a 51/50, he tells me. I reach the hospital at 7:15pm. The officer waits with me until he gets bored, around 9:00pm. "You have to promise me you won't run away," he tells me. "You don't look like a runner (little does he know), and you seem real nice, but you still have to promise. If you do run, I will have to come after you and put you in handcuffs, which I don't want to do." I promise not to run, although it sounds tempting.

So now I'm alone, unwatched for another hour and a half. What kind of 51/50 is this, anyway? The ER doctor finally sees me, and acknowledges the cuts are superficial, but I must be transported across the street to the psychiatric unit now that I have been deemed a danger to myself.

Once at the psychiatric unit, I am told to wait in a room, that it will be about 45 minutes before I can be seen. The room is dirty and smells of urine. I stand in the doorway most of the time just to keep from breathing in the stench. This place is a hellhole.

One of the nurses or technicians working here comes out of a locked door, which leads to an inpatient unit. I watch him as he stands in the open doorway, looking back from where he just came. I hear a female patient pleading for "freedom." He stands there with a grin on his face as she comes closer and closer to the opened door. Just as she gets to the door, he slips the rest of the way out and shuts the door in her face, looking through a small rectangular window to be sure to catch her disappointed reaction. A security man is also watching the scene. "Don't tease the animals," he says to the other man, as they both laugh.

I can't believe I just heard him say that! I feel like I'm thrown back in time several decades. People in mental hospitals are supposed to be treated humanely!

I think of St. Theresa and how much nicer it is. I am grateful for being there when I needed it most, and not having to be here.

I continue to wait…45 minutes…an hour…two hours. I see another patient come in the waiting area. He is probably around 40 years old, and he is extremely filthy. He has no shoes on, and his normally white skin is brown and crusty around his feet and toes. His hair is stringy and greasy, not having been washed in weeks, it looks like. His jeans are practically held together with dirt and grime.

The urine smell in my room is really getting to me, so I occasionally go to the restroom and over to the front desk to see how much longer it is going to be. I notice the grimy man staring at me every now and then, so I keep my distance. I stand back in my doorway. He approaches me, then turns and goes into the room across from mine. I know he is up to something, so I close the door to my waiting room for the first time.

The woman at the front desk said earlier she would bring me some food, so when I hear the doorknob turn, I figure it is her. Wrong. Grimy Man steps into my room and closes the door behind him. *Any second now, someone will come bursting in and kick him out*, I think to myself. *Any second now*. My heart starts racing. I know they have cameras all around for protection. They will protect me.

Grimy Man sits down next to me on the sofa and says hi. "Hi," I say back to him. I also have the strangest notion to ask, "So, what are ya' in for?" *Any second.* He takes his grimy hand and begins caressing my neck and tells me I'm so beautiful. At that, I jump up, race to the door, hoping he isn't the type to prevent me from leaving, and run to the front desk. They still don't realize he is in my room.

"There's a man in my room, and he's touching me!" I say, sounding like a little girl.

"Okay, just stay here," the woman at the desk says.

The nurse on duty that I've been waiting to see comes out and tells the guy, "She's got problems of her own. She doesn't need to be dealing with your crap, too. Understand?"

The woman at the desk tells me to now go back to my room. "It smells like urine," I tell her. She doesn't seem to believe me. She walks into my room with me.

"It sure does," she says. "These rooms need to be cleaned." I have to stay in the room, anyway.

The incident with Grimy Man is almost too much. I feel like I might lose it. I just want to get out of this place! I feel like I cannot hold up the mask for much longer, the mask that shows everyone that I'm fine, that my being here is the result of a big misunderstanding. I'm okay, really. I'm not insane. I'm not even a danger to myself. My eyes begin to tear up. The woman at the desk comes in with a bagel. My mask flies back up. Whew!

I finally speak to the nurse on duty. I tell him how the razor cutting was not serious, how I had no intention of seriously hurting/killing myself. I just wanted to feel. It didn't work. I'll never do it again. It is just a minor set-back is all. I mean every word, and he believes me. My next scheduled appointment with Terri is not for three weeks. He wants me to make an appointment before then, but I can't. With midterms and work, our schedules do not match up for three weeks.

The worst part of the whole incident is not the cops, nor the hospital, nor even Grimy Man. It is the destabilization in the relationship with Terri that I feel. A few days after the incident, I have an epiphany.

Despite feeling that Terri was extremely unhelpful and rude and betrayed me, no, perhaps *because* of this, I am forced to rely on myself. Over the next three weeks, I gently guide myself through the turmoil. My own strength becomes more apparent.

The last couple years, I have had my therapy sessions sometimes in Terri's office, sometimes in the conference room, sometimes split ½ and ½, all depending on how I was feeling and acting. The last several months, the sessions have been in the conference room. The session that meets after the three-week period is ironically in Terri's office. It is my 4-year anniversary of being in therapy. "If you had enough control to make it through the past three weeks," Terri explains, "then you have enough control to leave at the end of each session." True enough. Our sessions, though, are now made for every other week. Believe it or not, I am getting better.

Me: "Terri (gulp), do you love me?"

Terri: "Yes."

Me: (pause)

Terri: "You surprised?"

Me: "I'm surprised that you answered so quickly. I expected some long, drawn-out answer explaining the different kinds of love, etc."

Terri: "Intuitively, I knew what you meant. I could have gone into the different kinds of love, but I think I knew what you meant – on a spiritual level and on a human level, right?"

Me: "Right."

Terri: "I wouldn't have hung in here this long if I didn't."

Me: "You can care for someone and not give up."

Terri: "Yeah, well, you've really gotten on my nerves at times…" (grin)

Chapter 17

Both my parents died long before I was born. I don't know exactly *when they died, though, for they cannot tell me, they are dead.*

It's not easy being raised by parents who have left the land of the living. At best, it's quiet and lonely. At worst, it's murderous. The death cloud that surrounds them is large, and it grows larger each passing year. After a few years, just to keep out of the cloud's reach, I am pressed against the furthermost wall, palms flat, standing on the tips of my toes, daring not to breathe. My head pounds, a result of the pressure I am exerting on the back of my skull. Little beads of sweat gather on my brow and upper lip. The cloud is so close I can smell the stench of rotting flesh, and I know that if I cannot find a door or even a window soon, that cloud will suck me right in and I will be just like them – a newly-converted soul to the dead.

My biggest fear throughout my childhood was hearing the death rattle in my own breast, that sign that tells you the end is near and there isn't a damn thing you can do about it. I had to witness that sound four times in my four siblings, that gurgling disturbance that emanated from the hollow behind their ribs. But that wasn't the worst of it. When rigor mortis sets in in my own kin, my own flesh and blood, when all is stiff and hard, scarcely resembling anything once human, it becomes sickeningly apparent that it can just as easily happen to me.

I sit on the cold, hard floor of a dimly lit room. My legs are folded under my body. The circulation is being cut off in my lower extremities. First sign of death — no feeling. I am leaning forward, my head touching the floor. My arms are pressed tightly against my abdomen as the fingers of each hand clasp around the opposing elbow, an attempt to be balanced, to remain stable. Pain wracks my body, invisible waves of pain pouring out of every orifice, out of every tiny pore of my clammy skin.

I unclasp my fingers from around my elbows and clench them tight into fists. It is with these instruments that I pound out my pain, and pound long and hard, I do. After striking the hard floor one too many times, a bone in my wrist breaks. My body couldn't withstand the intensity of pain I desired to unleash. It broke. I broke. Tears gush out. Not because I broke, but because I could no longer pound out the pain.

I am taken to the hospital eventually, and a brace is placed on my wrist. "I don't know how she did it," my mother says to the doctor, "she was just playing by herself in her room."

%%. %%. %%.

Dream

I am face to face with a dark-haired, little girl of four or five years. I am lowered to her level. I do not really know her, but I sense something so familiar in her face, like looking into a mirror.

The little girl is embarrassed about what she is telling me. Slowly, she speaks of someone touching her. I hold her now, still facing me. She tells painfully of things I can't recall. She tells of touching herself "down there," then bringing her hand up and seeing blood on it. The little girl is careful to not disclose the person's identity, not even the gender.

As she tells me of the things the person has done, I am careful to remain calm, to not get upset, in order to facilitate more disclosure (the little girl might also interpret getting upset and angry as being upset and angry at her). "Who is it?" I ask. It is hard enough for her to tell me the what, impossible *to tell me the who. I tell her I will not tell anyone. I know who it is. "Is it your stepfather?" I ask.*

She begins to whimper, not wanting to say, not wanting it to be true. "Yes," she answers. I did not want to put words in her mouth (or later be accused of doing so), but I knew *who it was, and it was too hard for the little girl to come out and say it herself.*

I walk while holding her to try to find help. She is resting her head on my shoulder, exhausted. We are in a place I do not know. There is a lot of walking and searching. Many unknown people are gathering around.

We are now in the yard of my childhood home, still searching. In a group of people who are standing and talking, I see Mom. I motion with my finger for her to come to us. While she is walking towards us, I tell the girl that I have to tell my mother what is happening to her. The girl begins to cry. She doesn't want anyone to know, and I am breaking her confidence. No matter, it's more important that she be kept safe.

Mom approaches. The girl puts her head back down on my shoulder. Mom is frustrated. She asks what I want in an irritated tone, like I have interrupted something important. She says, "I hope you're not wanting me to take part again in one of your studies, especially that one about molestation. If this is another thing about molest…" she threatens. I frantically try to interrupt her spiel. I mouth to her to stop (mouth so the girl doesn't hear).

"Stop, just stop," I mouth, also gesturing with my one free hand.

Mom is still talking. I mouth, "She is being molested." I repeat the words a few times before I catch her attention. Once she understands what I am saying, there is a long silence. I mouth the words again. Mom and I just stand there looking at each other for a few seconds. I wonder to myself what the little girl thinks is happening in the silence.

Mom finally understands my words. I fully expect her to feel awful, to want to help all she can, to want to help this little girl so no more bad things happen to her. "Well, she seems fine now," Mom says.

"What?!" I can't believe what I have just heard. My mouth stands gaping.

"She's holding it together," Mom reiterates.

I lose it. In a raised voice I say, "No, she's not alright! I tried to kill myself when I was, what, 15, 16, 19…19!" I know the words are harsh for the young girl to hear, but I have to get through to my mom so I can get her some help. Unfortunately, the words fall on deaf ears.

Teenagers and children gather around. I take off running with the girl still in my arms, pushing my way through the crowd in an attempt to get to someone in time who will really help. As I run, I hear a teenage girl telling of her own suicide attempt.

An older teenage boy is in the crowd. He is bad. He has beheaded a girl for telling about and trying to get help from molestation. He wants to do the same to me.

The crowd has become too congested, I can't get out. I don't know who to go to for help. I turn to the little girl and tell her that I have to tell someone, I have to get her some help, I have to stop her from getting hurt.

I know the teenage boy is coming to behead me, and I have no way out. I am not scared, though. Before I am taken away, I look straight at the girl and say, "I love you." I hold and comfort her as she cries. Her actions let me know that she forgives me for breaking her confidence. I continue, "You deserve more." I turn to the crowd of children and teenagers who are being and have been molested and say, "You all deserve more. You deserve one day without feeling pain and anger, disgust, guilt, shame, and sadness. You deserve one day and 10,000 times that…" Dream ends and I wake up. My hope is that one of the older children will take the little girl under her care and find her help, protect her. At least she knows someone cared and wanted to help end her pain.

※　※　※

My parents decided to move back to California after only a year or so of being in Arkansas. I hardly noticed their absence. I'm busy with work and school and therapy, but I drive to their place for a visit every now and then. I also visit with my sister in Littleton and see my nieces and nephews. Mainly, I go to my sister's house to visit the kids. I love the kids. I have a difficult time around the adults.

I will feel really good, then I go for a family visit and start feeling sick. I feel nauseous and get a headache. Sometimes I feel really groggy, like I have been drugged. I cannot even hold my eyes open. When I leave from the visit, I feel sick for several days afterward.

There is the dysfunction of the family. They do not, and apparently cannot, feel. I have been opening to feeling, oftentimes in a very intense way. They cannot acknowledge this, reflect it, or support it. I also have a difficult time being witness to how my sister and her husband treat my nieces and nephew, and just the relationship dynamics in general. Nobody seems to have a healthy relationship.

There is more. I am going to college, a forbidden thing. I'm also living with Karen, a woman who is not a Jehovah's Witness, so obviously she is considered a "bad influence" and must be "corrupting" me in some way. I am still in therapy, which I haven't fully divulged to my mom, because she was never in support of it to begin with. And now 4 years, I'm still going! Preposterous! Of course, Terri is "corrupting" me, no doubt about it.

The main thing is I do not hold to their religious beliefs anymore. They make frequent comments or attempts to get me to go back to the meetings. It feels like a bombardment. I'm disassociated from the organization, but not "disfellowshipped", which is worse, I guess. There is the "Big D" and "Little d". People who get disfellowshipped are those who have sex when they're not supposed to, or do something else against the belief system, but still claim to be a Jehovah's Witness and act as if nothing has happened. I, on the other hand, went against the belief system but do not still claim to be a Witness. I have separated myself from it. There is more hope, from the viewpoint of my Jehovah's Witness family members, for someone like me. I am a lost sheep, just confused and wandering in a far-away pasture, needing to be beckoned home.

Add all of these things together, and it equals that my family absolutely cannot relate to me or support me. The result is me feeling sick in their presence, and I realize I want to see them less and less.

But I would like to talk more about my family's (particularly my mom's) highest disappointment with me – the religion. Oh, there were such high hopes for me!

I had such high hopes for God. Here God was supposed to be this caring, loving father figure. But really, how loving could this God be? He sits up there in space, completely distanced from all of us. If he were truly a God of love, he would not allow horrible things to happen to his "children." He would not sit idly by allowing his precious ones to be tormented and hurt night after night. Would he not hear the incessant cries from the millions of innocents? God could not be so cruel and abandoning. Therefore, there is no God. Or, if there is, it is something completely different from the Jehovah's Witness view of it. It must be some vague, energy form that is not personable or involved on any meaningful level with humans.

I've taken several classes on religion and spirituality, which I find fascinating. I love studying about humanity's many beliefs. I am particularly drawn to eastern beliefs around the nature of reality and creation and life and death. Different cultures view the Higher Being in many different ways, none of which, most likely, is the "real" way, whatever that means. I want to know, not what the "real" form of God is, because, obviously, that is not for us to truly know, but I want to know *something*! I don't care what *It* is, but what am I? I don't want to know the "proper" way to be a servant, especially to One I cannot fully know. However, what am I supposed to do with this life that I didn't ask for? Help others? Fine, then what?

Why do people have to suffer? To learn great insights into life and human nature? Fine, but where can all of this wonderful information be put to use? In death? This is sickening to me! "Life is hard, and then you die," Karen said to me once. Wow, I'm sure glad I'm alive! Look what I have to look forward to! I kind of like the idea of reincarnation. I wouldn't mind being a cat in my next life, a cat that lives in a nice home. I could just sun myself in the window each morning and sit on laps to be petted. Or, maybe I would be a cat in the jungle. That would be cool. But where is the meaning? What is real? What is my purpose?!

Various religions and psychological theorists try to tackle the question of reality and purpose. Once the defenses have been peeled away, the true self can shine through, supposedly. What if the defenses are part of who I am? You take those away, you take away pieces of me. I will never be the same as I would have been had the abuse not taken place…I have to live with that. I look at it, though, not as a loss, but as a gift of sorts. I feel I will be a better person for what I have suffered, better able to assist others. The "true self" cannot shine through, for she is no longer there. She was forced to change, to integrate defenses into her personality. Her personality and defenses became one in the same, inseparable.

Can defenses be altered or be totally substituted with healthier, more adaptive coping mechanisms without destroying the self? In other words, can the self ever be completely rid of defenses, and would it be wise to get involved in such an undertaking?

I wrestle with these questions, because I feel I am living a life that is not in my control, one constantly manipulated by childhood experiences. Is there a way to cut these puppet strings, and if so, why haven't I figured it out?

Some say religion developed because humans fear the unknown of death and must come up with a way to comfort themselves. I tell you, there are things worse than death. Having your life ripped from you while your heart remains beating is one. Having to pick up the rubble in the aftermath of a raping of the soul is another. Living an emotionally comatose existence is yet another. I would love to see my true self shine. I would love to experience my highest potential. I would love to connect deeply with others, even with God, if there is such a thing.

⁄⁄   ⁄⁄   ⁄⁄

My friend, Justin, invited me to watch a movie. He said he already saw it, but he wanted to see it again and thinks I would also really like it. "Sure, I'll go," I said. It was *The Matrix*. I was fascinated by this movie for more than one reason. First, I could not stop staring at Carrie-Anne Moss in that tight, black, leather outfit totally kickin' butt. Why am I so enamored by her? Shouldn't I be drooling over Keanu Reeves? Second, the whole nature of our existence and what is "real" is portrayed so interestingly in this movie. It is just like I have been feeling lately. I feel like I'm stuck in the matrix. How do I "unplug"?

⁄⁄   ⁄⁄   ⁄⁄

The phone rings. It is my nephew, Rick. He tells of how his sister, my niece, Maddi, is in the hospital. After speaking with him for about 20 minutes, my sister, Melissa, comes on the line. She begins telling me of her current stressor.

"Maddi was high on drugs and was threatening to kill herself, so she got hospitalized," she says. Melissa mentions how she's trying to get Maddi into counseling. She mentions funding for her counseling and how Maddi is in the Victim Witness Program.

"How is Maddi in this program?" I ask.

"Well, she's been molested by her dad the past three years." When Maddi was around 13 years old, she got very "difficult to handle" by my sister. My brother-in-law and Maddi also did not get along at all. My sister felt the best thing at the time was to send Maddi to live with her biological father, Marty. Maddi is now back under the guardianship of my sister.

My stomach turns. Melissa says, "Yeah, she was molested really badly."

"Do you know if Maddi was molested by him when she was younger?" I ask.

"It probably began when she was a baby," my sister says matter-of-fact. "Then, when she went to live with him at age 13, it started again."

"Can I tell you something?" I ask. "I think Marty molested me when I was little, also."

"Do you think?" she says, "I wouldn't doubt it," then resumes talking about how stressed out she is with Maddi.

After a break I tell Melissa that my molestation involved penetration. She says that with Maddi, the molestation involved anal and vaginal penetration and oral sex.

The last two weeks, Melissa has been trying to get Maddi to report it to the police. Maddi does not want Marty to go to jail, though, so she is refusing. She accidentally let it slip out at some point to a police officer when she was high. Once learning that they would be picking up Marty and taking him to jail, Maddi "came unglued," according to my sister. "She threatened to kill herself and burn down the house, and she had the guts to do," she continues.

Melissa says they have felony charges against Marty, including supplying drugs to Maddi. However, he has taken off and left the state. Melissa is trying to get a restraining order on Marty on Maddi's behalf.

Melissa continues to tell how Marty was very controlling of Maddi, preventing her from going to school. For a time, he even masqueraded Maddi around as his "wife". She says Marty would watch pornography, then experiment with the newfound acts on Maddi.

"I'm glad, in a way, that you told me what you did, because I didn't know how much of what Maddi said to believe," Melissa tells me.

Believe all of it. How can you not believe your own daughter? I think to myself. But that is the pattern in my family.

Melissa tells me of how Marty raped her and of her considering putting Rick up for adoption. "I cried myself to sleep every night and felt so bad for Maddi who heard me." Maddi was then 2 ½ years old. So my sister did feel at one time, I realize.

"I'm sorry this happened to you, too," Melissa finally says to me. "A lot of the stuff you've been going through makes sense now."

Melissa says she assumed that Maddi's early sexual "acting out" was the result of the incidences that happened with my cousin. But now she realizes it was "stuff she learned from her father."

After I hang up the phone with my sister, I just cry. Everything feels dream-like. Did I even have the conversation with her? *Wow, I really was abused*, I think to myself. I picture my little girl body having these things happen to it. I feel very sad for myself and for Maddi. I then think of pictures I've drawn, my bodily memories and my dreams. I think particularly about the dreams that felt different, felt more real or like visions.

I still want to doubt it all, though. I don't have any movie-picture memories! There is no *proof*. I'm going to tell Mom that I was molested and see if it feels any more real. I'll see if she has any information about it, something to validate my experience.

I decide to pick up the phone and call her. I check with her to see if she is aware of what has happened with Maddi.

"Have you talked with her since she's been in the hospital?" I ask her.

"Yeah, I talked with her yesterday, and I talked with her just before you called," she replies.

"I want to tell you something related to that," I start.

"Okay," in a tone that sounds like she already knows. Does she? Has she spoken with Melissa? They are always talking on the phone together.

"Marty molested me when I was little, too."

"He did," she responds immediately. Not a question, more like a fact. "Hmmm...(pause)...that's terrible," still with very little feeling in her voice. "Wish I had known about it then."

"Yeah, I wish that too," I reply.

"Well, anyway, um, what's past is past. Nothing can be done about it. Except I hope he goes to prison for the rest of his miserable life...Well, anyway, let me know when a good time is to come down to take your car to get the oil changed. You said you're off the 24th, 25th and 26th?"

"I'm off school, but I have to work," I reply.

"Well, I know you have to work."

"I'll probably just get it changed before then," I really have no desire to see her.

"Alrighty. Well, we'd like to come down and see you before too long…it's been a while since we saw you…"

I don't respond. I feel like more needs to be said. How dare she change the subject so quickly!

"You know?" she asks, encouraging a response out of me.

"Yeah, I know," I finally reply. My heart is pounding. I need to say more! "Mom, I want to talk more about what happened," deciding to press forward.

"Okay, okay, go ahead," she says.

"It's not just 'what's past is past'."

"Okay," she replies in a sing-song voice.

"It affects my entire life."

"Well, of course it does." How would she know? Or, maybe she *does* know and that is the issue.

"I think it would be good to talk one-on-one instead of over the phone…but whatever you want. Was it more than once?" she inquires.

"I don't know. I have snippets of memories. I don't have a whole series of well-laid-out pictures in my head."

"Where was I?" she asks. There is a hint of feeling coming through those words…but only a hint.

"I don't know," I tell her. "I told Melissa, and, uh, I can tell you some of the stuff that happened, if you're ready to hear that," I say with a nervous laugh.

"Well, I'd rather wait for us to be in person to discuss it."

"Okay."

"Let me know a day I can come down."

"Okay," I agree. "I'll see you later, then."

I decide to invite Mom to a therapy session with me to discuss things further. I feel I need support to be able to be in the company of my mother and to discuss the difficult topic. My mom sends me an email telling me how I need to "return to Jehovah." I feel that her message is a type of defense. This information is too painful for her, so she generalizes it into, in essence, bad things happen and you just need to return to God. This way, she doesn't have to feel anything, nor does she have to take any responsibility. It will all be made better if I "return to Jehovah."

While trying to fall asleep, I imagine the following scenario: I am at the session with Mom and Terri. I tell Mom of the abuse. No response. In an attempt to get her to feel, I begin to go into dramatic detail of what transpired. "He sticks his man-size penis into my little girl-size vagina and thrusts, and with each thrust says, 'You fuckin'…little… bitch!'" At this point I am crying hysterically and writhing in pain, and as I look at my mother I see a stone statue sitting there, incapable and/ or unwilling to let these words and feelings penetrate. I feel frustrated and angry, immensely sad and abandoned. There is nothing I can do but cry.

I feel a tremendous amount of anger towards my mom right now. I try to think of her reaction in terms of defenses so that I can somehow deal with this anger and hatred, but that too is a defense. I hate her because she does not feel. I hate her because she does not want me to feel. In her email she stated that I am an "intelligent, reasoning person." I do not merely consist of a head, mother! I have a heart, too.

I fear my actual reaction during the session. I fear I will disintegrate and not be able to pull myself back together. I fear my hatred will eat me alive.

I find it interesting that as I was reading her e-mail, and as I was feeling this anger, I wanted to turn it towards myself. As I thought,

"I hate her!" I had the impulse of taking my nails and ripping and tearing at my skin. Like some savage animal, shredding myself, seeing the blood pouring all over my clothes and the floor, leaving myself for dead. I guess it's easier (and safer?) to hate myself than it is to hate others, particularly her.

She joins me in a session with Terri. It doesn't go anything like my imaginings, except for the stone statue part. No hysterics. I tell her of the abuse, and how I feel it took place mostly at nighttime, which is why she never knew.

We also speak of spiritual beliefs. I get the sense my mom doesn't think it is appropriate to be discussing such things in front of this outsider, Terri. "I just want to be loved and accepted for who I am, unconditionally," I tell her. I know it's not possible for my mom to do this for me, but at least I voice it. I let her know I accept her belief system, and would like it if she could respect that I do not believe the same. We have to agree to disagree. For Mom, there is no accepting any other belief system, because there is only one Truth, and that is where she is coming from.

%%   %%   %%

Some time passes. I call out to Little Kristi. I hear her whimpering. I yearn to hold her close now, but she is still lost. "Kristi! Kristi, where are you?" I cannot see her anywhere, all I see is the darkness in which she travels.

A jaguar arrives from off to my right. She is a magnificent creature – sleek, powerful and beautiful. Her green eyes are mesmerizing, able to pierce through any darkness. Jaguar nods her head to me then goes in search of Little Kristi. She finds her very quickly. Little Kristi is so happy to be with Jaguar. Jaguar invites her to crawl up onto her back. Little Kristi does not hesitate; she immediately crawls onto her, more than ready to be carried away from this place.

Jaguar sees for Little Kristi, sees the path that leads towards the light, to where I am waiting. They both approach me. Little Kristi slips off of Jaguar's back and walks up next to me. Jaguar waits just a short distance away. I yearn to hold Little Kristi, but I cannot. I can only look down at her. Her pain frightens me. I don't know what to do with it. I feel disconnected from her, like I don't even know her anymore.

Chapter 18

The most destructive cultural conditions for a woman to be born into and to live under are those that insist on obedience without consultation with one's soul, those with no loving forgiveness rituals, those that force a woman to choose between soul and society, those where compassion for others is walled off..., where the body is seen as something needing to be 'cleaned,'...where the new, the unusual, or the different engenders no delight, and where curiosity and creativity are punished and denigrated instead of rewarded..., where the soul is not recognized as a being in its own right.... When an individual's particular kind of soulfulness, which is both an instinctual and a spiritual identity, is surrounded by psychic acknowledgment and acceptance, that person feels life and power as never before. Ascertaining one's own psychic family brings a person vitality and belongingness.

-- C. P. Estes, *Women Who Run With the Wolves*

※   ※   ※

I'm standing in the peanut-butter aisle at Safeway, doing my weekly shopping. I'm contemplating all the many choices in peanut butter. There are much too many. A woman walks up from my left, pauses, and starts contemplating the instant oatmeal choices, which happen to be next to the peanut butter. I am approximately six feet to the right of her and about 3 feet behind.

I switch from contemplating the peanut butter to contemplating her. I am, for some unknown reason, fascinated by her and cannot take my eyes off her. *Why am I drawn to her?* I ask myself. It's an unusual feeling. *Is it her hair? Is it her clothes? Is it her face?* I continue to self-inquire. I cannot even see her entire face, only her right cheek and jaw. I don't know what it is. *It must be her hair. I really like her hair.* She chooses an oatmeal, and no doubt feels my silent inquiry in her direction. My heart rate quickens.

As she turns to the right to continue down the isle, she glances at me and smiles a friendly smile. I make brief eye contact and smile back. At the very moment of eye contact, I feel it. I feel a warm, butterfly feeling running a quick, straight line from my neck, through my solar plexus, down to that dangerous little region between my legs. Whoa! What the hell was that?!

I get home and immediately ask Karen, "What does it feel like to be attracted to somebody?"

"Well," she starts, "you feel it in your body," she then hesitates, trying to find the words.

I interrupt, describing the encounter with the Peanut Butter Woman. "Yep, that's about it," Karen confirms. Karen is extremely supportive of me in general. She is like family to me, so there is support in this experience as well.

I begin to explore the possibility of my sexual orientation being inclined towards women. I meet up with a group from a calendar listing in a local newspaper. It's a group for lesbian and bi-women. There is an event coming up with members of the group going on a nature walk. That's perfect! I love nature! I'm going to pretend to be lesbian-for-a-day and join them on this walk.

I meet with the group. It is a small gathering. There are three women and a 4-year-old grandson of one of the women. As we talk and go on the walk, I feel extremely comfortable with them. I usually feel very shy and don't feel like talking much with strangers. I am surprised by my own outgoingness and comfort level.

I decide to continue to meet up with the group in other activities – board game nights, movie nights, etc. In all of the events I have the same experience – comfort. This comfort comes from a feeling of familiarity. A familiarity not felt with my own family.

I talk with Terri about my grieving. I feel I am grieving so much. I am grieving a lost childhood. I am grieving the loss of parents that I never had, that I wished I had. I am grieving the invasion of the body snatchers, grieving the invasion of the soul snatchers. I am grieving being raised a Witness. I am grieving a possible repressed sexual orientation. I am even grieving things that have not yet transpired, if that is possible. I am grieving the discontinuance of therapy, which is coming soon. I am grieving the death of the "patient".

I am grieving for my niece. I cannot comprehend how my sister could have let Maddi go live with the very man who raped her. Melissa also tells me that one of the women Marty cheated on her with during their short marriage was no woman at all. She was a 14-year-old girl. And yet, she allows her first-born, her own daughter, to go live with him!

The abuse started from day one, when Marty picked up Maddi. It continued thereafter, day after day, for 3 years. Maddi had the courage early on to tell Marty's second wife what was happening to her. His wife called Melissa and told her. Melissa didn't believe Maddi's story. "She's just a problem child," I heard my family say over and over again throughout the years, in reference to Maddi. Maddi, too, was abandoned. The mothers don't listen, don't want to hear. They are stuck in their own worlds, disconnected from anyone else, including their own children.

It is revealed that Marty has also abused his daughter from his second marriage. There are countless others this man has hurt. It is the lack of connection, communication, the code of silence, in families that enable these heinous acts to continue and proliferate. Abusers depend on it.

Yes, I am grieving a lot. I am grieving those lost aspects of self. I hate the fact that there is still so much trapped in darkness behind a closed door. It is like I am forbidden to have access to my own life, to really know myself. I see a division in my mind – one side light, the other dark. The dark half belongs to me too, so why can't I have it!?

I want those hidden, those "forgotten" pieces of my life. How can I explain to someone the craving for a whole, complete existence when she has been whole all along? How can I help her understand this undying need?

"What's so important about having to know everything?" Terri asks. I'm not sure, but I can compare it to an amputation. Somehow, though I may not be able to see it, I can FEEL the ghost image of when I was whole, the residue of the experience that has managed to trickle down through all these years. My legs were cut off, I can feel their absence, and I desperately yearn to have them back so I can walk again, and run and skip and jump. I am simply unwhole. To experience life fully I need those missing pieces put back in their proper place. Then, and only then, will I no longer miss that which I so long ago experienced.

I'm sliding down a hole towards a puddle of sadness made by the tears I've cried during my descent. The closer and closer to the bottom I come, the deeper and sadder I am. Eventually…no, not eventually… *soon*, I will splash into the salty water. I will be drenched in sadness. I cannot tell as yet whether I will breathe in the water and drown, whether I will breathe in the water and live (reverting back to an embryonic state), or whether I will crawl out in time in order that I may take in a breath of air.

The water glistens, a reflection of the tiny circle of light high above. Its surface is smooth, slowly taking in with utmost care the droplets of salty water which run down the sides of the dirt and stone wall ahead of me, the droplets which meet the larger body, the mother.

I'm writing an email to my mom. This is how it reads: "Hi Mom. Mom, I think I should tell you something. Perhaps this would be more appropriate in person than via email, but it's easier for me this way. I'm not sure how you will take this, probably not well, but you mentioned to me before that you will love me no matter what, and I hope this is true. So, I'll just come out and say it – I'm a lesbian. Love, Kristi."

It doesn't really matter that I'm not 100% sure that I'm a lesbian yet. I'm 90% sure, and that's close enough.

She responds to the email in the expected way. "Returning to Jehovah's organization is what is necessary," she writes. "I will not and cannot accept what is perversion, and neither will anyone else in our family." She talks of how I need to move back home, how I need to remove myself completely from the environment I am in. Yes, my environment. I am surrounded by friends who love and support me. Indeed, a hostile setting. "I pray that you will correct your thinking. Until you do there will be no further communication," she concludes.

So, my mother abandons me once again. There has been emotional abandonment since I can recall. I would attempt to describe my family life to friends of mine as a child and teenager, and I eventually realized they would never be able to fully grasp the solitude I felt, the cold, distant parents. They could not see it. After all, my family life looked intact – mother, father, siblings, all living under one roof.

Then, more recently, there has been my mother's spiritual abandonment. She cannot accept a belief system different from her own. Her constant attempts at reconversion are evidence of that. There is no such thing as unconditional love in a Jehovah's Witness household. That abandonment was quite a blow.

So, now, my mother has merely gone one step further and abandoned me physically. To me, her abandonment feels familiar. It is consistent with her past actions. It is just how my mom is.

Finally, after some time, I kneel down on one knee in front of Little Kristi, bringing myself to her level. I speak softly to this 5-year-old, shy, blonde girl. "Do you know who I am?" I ask her. She nods her head yes, while keeping her solemn, blue eyes pointing towards the ground, too shy to make eye-contact.

Jaguar now walks up and sits right next to me. "Would you like to pet her?" I invite Little Kristi. A light sparks in her eyes, as she now peers up at me. She nods again. "Jaguar really loves you," I say, as she pets her head.

"I really love you, too. Do you know why I am here?" I ask. Little Kristi shakes her head no. "I'm here to keep you safe. I'm here to let you know that no more bad things are going to happen to you. I'm always going to be here for you. You never have to be alone again. I'm also here to give you a big hug. Would you like that?"

"Yes," she replies, using her voice, which is clear, no difficulty whatsoever in being understood. I give her a hug.

"Would you like to stay with me?" I ask, as we separate from our hug, my hands resting on her shoulders.

Little Kristi looks in my eyes and sees that I am a really nice person, fun and also very loving. "Yes," she replies.

"Okay, here we go then. It'll be an adventure!" I say with a glimmer in my own eyes. Little Kristi smiles and feels a sense of belonging and connection, a sense of hope and future, looking forward to the untold magic that lies in store. She then takes a step and walks into me and disappears in a flash of light. I then feel a warm, glowing sun in my heart and one in my womb. With that, I feel I am whole again. A smile spreads across my lips, and a healing river of love runs forth, cascading like a waterfall.

※   ※   ※

On the 5th year anniversary of therapy, I send a letter to Terri. "You have always been so accepting of whatever course I would choose to take, and you refused to give up on me despite my many and desperate attempts to get you to do so.

"At times I wonder why you didn't walk away. Most people probably would have. I think that possibly it is because you have x-ray vision and are able to see through to a person's very soul, able to see through all the refuse that I had built up around me to the naked and needy little girl at the center of it all. You were able to see beauty where all I saw was ugliness. You were able to envision a bright future full of potential where all I observed was a dark and oppressing past and present. You passed on your gift of sight to me and for that I will be forever grateful. I'm not sure how you did it, and I'm not completely sure how I got from there to here. One thing I am sure of, though, is that being real is what it's all about. You have always been real with me and from you I am learning to be real, with others and with myself. With this reality comes a strength and a freedom. For the first time in my life I feel I am living for myself. What an amazing feeling! My family cut the ties; I'm free to go and I'm ready to fly!

"Terri, you mean so much to me. Certain experiences cannot be expressed in words. The darkest moments of despair have no words, and then there are things so great and so powerful that words cannot encompass them. The appreciation I feel for all your hard work, the gratitude I feel for your giving of yourself, is one such experience. To reduce it down into an overly simplistic form, you helped me to grow. Where I was once a tantrum-throwing infant, I am now a verbal adult. From pieces to wholeness, from death to life, from being numb to being able to love. Happy anniversary."

*% *% *%*

This year is one of completions. I graduated from college with a B.A. in Psychology, Summa Cum Laude, for which I give myself a big pat on the back. I also completed therapy with Terri after 5 years and 5 months, also deserving of a pat.

In addition, it is a year for new beginnings. I am starting a Ph.D. program in the fall. I have started a relationship with a woman, Lisa.

Currently, I do not identify as a lesbian. I have been smashed into categories and labels all my life. It is much too cramped a place to be. I want the freedom of simply being me. I don't have to affiliate myself with being lesbian, or bi-sexual, or straight. The beauty in life is we really don't have to categorize ourselves if we don't choose to. I am simply Kristi.

This year of endings and beginnings is indicative of life in general. When I was in therapy, the same issues kept circling around, time and time again. Mostly the issues were Mom, Abuse and Spirituality. Terri likened it to a spiral. At the time, the spiral metaphor illustrated how I dealt with the same issues, but was able to spiral upward from them, gaining a new, broader perspective each time they circled back around.

There is the life and death circling as well. I have regained my life, but my father is losing his. I decide to visit him upon learning that he has been diagnosed with cancer. I haven't spoken to any member of my family in over a year. My father has said he would like to have a connection with me. He is not a Jehovah's Witness, so that connection is possible. However, I feel I really do not know him. But here is an opportunity to get to know him.

I arrive at my parent's home to find a very tired, rapidly-aging, pale father lying on the couch. He rises slowly to his feet, smiling, to give me a hug. I realize the effort it takes for him to do this, and I love him for it. Mother is nowhere around. Maddi is here with her new baby, Hope. Maddi gives me a hug.

Mom is lying down in the bedroom, I hear, sick with a sore throat, some minor cold or allergy reaction. She emerges a while later, not to greet me, but to feed Hope. She makes no eye-contact with me, nor does she utter a word. I am invisible.

I speak with Dad a bit about doctors and tests and the probable fatality of his cancer. Large growths were discovered on his liver and spleen about 4 weeks ago. Mostly, we just sit together in silence, communicating without words.

Melissa pulls up in the driveway with a Jehovah's Witness friend of hers and her two younger daughters in the backseat. I am holding Hope in my arms when Melissa enters the house. Dad is sitting on the couch. I stand a few feet from the front door. "Hello," I say to her as she passes behind me. Melissa stops, turns towards me.

"Hi, Hope," she says, giving a little tickle to her belly. She walks on towards the bedroom where Mom is lying down once again.

Maddi suggests that perhaps now is a good time to visit my grandma that I love so dearly, who now lives about an hour away. We head out the door, by necessity passing Melissa's car where the friend and my nieces, Cassie and Jasmine, wait. The door where Jasmine, the youngest, is sitting is partway open. She looks at me. I smile. She makes a motion towards me, standing half-way in the car, half-way out, when she stops and remembers that she is not to touch me, not to talk to me, not consider me her aunt any longer. She sits back down on the car seat.

I continue walking, remembering how, at each and every visit prior to this, my nieces and nephews would run to me and hug me so hard I would practically get knocked over. The confused, hurt look on Jasmine's face just now is burned into my memory forever.

Once I am in my car with the door fully closed, I see all three exit Melissa's car and head inside the house. No one looks back. It is safe now that the big, bad, evil, dirty aunt is going away. The big, bad, evil, dirty aunt that used to play with them when they were lonely, hold them when they needed comfort, and listen to them when they needed support and understanding.

Maddi and I drive to my grandma's house. Maddi is fuming. I try not to show her too much of my pain and anger, but I let her know it is there, that I do feel. Maddi has a mind of her own and doesn't listen to her mom or my mom in their attempts to have no family member interact with me. Maddi is strong that way.

At Grandma's house, I am welcomed, as always, with open arms. Nothing ever changes with her. She is loving towards me no matter what.

Later, Maddi and I return to my parents' house to find my brother, his wife and kids there on the patio area. They are also Jehovah's Witnesses. Maddi and I walk up. My brother's son looks up at me and smiles. I smile back. I don't speak first, like with Melissa, for I need to get a less abrasive feel for things this time. I wait for my brother, Dean, the only sibling I really grew up with since he was closest to me in age, greet me first. He speaks…to Maddi about slacking on her lawn-mowing job, jokingly. A few seconds of idle chit-chat about some upcoming BBQ they are going to. Then, "Well, we better get going…" he says.

I sigh and head into the house. As the door closes behind me, I hear Dad call Dean to him. Not thinking anything of it, I head to the bathroom. I finish using the restroom and head into the kitchen when Maddi stops me saying, "Don't go out there! Your dad is talking to Dean, and he's crying saying, 'You're tearing apart this family…'" I wasn't planning on going back out there, but go Dad! I was proud of my dad standing up for something, even if it was just this dysfunctional family.

They remain talking outside for a few minutes, then I hear Dean and his family drive away. Dad does not immediately enter the house. I figure he is composing himself. Once he comes in I notice his reddened eyes. He sits next to me. We continue to converse in silence.

After some time has passed, I head outside. Dad follows me. We set up a couple of chairs on the front lawn in the shade. Mom is still in the bedroom. Maddi asked earlier if she has been in there the entire time. Dad replied no, she came out a while ago (while I was gone). The tone in his voice was one of irritation.

Dad and I just sit for a while. He then asks, "Are you and your mother ever going to work things out?"

"There's nothing to work out," I say. I am unsure what he does and does not know. He and Mom never really talk, so I don't know what she has told him, if anything. I think to myself, *It would be relatively easy for me to regain my mother's approval. I would simply have to slough off pieces of myself in the process of cramming myself back into a box in which I never truly fit in the first place. It could be done, but then I would be, at best, unhappy and unreal. At worse, I would die, probably even physically, but definitely mentally, emotionally and spiritually. I would die because what would be sloughed off are my mind, my heart and my soul. One's true self cannot survive without these, and, unlike some people, I do not want to live an existence devoid of essence.*

But I keep these thoughts to myself, and just give Dad the simple version. "Mom is ignoring me because I'm no longer a Witness and so does not approve of me." I add that I do not feel it is right, though, to shun me and for other members of the family to shun me.

Dad wholeheartedly agrees and says, "I would not belong to a religion that treats people the way you are being treated."

"That's partly why I don't belong anymore," I reply.

"I've tried to talk with your Mom and reason with her," he tells me.

"You can't reason with her."

"She won't even talk to me about it," he continues. "I talked to Dean and probably made him upset, but I don't care. The family is being torn apart."

I started seeing the family through his eyes. He sympathizes with me, but he has also seen the family as a cohesive unit prior to this. I never really saw it that way.

"The adults are keeping the children away from me as if I am some monster. I am still the same person I always was (sort of). I'm not a bad person."

"I know. I know," Dad says.

I realize this is the most my Dad and I have spoken in my entire life. We are speaking more than all the other times we have spoken *combined*. I feel it is his fatality that is encouraging this, allowing him to open. He wants the family to be a unit and be together after he's gone. I take a deep breath. "Thank you for being there for me," I say to him, as I try to keep my voice from sounding too shaky. He nods. He thanks me for coming down to visit him.

As I prepare to leave from my visit, I give Dad a hug. Mom makes an appearance and is holding Hope, much the same as I was holding her earlier when Melissa came in. I say bye to Hope and give her a kiss. I am careful to not make invisible the person holding the baby. "Bye, Mom."

"Bye," she says. The amount of disgust, or perhaps it's just disappointment, I hear in that one little word is overwhelming. I have to go *now*. Dad walks me to my car. We say bye again. It appears he wants to say more. I want to say more, too, but I don't know what at this point. I drive away.

When I arrive home, I cry all the tears I had been holding in all day. I am just beginning to form a relationship with my dad. His cancer has drawn us together. The very thing that is drawing us closer will soon be separating us forever.

On another visit shortly thereafter, Dad seems to have a clearer picture of the family, and how the religion separates us. I feel he understands that I have to be true to who I am. And the rest of the family will be who they are. Things probably won't change. He says to me, "You know, after I'm gone, your Mom, Melissa and Dean will still treat you the same way."

"I know…it's okay, I'll be alright," I say, as I start crying. I get up from the chair I'm sitting in and walk to him and sob on his shoulder. He is crying now, too. I kneel down, wrap my arms around his belly, resting my head under his arm and just cry and cry.

A year and a half later, Dad passes from this life. I am able to be with him at the moment of his passing. I sit by his bed and witness his last exhale, the final release of that which our bodies find unnecessary. No inhale follows this release, the indication that this physical life is once again renewed, reborn. A lifetime showing itself to be nothing but a single breath cycle – enter, breathe in…exit, breathe out.

And in this circling nature of life, where I have, after much time and effort, found contentment and understanding with the issues of Mom and Abuse, the issue of Spirituality decides to come around once again.

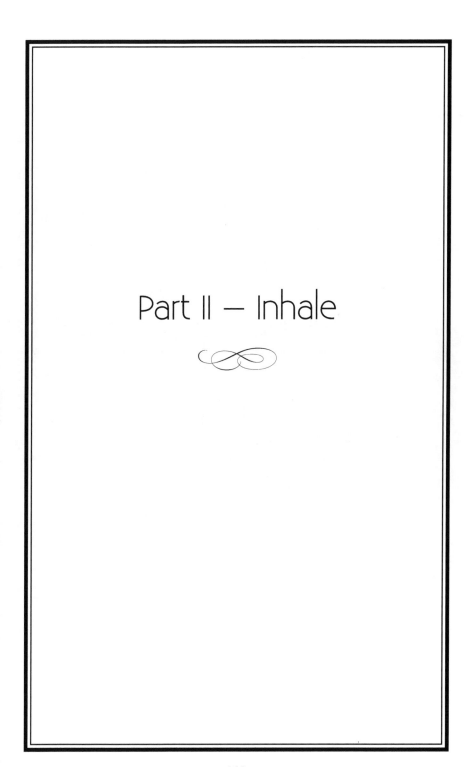

Part II — Inhale

Chapter 19

I love the dark hours of my being in which my senses drop into the deep. I have found in them, as in old letters, my private life, that is already lived through, and become wide and powerful now, like legends. Then I know that there is room in me for a second huge and timeless life.

-- Rainer Maria Rilke

% % %

I'm watching *The Matrix* again for the 10th time or more. It's my favorite movie, at least in the sci-fi genre. I'm watching it with a couple of my friends. As we watch the movie, we converse about the nature of reality, a topic with which I'm continually fascinated. As Neo has just awakened to the "real" world, Morpheus is talking with him about how we base our view of reality merely on what our senses convey to us.

Similarly, here I am, looking at Keanu Reeves and Laurence Fishburne, thinking they are real people. In "reality", though, they are simply tiny dots of color on the screen that my mind is interpreting as pictures of people who exist. I recall sticking my face right on the TV screen when I was a young child and seeing the "truth" to the picture before me – just thousands of dots of red, blue and green. Going another step further, my mind is also interpreting the television that displays the tiny dots, the furniture around me, my friends in the room, as "real". But they are images that the camera-like lens of my eyes are taking in, creating electrical signals that my brain then interprets. Similarly, the chair in which I am sitting, the sensors in my skin are creating signals that my brain then interprets as tactile feeling.

So if the scene around us is just signals that our brains are interpreting, what lies beneath the layer of perception? How many times do we dream and truly feel we are experiencing that scene? We do not realize it is not "real," that we are merely dreaming, until we wake up.

Amidst these ponderings I think of Siddhartha Gautama, the Buddha. When he walked the earth, many people inquired who or what he was. They asked if he were a god, an angel, a saint. Siddhartha answered no to all of these. "Then what are you?" they yearned to know.

Buddha answered simply, "I am awake."

This is what Buddha means. The Sanskrit root *budh* denotes both to wake up and to know. The Buddha, then, means "Enlightened One," or the "Awakened One." While the rest of humanity existed in a slumbering consciousness, dreaming an existence believed to be the waking state, Siddhartha opened his eyes, seeing the dream for what it is, and experienced true awakening.

I think about all of this as I watch *The Matrix*. The movie takes on much more meaning than it had up to this point. It is no longer just a really well done sci-fi film with a hot woman in black leather. It is a springboard for leaping into the unknown, an expanded perspective. Neo woke up. The Buddha woke up. Have there been others? Can anyone wake up? Can *I* wake up? If so, how? And what does this awakened state feel like? The Buddha sat meditating under a tree until he woke up. I have not taken meditation very seriously, but now, I'm curious. Does meditation allow one to tap into another state of awareness, one that is more "real" than this existence?

All of these questions feel huge and overwhelming. My mind feels like it is being blown wide open with possibility.

%%   %%   %%

(Intermission) To you, the reader. If you have not yet seen *The Matrix*, you may want to do so at this point in my story. Yes, I mean it. You may take this time before you read on (because it *will* keep coming up) to drive down to the video store, rent it and watch it. Or, buy it, since you might want to watch it more than once. It is one of those movies that one can watch several times, gaining a deeper understanding of the story with each viewing. It is chock full of beautiful, intricate layers.

You may also want to rent or buy *Matrix Reloaded* and *Matrix Revolutions*, the second and third movies, as it is a trilogy. If you simply watch the first one, you will not get the complete story. It would be like watching *Lord of the Rings: Fellowship of the Ring* and never watching the rest of the trilogy. You would never find out if Frodo deposits the ring back into the fiery depths of Mordor. Similarly, if you don't watch all three *Matrix* movies, you won't know what happens to Neo and if he ever understands his true state of being.

%%   %%   %%

Four years ago, I decided to drop out of grad school after only one semester. It didn't feel right. The entire month before I made my decision, I had an uneasy feeling in the pit of my stomach. I had just completed almost 5 ½ years of my own therapy, and all of a sudden I was learning how to be "on the other side of the couch." I needed a break. I didn't feel I could sit day after day in a room listening to people's issues. I was tired of issues. I felt I would go back to grad school and become a therapist and teacher at some point, for I still desired to help others through these means, but at that particular time I needed to do something that I viewed as more fun!

I got a job at the local YMCA. Being a lover of learning, I didn't abandon school completely, of course. I took classes at the Junior College like karate, guitar lessons and sign language. It was just what I needed.

I am now the Director of Membership & Communications at the Y, and I'm flying on a plane to Virginia for a work-related training. I've been practicing meditating for a few months. There's not much to do on the plane, so I decide to just sit quietly and relax. I allow my breathing to slow, and I work on brushing away thoughts as they arise.

After a few minutes of this, an image appears in my mind. I see the image of an eye. It is at the level of my brow, and it is purple. It is actually just a purple outline of an eye. The background is black. The eye is blinking. I open my physical eyes in curiosity. *What is that?* I wonder to myself. I close my eyes again, trying to go back into that space, but cannot. It's gone now.

While in the hotel room during the training, I have the following dream:

I'm taking pictures of dead people. I have fond memories of them. Someone asks me what I am doing. "I'm trying to come to grips with a difficult concept," I reply, referring to death.

The dream shifts and now I am in a great deal of pain, but it is a means to an end. I am giving birth. I am simultaneously the one giving birth and the one being born. I feel an immense amount of pressure and urge to push. I am squatting at the foot of a bed with my arms up on the bed for support. I also feel extreme pressure surrounding my head and body as the one being born. It is tight and cramped.

I'm crying. It's so painful. I start pushing...then breathe...push... breathe. I am almost out. I scream out with one last painful push, the last necessary step...and I emerge. Then I wake up.

I check the clock and it reads 3:33am. I am sharing the room with two co-workers. I don't want to wake them, but I need to write down the dream, for it feels of great importance. It's pitch dark, as I crawl out of my bed, trying to make as little noise as possible. I must find paper and a pen, so I make my way towards my purse, tripping over shoes and furniture in the process. Eventually I retrieve a pen and an envelope that had accompanied my paycheck. I feel my way into the bathroom where I can turn on a light to begin recording the dream.

A month and half ago, I ended the relationship with my partner, Lisa. We were together 5 years, 7 months. We had a commitment ceremony. We even got married when Mayor Gavin Newsome opened up San Francisco City Hall for same-sex marriages. We had a nice home and two kitties. However, neither of us fully accepted the other for who she is. There was much love, granted, but there was something lacking, a disconnect. I felt our world views were very different. Most of all, I felt like I had a spiritual need, a seed, that could not find fertile ground and bloom in the relationship. She did, though, gift my life with many, many things during our time together, and I am very grateful to her.

This dream, then, arrives at an interesting time. I am birthing myself, coming into a new life, one of greater self-discovery.

For better or worse, I do not wait long to get into a relationship again. I do not intend to get into a relationship so quickly, but it happens. It is with Nicole, one of the friends with whom I was watching *The Matrix* and having the in-depth discussion. I feel there is a spiritual connection with her. She provides an environment for me to continue to grow in search of my spiritual truth.

Nicole invites me to go on a trip with her and a group to Teotihuacán, Mexico, and I decide to go. The group consists of about 30 people, coming from professions ranging from artist to business executive to engineer to mother. It is a spiritual "Power Journey" led by Heather Ash Amara and Raven Smith. Thousands of years ago, the city of Teotihuacán was a spiritual epicenter for the Toltecs, a group of individuals from a variety of tribal groups who achieved a level of spiritual enlightenment. Teotihuacán is "the Place Where Humans

Become Gods." I am interested in how thousands of people still come here with the intent of self-exploration and healing.

As soon as Nicole and I arrive in Teotihuacán (Teo, for short), we take a quick nap in our hotel room. We had gotten up early, and the trip was a bit tiring. I notice immediately how the quality of my dreams is different in this "power spot." The line between waking and dreaming feels blurred, the line between the "dream world" and the "real world."

The structural layout of Teo is in such a way as to facilitate shedding the layers of fear, guilt and whatever other obstacles we hang onto that keep us from experiencing our joy and true nature. Heather Ash and Raven include exercises, meditations, and rituals throughout the journey to facilitate this releasing as well.

Heather Ash also teaches yoga to the group each morning. Prior to this, I had only taken yoga a handful of times at a gym, and did not have much interest in continuing it. On this trip, though, I am really enjoying yoga. I set a plan to start taking yoga minimum 2 times per week once I return home.

There is a point amidst the ancient ruins where we walk down the Avenue of the Dead in the plaza towards the Pyramide de la Luna, Pyramid of the Moon, which is a representation of feminine energy. In this particular exercise, it is here along the avenue that we are to face the Angel of Death, which is, in a sense, embodied by two members in our group. These two individuals will look into our hearts to see if we are ready to walk on towards the Pyramid of the Moon, if we are really ready to surrender our baggage and take the next step in discovering ourselves. This exercise is a reenactment of the same one Toltecs participated in during their spiritual journey thousands of years ago.

I have a bit of anxiety as I make my way towards the Angel of Death. I think about angels and demons. Since childhood, Mom instilled a deep fear in me about not letting myself be open, perchance demons would come into me and take over. I would hear stories about the ill fates that befell those who had been possessed.

A couple of my brothers had experiences my mom claimed were of a demonic origin. One brother heard footsteps throughout the house but no other family members were awake and walking about. When he verbally called out the name Jehovah, the footstep noises reportedly went away, but it was a frightening experience for him. My mom felt it was linked to a pair of motorcycle boots that my brother had been given. The boots came from Marty, interestingly enough. I cannot recall my other brother's experience, but my mom believed it also was related to an item given to him by Marty. No further incidents occurred after these items were disposed of through burning them.

My fear around demons grew stronger after hearing of my brothers' experiences. I would have nightmares of my brother being possessed and trying to knock down my bedroom door to attack or kill me. I would listen to the tiniest of sounds in the house, checking to see if they sounded like shuffling footsteps, doing all of this, of course, with my head under the covers. I never came face to face with any demon as a child, unless you count the human form.

Still walking down the gravel pathway to the awaiting Angel of Death, I think about my time during the last few years of atheism/agnosticism where I lost that fear of demons. Since there was no God, there could not be any angels or demons in my mind. But now, once again, I'm thinking there is some form of God or Source, so then there may very well be demons. The Angel of Death requires a surrendering. But if I surrender, I will be open to those dark forces to take root. Surrendering is doing so to the unknown.

I continue to ponder how my brothers had the "demonic" experiences. Perhaps they had some unconscious realization that the "demon" was Marty. Again, I reassure myself, I did not ever experience any invisible demon. If I stay closed off to the darkness, would I not also be keeping myself closed off to the light? I decide to take the chance. I no longer want to live in fear, including fear of the unknown, and I don't want to be closed off to all that is good. I now stand face to face with a man named Jai, as he embodies the Angel of Death. As my heart races, I look at his kind eyes and warm smile, and I simply feel pure love pouring in through this angel. I surrender and allow him to look into my heart and see its willingness. He then says to me, "You may pass." Like my dream, where "I'm trying to come to grips with a difficult concept," I let go of my fear of Death.

There is an opportunity to release yet even more of what we carry that holds us back from experiencing our potential. This opportunity lies in a place in Teo simply referred to as the Women's Temple. It is underground, in the coolness of the earth. In one room of this temple is a very deep hole, which sinks even further into the earth. It looks similar to a well. It is into this opening that one can let go of sadness, grief, fear. The earth will take it all in willingly, without complaint, allowing us to be rid of it. Though I am not one of them, there are several who shed tears in this nurturing place. It is a place facilitating much healing, it seems.

At the end of the trip, several tell of their experiences, many of which have not been shared until this point. Some tell of visions they had. Raven tells how he saw the ancient deity, Quetzalcoatl, come out of the earth and fly over to the Pyramid of the Sun. He says it then began to consume itself, eating its own tail. There was also a wide, bright ring around the sun. The ring around the sun was not part of his vision. He looked up and saw it in this physical reality. The ring around the sun, I've read, symbolizes the "hierosgamos", or the "sacred marriage," union of male and female energies.

A woman named RMaya shares her experience. While in the Women's Temple, she felt a "snake-like energy" swirl through her. She felt like she represented a chalice, holding female energy and wisdom. She heard the words, "It is the woman who determines when the time is right for the seed to be planted, and the time is now." After the Women's

Temple, we went up to the Pyramid of the Sun, which represents masculine energy. She says that when we were on the Pyramid of the Sun, she, unbeknownst to anyone else, emptied the energetic chalice at the top.

Finally, another person, Jai, tells of his vision. He says that when we were all on the top of the Pyramid of the Sun doing the ceremony, there was a point when a large beam of sun energy came from the sun to the top of the pyramid. Then, within that beam, a flash, like a lightening bolt, came through and touched the Pyramid of the Sun. He says he got the feeling that this lightening bolt was a "fertilization" of sorts. Now it makes sense, he says, given the information from RMaya.

At this point, another member of the group, an artist, pulls out a picture that he drew several months ago and shows it to the rest of us. The picture illustrates the Pyramid of the Sun and Quetzalcoatl, a chalice and a ring around the sun.

I am in awe, and admittedly a bit confused, how there are several, completely separate, accounts that all seem to be part of a bigger picture. I'm not really tapped into the whole "vision" thing, but I keep an open mind. It is interesting, to say the least.

Chapter 20

Returning home, I continue my meditation practice and explore meditating with Nicole. During one meditation experience I sit on the bed, and Nicole puts some music on and sits behind me. She puts her arms around me and rests her right hand over my heart. I place my left hand over her hand. I close my eyes and relax. We just breathe and meditate together.

I then feel like I go on a journey unlike anything I have experienced before. I feel ecstasy swell in my heart one moment, then the sadness and grief of the entire world weighing on my shoulders the next. I feel so weighed down, and I realize my body is starting to slump forward. I open my eyes. I feel sobbing inside but it doesn't make its way out. Then…ecstasy and lightness again. I sit with these feelings for a while, simply experiencing how they feel moving through my body.

I close my eyes again and breathe. I now imagine or "see" Nicole and I, but as an energy bubble and in the midst of dark space with only a few bits of light around, like far-away stars. We are one bubble, and there is a smaller, intense light within the bubble in the same place as where my heart is, our hands are, in the physical realm. The bubble is light-energy of some sort, thin-banded, yellow. There is a feeling of space, of being in great expansiveness.

Shortly after this, I feel like I "wake up." It is only a brief moment of this feeling. But in that moment, I feel with every fiber of my being that I have some kind of enlightenment experience. I also know that after a few more moments pass, I will doubt myself.

I will say I had an enlightenment experience, but not *the* enlightenment experience, whatever that is, or the full awakening. Perhaps it is more like walking through doors. Ultimate reality, or truth, whatever you wish to call it, is always here, but we have to remove each of the veils or layers to truly see it.

I understand it like this: A person sees life through, let's say, 7 layers of clouded glass panes. Looking through these panes cause this person to see life only as fuzzy forms of grayness. He or she does not realize the world looks very different from what he or she is seeing. Through some means, one pane of glass gets lifted. "Oh," this person exclaims, "look at that! I see shapes." Another pane lifts. "I see edges. I didn't know objects had defined edges." A couple more panes lift off. Now there are colors visible, and so on.

Early in life, we see through all 7 panes. One, we don't realize we see through panes. Two, we don't know there are 7. Three, we don't know that if we keep trying, we can see the world completely unveiled, in its true state. After the first or any subsequent pane is lifted, we may very easily think we are *now* seeing the world as it truly is.

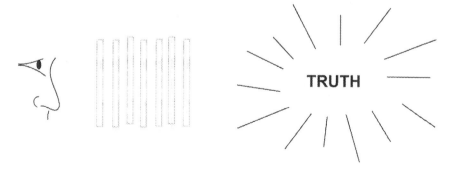

So in my meditation experience, I feel I experienced an awakening. But I will keep trying, through meditation, yoga and regular day-today living, to seek ultimate truth, for I most likely have 6 more doors to go through (or panes to be lifted), or 4 or 10.

% % %

It has been a month since being at Teo. I'm looking through my journal, and as I read over the last part, the "vision" of RMaya and the others, it becomes very clear to me that the "fertilization" that took place resulted in a female child, which symbolizes that an era or time period in the not-too-distant future will be focused more on feminine energy. This is not to say that we will all be going back to a matriarchal society, but to an appreciation and respect of the creative, nurturing, and intuitive spirit. I have no idea why or how this becomes clear to me, or where it comes from, but it is my experience.

% % %

Currently, most areas of my life are going very well and feel "easy." But not the area of romantic relationships. I feel very disconnected from Nicole, on the verge of breaking up. We make a point to come together, and we have a truly amazing conversation. During our conversation a chord is struck inside me, one that resonates deeply. It is as if a mirror is held up to me, and I am able to more clearly see the effects of my wall.

My wall, that thing that has kept so much inside over the years. That thing that has kept me from being fully open, communicative, and able to connect deeply with others. The effects of the wall still show up, particularly in my romantic relationships. I'm seriously tired of having it. "Wall?! Are you listening? I'm talking to you. Thanks for being there. You served your purpose well. You protected me and guarded me from further pain and disappointment after experiencing quite enough. But now, you no longer serve me; you are no longer an asset. You are a hindrance and a barrier to healthy closeness. Please be gone. I can go it alone, exposed." The wall responds to my tirade in the dreamtime.

Dream

My supervisor from work is with me, standing outside a building, perhaps a house. I feel sick, but in an odd way. There is a substance in my mouth. It looks like and has the consistency of wet sand. It builds up in my mouth, and I have to use my hand to scoop it out and throw it on the ground.

I'm talking with her, trying to explain something, or perhaps trying to get assistance from her for this odd thing happening to me. It is nighttime and late, and she seems tired. At one point, she seems upset at me because I have "ruined" her evening that she planned with her husband. She now feels obligated to stay with me, though.

For quite some time, this substance builds in my mouth, and I have to scoop it out and toss it away to keep from gagging. I do this over and over. Finally, it occurs to me what is going on. At this moment, I become lucid in the dream, realizing I am dreaming. I realize this sandy substance is part of my wall coming down, my internal, figurative wall that is no longer useful. It somehow has to get from the inside out, and what more appropriate way than through my mouth — the very means with which I keep the wall constructed or destructed — through not talking or talking.

At this lucid time, I just start laughing in the dream. I find it quite humorous. I laugh so hard, then I wake up in this reality with a smile on my face.

Despite my newfound understanding of how my wall still plays a role in close relationships, and even though I feel it is crumbling, I still decide to break up with Nicole. I start having doubts about my sexuality. You would think I'd have it all figured out by now, given that I'm 30 years old. I love being with women, no doubt there. But could I also be with a man? I have fantasies about being with men, but it seems different in person. But now that my wall is dismantling, perhaps I could be physically with a man. Perhaps that would be a breakthrough.

So I try it. I tell a very good male friend of mine, who has expressed feelings for me, that I am ready to date him. I forewarn him, though, "You know, there is a strong possibility that this won't work, that I only like being with women, and I end up breaking your heart." He is willing to take the chance. We kiss at the end of our first date.

The following day I get a voice-mail message from my ex, Lisa, that my beloved grandma is in the hospital and not expected to make it long. She's had a stroke, and now she has a staph infection and other major health issues. My sister-in-law, who didn't realize my phone number had changed, left the message on Lisa's machine, thinking I still lived with her. I call Lisa, after not having spoken with her in a year, and get the details about the hospital and such. We talk on the phone for about a ½ hour, shedding a few tears. We then set a day and time to have lunch, just as friends, to catch up.

The following day, on the 3-hour drive to visit my grandma, I think about my current situation. I do not feel good about kissing my friend. I feel it is a mistake that I am trying to date him. I just broke up with Nicole a very short while ago. And then I spoke with Lisa, for whom I still seem to have some feelings. Now my grandma is dying, the only family member who continually showed me so much love, my escape from my depressing, stifling childhood household. I feel overwhelmed.

Once I see my grandma, I know she does not have much longer to live. I don't know if she even realizes I am visiting her. She is highly medicated. I know it is not the way she would prefer to spend her last days. She would rather be at home in her favorite chair, or lying in her own bed, no medication, pain or not, no doctors or nurses, just family around.

I return from visiting my grandma and talk with my friend. I let him know it is a mistake to date him. I let him know in the scaredy-cat way of email. I still feel like crap for being in this situation, but I feel a bit better now that I have moved towards changing it. We talk in person about it a couple days later. We both feel it should have been left the way it was, just friends.

A few days later, I'm text messaging him. I then step into a teasing, flirtatious, seductive role. I invite him over to my place. We mostly just talk and sit on the couch. As he gets ready to leave, I ask if he wants to spend the night. "Sure," he says. I then lean over and give him a hug, then a kiss. More kissing and making out...clothes start coming off... all I have left on is my thong underwear. He has his pants on. We stop. I don't want to have full-on sex. He stays the night, but I don't think either of us sleeps.

The following day I feel very uneasy. I feel it in the pit of my stomach. It is that feeling that tells me I am not doing what I want to be doing at this time, the same feeling I experienced when I knew I had to drop out of grad school. The timing wasn't right for me. It is also the same day I scheduled to have lunch with Lisa. The lunch goes well, but *what am I doing?!*

There is SO MUCH NOISE in my head right now! I have to change whatever it is I am doing. I feel I'm hurting my friend. I also feel I'm hurting Lisa by giving her the impression and hope that I may be interested in her again, but I know we are not right for each other. I feel I'm hurting Nicole, even though we're not together and she knows nothing of what is going on. It is as if I'm "cheating" on her somehow, and she is bound to find out sooner or later. I've dreamed myself into this mess, now I need to dream myself out of it. I literally feel like I am stuck in a nightmare and can't wake up. Wake up! Wake up! Wake up! Wake up!

Things have been really clear for a long while. I'm happy, successful at work, have great friends... It's just the last few weeks that things seem really muddled, particularly in that tricky area of relationship. Something has knocked me so hard that now nothing is in alignment.

Everything is in flux. It all seems very unreal. I want peace, integrity, love. I feel I had these things just a short time ago. Come back! I'm trying to be my own therapist. *Is it some deeply-buried abuse stuff trying to resurface?* I circle back to that again. *Is it because I asked the wall to come down, and now it is, pieces tumbling out haphazardly. So now, am I having to figure out how to live life free of restraints?*

Just before I broke up with Nicole, I expressed to her how things seemed to feel really jumbled and confusing. She said in response, "You know, there is another trip to Teo next month." Nicole said she would not be going. Also, this trip would be with a smaller group and only of women, which is a first. Immediately, it felt right. That alone seemed clear. Yes, I will go to Teo. I signed up. It's funny how my life is still flowing in that circular pattern. Now Teo is coming back around.

Heather Ash emails me, confirming she received my registration. "Jill is going again, too," she says. Oh, good. That way I will know someone there, besides Heather Ash, of course. Jill was on the same trip I was a few months ago, and though I did not get to know her very well on the first trip, I liked her. She was very interesting. It was the first time for both of us for a trip like that. Jill, though, had been learning from Heather Ash and Raven through other means. She had also studied with a shaman teacher for several years. Jill seems to be an amazing shaman herself. She is very "connected", able to see things most others cannot, and able to receive messages.

About a week before leaving for Teo, I get back together with Nicole. It is my pattern. I broke up with Lisa three times, then returned to be with her. The fourth time, I did not go back, but I quickly got into another relationship. Now with Nicole I am feeling that familiarity of back and forth, back and forth.

Chapter 21

Five days prior to leaving for Teo, I get the news that my grandma died. I feel a huge loss. I will not be able to attend the funeral, for I will be in Mexico. I do not feel I want to cancel my trip to attend. I will honor her in Teo. Besides, the service would be a Jehovah's Witness service, a belief system far removed from me now. Grandma claimed she was a Jehovah's Witness, but she never attended meetings or studied much in the religion. She even celebrated holidays with her grandkids, coloring Easter eggs and cooking a delicious turkey dinner on Thanksgiving. She cussed and had a mind of her own. Indeed, she was considered one of the "weak" ones of the faith. Boy, did I love her! Still do, of course.

I call my mom to let her know I will not be attending and to give her my condolences about her mother passing. "It's been a long time since I've heard from you," she says. "How are you doing?" Yes, it has been over 3 years since Dad's death, which is when I last saw and spoke with her. I am more taken aback by her asking how I am. This is a first. We speak for about 20 minutes or so. She ends the phone call with "I love you." This is also a first. She never ended a call with "I love you."

I recall specifically bringing this up to her one day as a child. I would overhear other mothers and children, husbands and wives, saying "I love you" at the end of a phone call. "How come you never say 'I love you'?" I asked her. "Oh, people say that so much it loses any meaning," she replied. *But, what does it mean if you* never *say it?* I thought to myself.

Journal Entries: Teo – Day 1

On the way to Teo, I run into Jill in the airport. We are both in the ticket line waiting to check in. I am not too surprised to see her, since Heather Ash said she would be coming. Also, she lives not too far from me, so we fly out of the same location. It's good to see her, and we talk a bit about our upcoming adventure.

As soon as I walk onto the grounds of Teo, specifically the Dreaming House, where we are staying, I start to feel nauseous. The location of the Dreaming House is on land that was part of the original Toltec spiritual city. Some would call the area "sacred land." The nausea feels different from usual. I feel it off and on. Thankfully it's not constant. It's just odd. I can tell it isn't caused by anything physical. It feels like it is caused by something energetic. I have no idea what, though.

Heather Ash usually "feels into" most every aspect of these trips, including the lodging. She figures out ahead of time who gets roomed with whom and so on. As we arrive at the Dreaming House, Alberto, the owner and good friend of Heather Ash, says he has it all planned out and assigns rooms. Heather Ash decides to go with the flow. Jill and I end up being the two left over at the end, which means we end up being roommates.

Teo – Day 2

Led by Heather Ash, our small group of 13 women goes to visit the Pyramid of Quetzalcoatl. On our way we think about areas in our life where we dishonor ourselves, symbolically put them into rocks, acknowledge how those things have previously served us, and then toss them over the edge of one of the platforms into the area known as Hell. My areas are 1. Not maintaining my boundaries, 2. Not being true to my sexuality recently, 3. Not being open with emotions, and 4. Having a wall, particularly in romantic relationships and love. I understand how each of these things has served me, and I toss them over the edge. It's time for them to be gone.

We get to the Pyramid of Quetzalcoatl, the "Sovereign Plumed Serpent," a creature part snake and part bird, representing the union of matter and spirit, earth and sky. It is here that we take a "leap of faith." This area has two parts. On one side there is a high platform. On the other side is the Pyramid of Quetzalcoatl itself. In between the platform and the pyramid is a drop off of about 30 feet. The distance between the two is about 15-20 feet. Back in the time of the Toltecs, a spiritual leader would lead a group to this area in the dark of night. He or she would then challenge individuals in the group to make the leap from the platform to the pyramid, leaping into the "mouth" of Quetzalcoatl. Many would be scared and not jump, knowing the distance before them. Some, though, would jump. Unbeknownst to them, the spiritual teacher filled up the chasm with water, allowing those who took their leap of faith to make it safely. "A true spiritual teacher will never ask more of you than what you are capable of," Heather Ash explains after recounting this story for us.

Currently, the Pyramid of Quetzalcoatl is set up for tourists with a metal fence around the platform so that you cannot walk (or fall) down to the bottom of the drop off or go crawling on the pyramid. So we take our leap of faith in our minds, which is where it truly is anyway.

After the visit at the pyramid, Jill and I are chosen by Heather Ash to work with the Angel of Death. I don't know what this means exactly, but I'm going to take another leap of faith and just go with it. I recall what a powerful experience it was for me last summer.

Heather Ash leads Jill and me away from the rest of the group to stand in a particular location. Jill and I stand a few feet apart with our backs to the Pyramid of the Moon. There is a river flowing beneath the bridge where we stand, a river flowing through us. The rest of the women stand in two lines, facing us, several feet ahead. They are to walk up, one at a time for each of us. Jill and I are then to simply be present, look into their eyes. We then allow them to pass if they are ready, or we turn them around to go back into line to approach the Angel of Death again. Heather Ash comes over to me, puts her hands on my shoulders, and gently asks me to simply open my heart, to open it more for each person and just be present. "The Angel of Death will know what needs to be done," she says.

Jill and I stand there as the women approach us. *Open, breathe*. At first I'm very nervous. Then I feel like I take a back seat while the Angel of Death takes control, though I have every capability of taking back control if I want to. Even as people are walking towards me, before they are eye to eye, I can feel their intent, emotion and even see into their heart. It feels like there is a line from my heart directly to the heart of the woman across from me, and the hearts alone are communicating, reading each other. It is an experience unlike any other.

After a couple women pass, one woman approaches me and I immediately feel she needs to turn back around, that she's not yet ready. I get nervous again and start questioning whether or not I can turn her back. At that same moment I see Jill has just turned someone back around also. Great, now they'll think I'm just copying Jill. Whoa! I tell myself to step back. Kristi just got in the way. Follow my heart… so the Angel of Death turns her back.

The last woman approaches me. It is the woman whom Jill turned back. We look into each other's eyes and hearts. I feel like I'm looking into my own reflection. "Open," is all the Angel of Death says to her through me. I feel her open and she continues on.

I feel an immense amount of love. I realize the Angel of Death is coming from a place of pure love. Last summer I felt this love coming from Jai who held the Angel of Death energy when I had to face it. Now I feel it from this perspective, just pure love.

Back at the Dreaming House, as we gather together as a group in the evening, we are asked to find the areas where we still feel blocked or attached, prohibiting us from experiencing our potential, or true self, and then find a person in the group to represent that area. I realize I probably still have attachment to The Big 3, as I so fondly call them: Abuse – Religion – Mother. The abuse is too big for this moment, and I don't feel that much attachment to the religion at this time, so I pick Mother. Through the help and role-playing of my partner, I tell my mother what I need to. Mostly, I just tell her how it would be nice if she could accept me unconditionally.

For another exercise, we are asked to identify a spiritual guide, and I immediately envision Jamie Sams, whose amazing book I am currently reading, *Dancing the Dream*. She is a Visionary, a Seer, from a Native American tradition. I envision her with a hawk on her left arm and her right hand is placed on my heart.

Later in the evening, back in our room, I ask Jill, who is knowledgeable about these sorts of things, what a hawk represents. She says it may be a message, either one for me or one that I have to give. I immediately think of the book I'm writing. I feel like the message is somehow tied to my book.

Tomorrow is the Women's Temple! I vow to bring to the Women's Temple complete openness and the final releasing of another aspect of The Big 3 – my abuse.

Teo – Day 3

Our group walks down the stairs into the earth, entering the cool, comforting womb that is the Women's Temple. Some of the women who have been working with Heather Ash for several months or years go into the part of the Women's Temple where the well is to secure and energetically cleanse the room. The rest of us wait in another room of the temple. While we wait, I place my hands on the ancient stone wall and feel maternal energy emanating from it. I think of Grandma and her loving lap. I miss her deeply. I also sense she may be here with me in some form. I feel the urge to cry, emanating from deep within my gut, as if the tears are pooled just below my belly button, awaiting the force of a geyser to bring them forth.

I keep feeling I want to be last, that this is going to be a major release for me, so I move to another area of the room, away from the doorway. I figure the women standing right next to the doorway are likely to be the ones led in first. *I want to be last.* Yet I go back to my original position near the doorway.

One of the women who helped secure the room approaches and gently guides me and one other woman towards the room with the well. We are the first ones. On the brief walk to the room, I keep doing double-takes, thinking I see snakes crawling on the temple walls and floors, or perhaps just pictures of snakes. Once in the room with the well, a woman named Diana stands behind me. Heather Ash stands behind the other woman. Knowing the routine from the first Teo trip, I lean over the waist-high metal gate (another protection for tourists) in front of the well, letting my arms dangle down towards the hole, gazing deeply into the earth. In feeling the gravity and weight of my upper body leaning over, it feels as if the earth is beckoning to receive whatever it is that needs to be released. I start crying almost immediately. Diana is making motions like she is sweeping energy downward from my hips and back into the well. I just keep crying. I stop crying after a minute or two, and Diana raises me back up to standing. *That wasn't too bad,* I think.

It's time to hand me over to another woman at the side of the room to simply be held. I can't let go of the railing next to the well, though. I start to go down on my knees, beginning to cry again. Diana keeps me off the floor. I feel Heather Ash come over to also hold me up. "Open her up," she says, as I am held fully upright and my chest area is opened, reminiscent of the scene in the hospital with Sarah. At that point, I just start bawling.

"There's so much inside!" I cry.

"Then let it out," one of the women says. I'm handed to a woman to be held. I just keep crying on her shoulder. Crying, crying and crying some more.

Heather Ash comes over and rubs the middle of my back, between my shoulder blades. She says, "It will come in waves. Just be open to them." I feel one of these "waves" hit me, and I raise my face to the earthen ceiling and start wailing and scream out. It is a raw, primal scream. I have no idea where the scream comes from; it surprises me. Then I cry again for a few minutes. Then another wave. I wail, scream and stomp my foot a couple times. It feels like I am exorcising my demons.

"I don't want it anymore, I want it out! I just want it out!" I scream in between the sobs.

I think about the little girl who was abused and various images come into my mind, but mostly I'm not in my head. It's just my body; it has a life of its own, and it's just feeling…and finally releasing.

I stop crying after a long, long while. The woman holding me gets me a tissue for my nose. I tell her I need to sit down. She guides me over to the metal tourist walkway. I'd rather just sit right on the temple floor, the earth, but I sit on the walkway. I just feel, breathe and try to get grounded.

Heather Ash comes over and touches my shoulders as if to move me. I'm having a hard time being present. I feel so out of it. I pull away from her touch, not wanting to be moved. She then gets a better hold of me under my arms and lifts. "Just for a minute," she says. I stand. She directs me to a corner of the room and asks me to sit there, facing out. That's *exactly* where I want to be, where I wanted to sit in the first place, so I sit down. She then takes her black shawl and puts it over my head and around my shoulders. I am a woman in mourning.

I again sense my grandma. She doesn't fully know what's going on, and doesn't fully understand the different state she is now in, but I feel her presence, support and love. I start to cry again. There is still more to come out.

I do not feel fully present, but I realize there are now large groups of tourists coming through the room on the metal walkway. I do not see them, but I can hear and feel them. No doubt they are bewildered, or perhaps they are intrigued by the show. The scene before them is one filled with at least two or three women crying and releasing and being held, a shrouded woman sitting in the corner with two "guards" in front of her, and other women standing at key points in the room, with arms out, protecting the space energetically. No one in our group bothers to stop what she is doing. There are much more important matters at hand than being concerned with what the tourists will think.

I vacillate between immense grief, calm meditation, feeling bombarded by so many people's energy, and disorientation. I am in the corner under my black shroud for an eternity. I am so grateful for the two women in front of me. All I can see of them is their shoes, but I feel how they are protecting the space around me.

At one point, Heather Ash comes over to me and places her hands on my knees. She then places her right hand on my chest over my heart. The image of my spiritual guide from last night, with her right hand over my heart, flashes into my mind. I quickly open my eyes, lean forward into Heather Ash's hand, and say with urgency, "I have to get out of here!" My voice is slurred and I feel groggy. There are more and more people coming through the place of the well. It's too much.

"We will be going soon," Heather Ash responds. "Can you just sit with that feeling for a minute? Why do you feel the need to leave?"

"Too many people," I get out.

"Can you be more specific?" she asks.

Not really. "Just too much energy," I say. I am so open and exposed after this experience of releasing. It seems I have very few filters remaining and can feel the energy of everyone, for a person's energy and presence reaches far beyond the physical confines of the skin.

"Okay, just sit with that for a minute," she says again.

"I need to go to the Pyramid of the Moon," I say, not really sure why I say it.

"That's where we're headed," Heather Ash replies.

I continue to sit there a few more minutes, our foreheads touching. I sink back into a meditative state, calm. Heather Ash gets up and asks one of the women if she can take me out near the tree. Yes, the tree! That's where I want to be right now.

I have loved trees my whole life. On any given day as a child, you could find me in a tree. Where I grew up, there was a very old and very large oak tree. My brother and a cousin built a platform up in the tree, about 15 feet from the ground. There were steps and a rope to climb up to it. From age 5 to the time I left that house at age 19, I crawled up in that tree. I would sit quietly on the platform listening to the wind blow through the leaves. I would sit quietly long enough that all the dozens of blackbirds in the tree would either forget I was there or get used to my presence and start chirping again. I would crawl beyond the platform, conquering any fear of heights or falling. I would at first crawl on hands and knees on limbs throughout the tree. Then, getting more brave, I would walk across them upright with no hands, 20 feet off the ground or more. I LOVED that tree! It would be my place to get away from everything and find myself. Even still, I need a good climbing tree nearby to just sit and contemplate life.

I stand up onto my shaky legs from the temple floor with some assistance. The woman proceeds to lead me out. There are *hoards* of people around now, more than I had realized. There must be busloads. They are blocking all the narrow doorways. We squeeze our way through, however. Likewise, all the metal walkways are full of people, so I step down onto the temple floor and head towards the exit. I feel ill and overwhelmed being that close to all the people.

Once we get outside, I can breathe again. I walk right towards the tree, step up and over the rock wall surrounding it without pause, and sit with my back against the tree. The woman crawls up and sits next to me. Ah, the tree is good.

Within a few minutes, the rest of our group comes out and joins us. Heather Ash comes up to me, puts her arms around my shoulders, and asks me how I'm feeling. "More free," I say, "and a little disoriented." She tells my mind that it's okay, petting my head. I don't have to try to understand what has happened. I just need to feel it.

I continue to try to bring myself back together, to get more and more grounded. I hand Heather Ash's shawl back to her, thanking her for its use. "Do you want to keep it for a little while longer?" she asks.

"Yes," I say and smile. It is comforting.

"I thought so," she smiles and hands it back.

After the Women's Temple, continuing our route along the Avenue of the Dead towards the Pyramid of the Moon, we go through a few more exercises, letting go of more of our physical, mental and emotional ties, to strip down to that core, spiritual self. The entire time we are doing this, the Pyramid of the Moon is beckoning me. *I'm coming.* We finally reach the platform in front of the Pyramid of the Moon, and then we are dismissed to be on our own until dinner.

I gaze up to the top of the pyramid and immediately begin the trek upward. The weather is warm and sunny, and the stone steps are narrow and steep. I feel winded, but I continue my mission with haste, onward and upward. I get to the top, take off my shoes, feeling stone connect with flesh, and just sit and meditate. I try to figure out what is going on with me and what happened in the Women's Temple. *I think I've just had so much happen in my life, so much shit, that I wanted it all out,* I contemplate. *My body purged it. It's funny, because mentally I've worked through these things time and time again. But in the temple, it was pure body working it out. The body was finally releasing.*

Maybe at some point my mind and heart will be aligned. I still feel like there's something hanging on, though, some sort of disconnection. Maybe I need all the memories back in order to fully be in alignment. No, that doesn't feel right. I feel that odd nauseous feeling again. I do not get answers to all my questions, and I don't know what lies at the bottom of that continued uneasy feeling.

Late in the evening, as we are together as a group wrapping up our day, we are asked to share our experiences. I am either the last or next to last one to share. I don't share much, only that I love the group and am still trying to figure out how to process what took place with me. Heather Ash makes a remark about not holding on, or something to that effect. Is she speaking to me or to the group? Yes.

Heather Ash shares a portion of the vision RMaya had on the summer trip with the group, and explains that tomorrow we will be bringing water up to the Pyramid of the Sun to pour out. She then asks that we bring into our dreams "ways that we can be of service to Teo." I have mixed feelings about that request. I love Teo, but I have a hard time being "in service" to something, and I'm confused about how to be in service to a place, anyway.

Our group is about to disperse, as it is getting late, when Jill approaches Heather Ash to give her information that is being conveyed or channeled through her. I walk away to give them space. I do not hear anything Jill says; it is for Heather Ash to hear. Jill announces out loud after she is finished talking with Heather Ash that there is something about a crystal. It is not one of the crystals on the altar in the room, which was created by a few members of the group the first day. A woman, Sarah, says she has a crystal in her room. Jill should check it out.

As I am about to head up to my room for the night, still feeling quite off after such an emotional day, Diana looks at me and says, "Are you up for an experiment?"

"Sure," I say. Why not? After today, I'm up for anything.

Diana has a meteorite in her hand. "It is only for women to hold," she says. "I'm supposed to give it to you for the night," Diana continues. The meteorite (or someone or something) is communicating this to her. "Put it over your heart chakra." So I accept it, thank her, and head up to my room.

I lie in bed on my back, holding the weighty meteorite on my chest. I lie like this for several minutes, still trying to figure out what happened with me today. Then I focus in on the meteorite. I envision and feel the meteorite attracting energy from above and funneling it downward into my heart. Interesting.

Feelings of nausea surface again. Just when I think the nausea is gone, it returns. It feels like something is in my abdominal region. *Is it another energetic form trying to take hold of me? Oh, I hope not!* I try to grab it, whatever it is, and pull it out, not really knowing what the heck I am doing. I lie with the meteorite some more.

Then it hits me! I know what I did! It took me all day to figure it out, but I finally got it! My intent was to take my abuse story to the Women's Temple and once and for all let it go. Well, I let it go, BIG TIME…but then…when no one was looking…I tip-toed back around and retrieved a small portion of it. Sneaky! I'm not sure exactly what portion I retrieved. Perhaps some last little bits of "victim" status or some piece of drama surrounding it, or just feeling the need to be in control at all times. I definitely didn't feel in control in the Women's Temple, and maybe that is freaking me out. Or, maybe I am simply hanging on to keeping it all in my head, trying to "figure it out," rather than just letting the experience be what it is, feeling the new openness in my heart. In any case, now that I realize that I had not completely let it go, I can do it now. Snip, cut whatever string I wanted to hang onto. Instantly, I feel lighter and much more free. It's amazing how that works!

Feeling joy and gratitude for this newfound freedom, I agree to dream how I may be of service to Teo. It's the least I can do, as this beautiful place provided the opportunity to release so much. I turn off the lamp, ready to get some sleep. I put the meteorite on the bedside table.

Dream

Heather Ash, Jill, me, and maybe some other people are on the Pyramid of the Sun. The three of us are standing on the top, bringing forth the energy from the bottom of the pyramid. Our arms are up in the air. I see us raising the energy, a lot of fire energy, higher and higher until it shoots upward into

the sky. I see people dancing on top of the pyramid. We are singing a song:
Wishi ta do ya do ya do ya/Wishi ta do ya do ya hey...

I awake in the middle of the night and think about the dream. It does not feel like a normal dream. I go back to sleep and dream the same dream again, *exactly*. I awake again. This happens 4 times throughout the night, having the same dream and awakening each time when it ends. I've never had a dream like this. I've never dreamed the same dream twice, let alone 4 times! Something big is going to happen.

Chapter 22

Buckle your seatbelt, Dorothy, 'cause Kansas…is going bye bye.

From *The Matrix*

*L*ast summer when I was here, RMaya and the others spoke of the pouring of the chalice over the Pyramid of the Sun and the fertilization. A month after I had returned home from Teo, I had felt the "child" would be a "girl," the feminine form.

%. %. %.

Teo – Day 4

Our group gathers together in the morning as usual. Before we eat breakfast, we talk some, and we sing some. We sing about 6 short songs or chants each morning, one of which is Wishi Ta, a Cherokee song, the one that appeared in my dream.

Apparently Jill and Sarah connected at some point last night while I was communing with the meteorite. The crystal from Jill's vision turns out to be one Sarah brought. It is a clear quartz crystal approximately 5 inches in length and about an inch in diameter, rough-cut, flat on one end and pointed on the other. Sarah has an epiphany, "Oh, *that* crystal!" and she now proceeds to tell the group the story of the crystal through a vision she had quite some time ago.

"There are world-changing crystals buried in various places around the globe," Sarah begins. "There's one off the coast of Italy, another one off the coast of Kona, one off the coast of northern New Zealand, one in the Baltic Sea just southeast of the island called Bornholm. Most are buried in the ocean. They are all connected in a network, or grid. And there's one buried in my back yard. I got a message that I should take a crystal, a particular one that I had in my possession, and place it in my backyard. By placing the crystal in my backyard, it would soak up, for lack of a better phrase, the energy of all the buried, network, world-changing crystals. So I did it. This crystal that is infused with the energy of all the global, network crystals found its way into my bag and here to Teo."

The crystal then found its way into Jill's vision, whatever that was. It is a very intriguing story.

After the morning ritual, our group heads to an adjacent building for breakfast prior to our day at the Toltec ruins. As the group is eating, Heather Ash walks into the dining room and asks if there is someone who can carry a large bottle of water in her pack. We do a lot of walking around, and it has been rather warm. I figure it is Heather Ash's drinking water that she cannot fit into her hip pack. I raise my hand and say I can take it. I have to do a little maneuvering in my backpack, but I make it fit. She then says it's the sacred water. Oh, okay.

We make our way into the park, getting our passes stamped at the entrance kiosk. It is Sunday, a day of free entry. A lot of visitors seem to be taking advantage of this.

We head to do a ceremony in a place called the Butterfly Temple. It is a ceremony of coming out of our cocoons and spreading our wings. After it is over, we "bless" the water I have been carrying by writing with a pen a loving word on the outside of the plastic bottle. We then exit the temple and come together in a circle.

While in the Butterfly Temple one of the women had been asked to "bring in the water" from all over Teo (the water, that the land showed, used to be all around when Teo was in full swing). This woman is pregnant and was asked to take a different role from everyone else in the temple. In our circle outside, she shares her vision that took place during the ceremony. She saw the women of ancient Teo carrying large urns of water from the Butterfly Temple to the Pyramid of the Sun. These women wore elaborate clothing, which she described in detail. There was lush vegetation all around, water flowed everywhere, and life. It is a beautiful vision, and everyone thanks her for sharing.

"Anything else to share before we start our walk?" Heather Ash asks. One woman states she sees dancing on the Pyramid of the Sun, our next destination. I nod my head in agreement, thinking of my dream. Heather Ash says there will be dancing. I feel the need to say something, but nothing comes to mind. One of the women points upward and says, "Look!" We all look up to see a ring around the sun, the hierosgamos, just like Raven saw during the previous Teo trip. We are then asked to walk in silence to and up the Pyramid of the Sun, unless there are things that need to be said in regards to the ceremony, visions that are seen and need to be voiced. The plan at the top of the pyramid is to do a ceremony and pour out the water.

We all, in silence, begin the walk to the pyramid. The only sounds heard are the crunch of gravel underfoot and the sound of one of the local women trying to get tourists to buy the goods she carries – an assortment of necklaces, wooden whistles, stone carvings in the shape of the large pyramids, and more. "Almost free, almost free," she assures all those as they pass by. *Almost free.*

As I bear the sacred water in my backpack and crunch along the walkway, all the parts I had been feeling and experiencing over the last few days all of a sudden come together into a cohesive, larger picture, an array of puzzle pieces perfectly clicking into place. Also, *new* information floods into me and literally stops me in my tracks. I stand motionless, feeling the information pour in, as the rest of the members of the group walk past me. The information is as follows:

The pouring of this water is not a reenactment of RMaya's experience, a joining of masculine and feminine energy and a fertilization. It is a continuation of it. This water represents new life, a birth or rebirth. The chalice is the woman. The water is like the amniotic fluid. This girl born will usher in a new era. We are here to be at this birth! The 13 women present in the group are like midwives, helping bring in this new life. All the women of Teo – past, present and future – are here to witness and give their blessing on this joyous occasion. They accompany us from the Butterfly Temple, where the water originated and new life was exemplified, emerging from its cocoon, all the way up to the top of the Pyramid of the Sun.

All the men of Teo are here as well, to witness and to guard and protect the space. They stay back and let the women move ahead and attend. That's also why only women are here on this Teo trip.

I see again my dream of Heather Ash, Jill and me, standing on top of the pyramid bringing up the energy, it then shooting out. I hear the Wishi Ta song being sung.

I feel like I need to tell Heather Ash of what I see/realize, but my heart is pounding. I can't break the silence, I feel at first, but I just know I have to. Becoming mobile again, I catch up to Heather Ash and put my arm around her. She looks at me and says, "Yes, what's going on?"

I'm silent a few moments, gathering my courage, trying to be open and not worry whether this is "crazy". Then I say, "I don't know if I can do this."

"Which part?" she asks.

"I don't know if I can carry this water. I don't know if I can be a part of this," I reply. "The water is like the amniotic fluid..." and I proceed to tell her about the realization – the birth, the girl and the new era. I tell her how I see the three of us and maybe other people on top bringing forth the energy. Then I tell her how I have been feeling nauseous since arriving in Teo and thought it was related to what happened at the Women's Temple yesterday, how it was connected to mourning my childhood and the loss of my grandma. But in actuality, I now realize, it is morning sickness related to this birth. Heather Ash asks if I feel the actual birth is somehow through me. I say, "I don't get that sense, no," with a hint of denial and fear.

I tell her I feel overwhelmed. She asks what makes it feel that way, "Is it the bigness of it?" Yes, it is the bigness. So she asks that I take that bigness and share it with the group.

She thanks me for sharing and we continue to walk towards the pyramid the remainder of the way in silence. Once we get to the pyramid I feel the need to remove my shoes and walk up barefoot, to be more fully connected with it. Our group spirals counterclockwise up the pyramid rather than walk straight up the staircase, as the majority of people do. At each level, we circle the perimeter, then move up. Circle, move up. Opening. As we get higher and higher, I feel the energy changing, the vibration in the air intensifying.

There are a lot of people at the top of the Pyramid of the Sun. Heather Ash has been here numerous times before and had people get upset when the center was occupied by the group. In the center, there is a small, metal circle that marks the exact center of the top. Many visitors crowd around this area, bending over to touch the metal circle, as if it holds some magical healing power. There is a lot of activity. So, Heather Ash motions everyone to make their way through all the people. "We have to do this quickly," she says.

Heather Ash guides Jill to sit down, then Diana. She sits me with my back to the Pyramid of the Moon, facing Diana. Heather Ash sits across from Jill, the four of us in the center, and everyone else in our group sits around us in a type of lotus flower formation. Diana and I have our eyes locked and Jill and Heather Ash, theirs. Immediately the crowd of people comes in and circles around us, growing very still and silent, waiting, respectful and yearning. They seem to sense something special is about to happen.

As I continue looking straight into Diana's eyes, I see Jill in my peripheral vision making a motion to place something in a silk bag in my lap. Similarly, I see Heather Ash shake her head no, so Jill pulls back. Jill then tries to put it in my lap again, but Heather Ash again shakes her head. So Jill trusts Heather Ash's instinct and puts the bag and whatever lies inside away.

We all place a hand on the knee or shoulder of the women next to us. Diana and I hold hands. We all start breathing in unison and bringing up the energy. The energy is brought up from the bottom center until it encompasses the entire pyramid and comes forth to the top. I can see it very clearly in my mind's eye.

Once the energy is raised to a certain point, Heather Ash asks Diana to pull out the chalice, and me the water, without letting the energy drop. I didn't realize they had brought a literal chalice. Diane retrieves a brass chalice from her bag, and I pull out the water bottle from my backpack. I unscrew the cap and pour water into the chalice until it is close to being full. Diana raises the chalice up in the air and I put my hands around hers. Our group continues to breathe, strong and together. The group of people around us is still, silent.

Diana keeps her eyes locked on mine. There is so much intensity that I have a hard time keeping my eyes on hers. A couple times I close my eyes for a second or two, or look away for a moment. At one point I look and see the number of tourists standing around, but I see them in my mind's eye as representative of spirits from all times and generations, all the people of Teo, witnessing this occasion, the bringing in of this new life, new era. And then Diana brings me back, drilling in those intense eyes. She keeps saying to me, "Bigger…bigger!" as in allowing my energy to continue to expand and allow my heart to grow. I don't think I can get much bigger.

Our group keeps breathing and bringing up the energy, higher and higher. Finally, at the peak of intensity, I see this huge shaft of light and energy, which is encompassing the pyramid and coming to a focus at the top, shoot upward into the sky.

With the energy now dissipating I look around to see many people in our group have tears streaming down their cheeks. It was, indeed, an intense spiritual experience.

The chalice is lowered and Heather Ash pours out a small portion of the water on the top of the pyramid. She then dips her finger into the water and places it on Diana's forehead, then Jill's, then mine, and everybody in our group. She asks Diana to now stand up and disperse the water to the rest of the people. She then asks me to stand up and also dispense the water.

I feel the stone of the pyramid and the water mix with my bare feet. I hear a baby cry, not from here. Mothers and fathers who are standing around our group gently push their children through the crowd toward us to be "blessed". The children, adults, locals and tourists alike, come forth to take part. The older women squeeze their way through and bring their crystals, amulets and rosary beads to us to have them blessed with the water. Some of them, too, have tears streaming down their faces. Many thank us profusely. The experience is surreal.

I feel an extreme amount of joy, and that seems to be the overriding feeling from our entire group. It feels like the joy that accompanies the entrance of a new life.

Heather Ash takes water to disperse and starts singing the Wishi Ta song. I had not mentioned that part of my dream and "vision" to her. Our whole group joins in. We all sing as we are spreading this new life to the people. I smile so big and feel in awe of and gratitude for this moment.

After making our way down the pyramid, I walk back to the Dreaming House with Heather Ash. I tell her some more of the things that I had seen earlier – how the women of Teo were accompanying us to witness and to give their blessing and support, and how the men were there to also witness but primarily to be the guardians and protectors, allowing the women to be in the forefront. She tells me she had a friend of hers join us, energetically, while walking up the pyramid and her friend said, "I've brought the men!" She then saw the men coming up and circling the pyramid behind the women, staying back. "There was no dancing, though," Heather Ash says. "There was dancing inside," I reply. Our hearts were dancing.

Heather Ash tells me about the Women's Teo trip and how it was completely unplanned, but she felt compelled to make it happen. Each time she sat down to outline what would take place on the trip, her page remained blank. She couldn't structure it; it had to stay fluid. She also says that she was at first thinking the ceremony on top would have to be quick, but then realized everyone immediately wanted to be a part of it. "That has not happened in a long time," she says.

I realize all the opening that had taken place in the Women's Temple yesterday had the purpose of opening me for this day. I strongly feel that if the events had not transpired as they did, I would not have been able to have the same experience. I also realize that each and every woman here in Teo on this trip is here for a reason, to be part of this, and for specific reasons of her own, and perhaps for something even greater.

I feel Jill and I are back here for a reason, too, though that is unclear. In talking with her this afternoon, we both said that we may be back yet again to continue the work, because it feels like there is more coming.

Later in the evening we all come together to talk about our day. People share their visions and experiences. Some saw what are called the "giants" that reside in Teo, standing guard on the four corners of the pyramid. Some saw the lush vegetation and life around the grounds from ancient times. One woman tells how she felt and heard a male dragon flying around and then a female dragon in the portal at the base of the Pyramid of the Sun. She realized, then, that the female dragon was pregnant and that there was to be a birth of some sort. Others say they saw/knew the women of Teo were present and how the men stood guard. Some saw angels standing guard. Lastly, I shared some of what I had seen.

Listening to these others' experiences and visions confirms that all of our stories are just part of the same, larger one. It is such a great honor to be part of this occasion.

Teo – Day 5

Our group goes to visit a hot spring, which is about a 3 – 4 hour bus ride from Teo. Heather Ash says we will be having "baptisms", half-jokingly. I feel a little nervous with that comment. I was baptized once already in a very confining religion. The thought only brings up uncomfortable memories. I don't ever want to or plan on being baptized again.

We arrive at the hot spring. I expected to see a small pool perhaps, but no. There is an entire hot river! The steam is floating off of it as it rushes down the mountain. The landscape is very different from that around Teo, a lot more greenery. In a way, it seems like we are in the tropics. In addition to the hot river, there are huge caves, which are really awe-inspiring.

We slip into our bathing suits. The weather is cool and rainy, and I shiver from the cold. We all quickly jog down the winding, muddy path to forge the river, with the help of a rope. The rain has made the river full and strong. It is precarious to cross it, but we must do so in order to crawl into the pooled area within one of the immense caves. It is one of the most amazing places I've ever seen.

Heather Ash leads us to a place within the cave where water rains down in certain places. A person can stand under one of these waterfalls and get a nice, heated back and shoulder massage. "Here, stand here," Heather Ash says to me at one particularly good place for a massage. Then others in the group join in.

"I thought we were getting baptized," one of the women asks.

"That was it," Heather Ash says with a smile.

Okay, I can handle that *kind of* "baptism," I think to myself. *Hmmm…baptized at 30 years old in a river, just like Jesus. Go figure.*

Our group then heads off further into the interior of the cave. There is no light other than the sporadic light from a couple tourists with a malfunctioning flashlight. When the light is off, the darkness is complete, and we must feel our way along using a rope. We tread slowly, for the rocks are slippery and the ground is quite uneven.

Eventually the cave opens up into another huge expanse. When the light flashes on, I can see that there are stalagmites and stalactites all over. It is otherworldly and so beautiful. There are also more places to receive a welcome water massage.

After an enjoyable day spent at the hot springs, we take the long bus ride back to Teo. Since tomorrow will be our last day, and everyone will be heading off to the airport, we do a brief closing ceremony back at the Dreaming House. We each pick a small stone that was collected from the hot spring river and write a word on it, something we want to keep with us, even back home. I write the word, "awareness." Sarah then pulls out her crystal and says she would like to pass it around. "If you like," Sarah says, "you can put an intention into the crystal." We each take a turn holding her crystal and putting an intention or loving feeling into it.

I'm going to miss being with the group. I had such a great time.

Chapter 23

*J*ill and I are in our room in the late evening before bed. Jill is sitting and talking with me. She brings up the subject of fairies. I ask, "Are they around me again?" I recall her mentioning she saw them around me last summer when we were here, and it looks like she is seeing them now. She says there are several around. "How many?" I ask.

"It depends on the day", she replies. "I don't know why I'm telling you this", she says. "I don't know why I'm telling you this," she repeats again. Jill proceeds to tell me how the fairies are the "gatekeepers." They open the door between this physical realm and the spirit one. They are the reason people see angels.

She continues to tell me how they are elemental spirits. She describes how she sees them – not solid, more ethereal. The fairies love symbols, usually simple ones. They will sometimes draw out symbols for her to help explain things to her. Jill mentions that objects like rocks, plants, and spirit forms, like fairies, have only one vibrational rate. However, humans have the capability of moving between various vibrational rates, or having various rates simultaneously. She says the fairies encourage me to keep drawing, if that's what I want to do. They also want me to keep working on my sight. "My sight? As in seeing?" I ask. Yes. I immediately think this is the case because the fairies want me to be able to see them.

As I pack up my belongings in preparation for leaving early in the morning, Jill sits on her bed writing in her journal. We are both very quiet. She stops and just sits for a few moments. She then says, "I have to tell you something. I don't know why, but I have to say this out loud."

"Okay," I reply.

She says, "I need to hold the crystal. I still feel like I needed to put it in your lap on the Pyramid of the Sun. I need to hold the crystal."

I respond, "Then you should do it." She immediately goes downstairs to Sarah's room to hold the crystal.

I finish packing what I can for the evening then go to brush my teeth to get ready for bed. It's been a full day, and I'm tired. As I brush my teeth, I keep getting the message/feeling that something is unfinished. The original "vision" I had seen for the ceremony on top of the Pyramid of the Sun – with Heather Ash, Jill and I – needs to take place. What happened yesterday wasn't it, I feel. I then feel very strongly that we have to get back up to the top of the Pyramid of the Sun to finish. *Is this for real? This can't be!* I question myself. *Just finish brushing your teeth and go to bed.* But the feeling is strong…and relentless.

I think for a few minutes about the logistics of getting back up the pyramid. I don't think we can sneak in tonight, but maybe really early in the morning the three of us can go. But everyone is planning to go to the Basilica. Neither Jill nor I have a strong desire to go the Basilica. I believe we are the only two who did not raise our hands to go when Heather Ash asked the other night. There must also be a reason for that; we're not supposed to go. We have to finish something. Maybe the three of us can find alternate transportation to the airport in the morning – taxi, Alberto, something. But everyone needs to have Heather Ash's "re-entry talk." How is this going to work? I shouldn't worry too much about that. It will happen if it needs to. I need to go down and find Jill and see if this sounds completely crazy to her, to see if we're on the same page.

I decide to go for it. I head downstairs to find Sarah's room. I don't know which one it is, so I listen for their voices. I hear them rather quickly and knock on the door. Someone says to come in. I open the door and Sarah says, "Are you here to hold the crystal too?"

"No, I just need to talk to Jill." Jill stops what she is doing and comes outside with me.

Once we're outside and a few feet from the room, Jill asks, "So you need to hold the crystal, right?"

"No, I just need to ask you something. What happened when you held the crystal?"

"Here, let's go hold the crystal," she says, grabbing my hand to lead me back to Sarah's room.

"Hold on," I say, getting a bit frustrated. "I just need to know what happened when you held it. Do you feel there is unfinished work?"

"Yes," she replies without a moment's hesitation. So I tell her how when I was upstairs I felt we needed to complete the ceremony on top of the Pyramid of the Sun, how I kept seeing Heather Ash, me and her on the pyramid.

"Are you sure you're with me?" I ask again, needing some reassurance.

"Absolutely." Then she says one last time, "Let's go inside and you hold the crystal." I acquiesce at this point.

I go in and sit on the bed. Jill tells me to sit how I want to sit, so I sit in the way I was sitting on top of the Pyramid of the Sun, cross-legged. Jill goes to put the crystal in my lap, then hands it to me instead and says, "You put it where you feel you need to put it." I hold it in my lap and close my eyes.

I feel instantly transported to another state of consciousness. "I am on the Pyramid of the Sun," I say. Jill asks me to lock into when we were up there, when I was looking at Diana.

"Yes, lock into Diana's eyes," Sarah says. I lock into Diana, but she quickly fades away.

"Who do you see across from you?" Jill asks.

"No one."

"Okay, what do you see?"

"I see a triangle, a golden triangle. It's the three of us, one in the same." I told Jill of my earlier dream/vision this evening after returning from the hot springs. Here again, I see Heather Ash, Jill and myself standing on the pyramid, the same as the vision. "Our arms are up," I continue, "and I see the crystal becoming the focal point for all the energy from the pyramid, which is used to transmit the energy around the globe." This crystal is the means to transmit the new life, new era, all over, not just Teo and our part of the world, I now realize. So we need to do it.

"Can we do it right now?" Jill asks.

"Yes, let's do it now!" Sarah says.

"Or does it need to be the same three you saw?" Jill interjects.

I sit for a moment. "It needs to be the original three."

Jill explains, "Okay, so that's Heather Ash and she's really tired, probably asleep now. Can it wait until morning?"

"Yes, it can wait until morning," I reply.

We leave the room and once we're outside, I ask Jill, "So we're on the same page?" just wanting to be sure.

"Yes we are, I support you 100%," she says. "So you need to talk with Heather Ash in the morning."

"Can you talk with her?" I ask, a little nervous.

"No, you need to do it," she says. "I'll be right there next to you holding your hand. You are supported."

"Okay," I say. I can do it.

Back in our room, I'm shaking from the cold, as the temperature drops considerably at night this time of year. I am also shaking from the energy running through me, so I stand right next to the small, portable heater. Jill sits on her bed with a serious look on her face. After a few moments she says she hears "click-click…click-click" over and over. She asks internally what that is and the reply is, "You're getting downloaded." She has no idea what that is all about, but she keeps hearing it.

I watch Jill very intently as I stand to get warm. I all of a sudden see an eagle headdress on her. I see this, not in my mind's eye. I see this right in front of me with my physical eyes! I've never seen anything like this before. It seems so unreal, yet I know it *is* real. It looks like some kind of special effects in a movie where there is one image superimposed upon another. Jill's head and face is the more solid, fleshy image, and the eagle headdress is more ethereal or like a hologram, but very clearly visible.

I tell Jill I see an eagle headdress on her. I keep watching her, and I start to see other animals appear superimposed over her face. The next one is an alligator. I tell her I see an alligator. Then I realize to just be quiet since there is going to be a lot going on. I continue to see other animals in her face – monkey, puma – then I see this gnome-type creature, then more animals. I see an old Shaman/Medicine Woman, from a very ancient, primal time appear. She remains longer than the others. The animals appear for a couple seconds then fade out. This woman has a headdress on, made out of various animal skins. The animal skins are light in color. The headdress covers the Medicine Woman's entire head and shoulders. Her face is small, her eyes set close together. She is older, showing wrinkles, and she has a dark complexion. I see her as clearly as I see the floor I'm standing on. This Shaman woman looks straight at me. She just keeps looking, knowing that I'm seeing her, looking back at her. Finally, she fades away. I just stand there witnessing this. My jaw is literally hanging open in disbelief. I close my mouth.

Jill turns to me and says, "You're light, you're an angel, and you are so supported." She repeats it two more times.

There is a lot of information being "downloaded" into Jill. She keeps telling me, "I don't know why I'm telling you this," and then talk about various things – astrological convergences, the coming of the 5th Sun, the Hopi – mostly things with which I have no familiarity. She then states that she needs to call in her Shaman teacher. She calls in her teacher and then says very clearly, "I know why I'm telling you all of this." I'm listening. "I know why I'm telling you this…because you're pure. You are so pure. You are so pure. You're pure light. The information gets conveyed only to pure light."

Jill then asks me to go get Sarah from downstairs. So I head off to get Sarah. I knock on her door and Sarah asks, "Now what?"

I say, "Jill needs you."

"Can't it wait until morning? It's late and I have to get to sleep," she says.

I think for a moment. *Don't you understand there are important things going on? There are animals in her face and an ancient Medicine Woman residing in her body, and she's being downloaded with information about astrological convergences!* I think to myself. No, it can't wait. "Can you please just come, even for a couple minutes?" I ask.

"Okay," Sarah sighs. "You just caught me up out of bed to blow my nose, I was in bed already." She puts a sweatshirt on and follows me up to my room.

We come into the room and find Jill still sitting on her bed. Jill says to Sarah, "Don't touch me." Sarah sits down next to her without touching her. Jill tells her about the clicking sound and the downloading of information. Sarah starts talking about how she can stop it if she wants to or slow it down. She keeps talking and Jill keeps shushing her to be quiet in order to listen to the downloading. After a few minutes Jill says to Sarah that she can go and thanks her for coming.

I crawl into my bed shortly thereafter, and Jill is trying to get her things packed in between the downloading. She tells me a little about a vision she had earlier, the one she told Heather Ash. "I kept seeing three people. I saw myself and Heather Ash, and I couldn't tell who the third person was, because this person was unsure. Now I realize you are the third person," she says to me. "Trust in yourself."

As she's still packing I tell Jill about the Shaman/Medicine Woman I saw. I describe her the best I can. Jill says she has felt her before. She doesn't know who she is, though.

"Did she say anything to you?" Jill asks.

"No."

"Are you sure?"

"Yes."

"Are you really sure?"

"Yes, I'm really sure. She didn't say anything," I say, laughing at Jill's persistence.

As I lie in bed, I write in my journal and think again about the ceremony on top of the Pyramid of the Sun. I realize the timing of the crystal was wrong. Jill kept trying to put it in my lap on the pyramid, but the timing was off. That's why Heather Ash kept telling her no, but I don't know if Heather Ash realized why. Now the timing is right. Everyone has infused her intention into the crystal. The conduit is now appropriately prepared for the healing energy to go out into the world.

Jill asks out of nowhere, "What did you write?" I don't know what she is asking about. What did I just write in my journal? "What did you write on your stone?" she clarifies, without me having to ask.

"Awareness," I reply. Jill says she wrote "surrender". I chime in, "And Heather Ash wrote 'trust'." I'm counting on Heather Ash trusting what will take place in the morning.

I'm still writing and, standing by her bed, Jill says to me, "You come directly from her."

"Who?" I ask.

After a pause, "Mary…it's the only name I can think of…the Fairy Mother." She says the Fairy Mother is here and wants to communicate with me. Jill asks if I would like to do that.

I think for a few moments. Part of me wants to, but not right now, I'm trying to write. "Can it wait?" I ask Jill.

"Yes," she says. "That's okay, you don't have to."

A second later, "No, she has to meet you," Jill says. So I crawl out of bed to meet this Fairy Mother/Mary.

Jill becomes the intermediary between the Fairy Mother and me. I go over and stand next to Jill. She stands in front of me and holds my hands. She tells me to close my eyes and try to relax. Again, I'm nervous and shaking.

I close my eyes, and I see this spirit woman with blue eyes and light hair. She is tall, very beautiful and dressed all in white, flowing clothing. She seems to have a regal quality about her. In a way she seems very familiar, like she is a part of me, or, rather, I am a part of her.

It's hard to stand because my knees feel weak, but I hold on. Jill speaks for the energy being. "She wants to introduce you into the fairy world," she begins. "She will show you how to enter. There is a tree in front of you." Of course, a tree. "Do you see the tree?"

"Yes," I reply. I see a large oak tree.

"There is a door in the tree, do you see the door?" I see the door.

"Open the door and go inside. What do you see?"

"Darkness," I reply.

"There is a staircase," Jill continues, "Do you want to go up or down?"

"Up," I immediately reply.

"Okay, go up the staircase and open the door. Where are you?"

"I am up in the branches."

"What do you see?"

"Little lights all over." I know they are small fairies in the branches, but I only see them as little bursts of light.

Jill speaks more for the Fairy Mother. "She has something she wants to give you…let me know when you're ready, 'cause there's more information coming."

I envision the Fairy Mother handing me a gold necklace with a large, round, gold pendant. The gold is brilliant. I cannot make out the detail of the pendant, some kind of symbol. "Okay," I say, to let Jill know I'm ready.

"She wants to know if she can show you around." Jill says. I at first think no, not now. But then I question when I will again have this opportunity (it's not like I know a lot of people like Jill; it could be a long time), so I agree. "When she's done showing you around, let me know."

I sense a lot of greenery around. Everything seems to have a sparkling, magical quality about it, but nothing really comes into focus. I am so nervous. After several seconds, I say I cannot see anything. "That's okay," Jill says. "Do you still see her?"

"Yes…she's smiling at me," I say and smile. "I'm not ready yet."

"That's okay," Jill continues. "It's good to know yourself, when you're not ready…She wants to know if you have any questions for her."

I think for a moment then say out loud, "Why now?"

"Listen for her answer," Jill says. I realize then that I could have just asked silently.

I hear, "Because now you've come into your light. Because now you've come into your light. Because now you've come into your light."

"Okay," I tell Jill, even though I'm not quite sure what that means.

"She wants you to know how much you are supported, and she wants to tell you how you can keep in touch with her." I am shown that I can keep in touch with her through trees, specifically oak trees. When I am around them, I can walk through the door or call on her.

I thank Jill for that opportunity and assistance. I tell Jill the answer the Fairy Mother gave me to my question. Jill says she heard, "Because now you are ready."

Yesterday, Jill said the fairies wanted me to continue working on my sight, and I had thought this was because they wanted me to see them. Now I realize it was primarily so I could see the Fairy Mother.

Teo – Day 6

It's after midnight and I lie in bed again with all the lights out, trying to get to sleep, knowing it's going to be an early morning. Jill asks, "Are you awake?" Of course I'm awake. Both of us have been on some energy high all evening. It feels like we are on a combo of speed and mushrooms, not that I've ever had a combo like that. But we are not influenced by any substance, just the magic and power of Teotihuacán.

"Yes," I reply. She turns the light back on and grabs her notebook.

"Do you remember the four structures and their positive side?" a reference to a teaching from Heather Ash earlier on the trip.

"I know some. I don't know if I remember them all." We go through them and between the two of us remember them.

"Okay, I'm going to say one of the structures and you give me a direction, i.e., north, south, east, west, that you feel it coincides with, first thing that comes to mind." So Jill goes through them and I shout out directions. Then she tries something and it doesn't really work the way she thought.

At that moment, the symbol on the necklace that the Fairy Mother gave me becomes clear. It is just a vertical line and a crossing horizontal line within a circle – the four directions. So I tell Jill about it. I still don't really understand the gift, but at least now I see what it looks like.

Jill and I have been up for several hours, bouncing back and forth. Both of us are just vibrating. My whole body is buzzing and I'm still shaking down to my core. It's very intense. Neither of us has a watch, but I figure we finally get to sleep around 1:00 or 2:00 am.

When I finally fall asleep, my dream is again about the Pyramid of the Sun ceremony. The dream has the same unique quality to it as last time. It is as if I am awake, difficult to distinguish if I'm truly asleep.

The content of the dream is almost identical to the dream two nights ago: Heather Ash, Jill and I stand on top of the Pyramid of the

Sun, our arms raised up, bringing up the energy. The energy shoots out. But this time it is with the help of the crystal. There is also information about the Medicine Woman, no detail other than that she is involved. I remember getting information that this woman has an unknown language. I still don't know if we have to go physically to the pyramid, but it feels like it probably can be done energetically. I also get the message that the space for the ceremony will need to be cleared. I wake up immediately after this dream/vision. It is again very clear to me that the completion of the ceremony needs to happen. I can't go back to sleep again for at least a couple more hours. Then again, I receive the same dream/vision/message.

After falling back to sleep for an hour or two, I am shaken awake by Jill. "I feel it's time to get up," she says. I get up, a little groggy. "I have to go see Tamara," Jill says, referring to one of the women in the group. Jill is still in that high-energy, high-vibration state. It doesn't seem like she has slept at all. When she leaves the room, I start questioning whether or not it is necessary that I talk with Heather Ash and to complete the ceremony, but I don't question long. Of course it is necessary. I can feel its truth in every fiber of my being.

I finish packing up the last of my things. *I wish I knew what time it was,* I think to myself. I don't think there is much time available for the ceremony. Once my items are all packed up, I head downstairs to find Jill. She told me last night that she is going to accompany me to talk with Heather Ash. I again start buzzing and vibrating, wide awake now.

I hear Jill talking in one of the rooms, and the door to the room is open. I open the door further and see her and Alberto looking at old Aztec artifacts that have been collected around Teo. The Aztecs occupied the area after the Toltecs. I go in and join them. After a few minutes we finish looking at the artifacts. Jill says she needs to go talk with Tamara, and Alberto tells me I can leave my suitcase out front. I drop off my suitcase, and when I return to the house, Jill is nowhere in sight. I don't know which room she is in, and I feel like I shouldn't interrupt them anyway. I just sit anxiously, waiting as the clock is ticking. I keep telling myself to not worry about the time. I've realized by this point on this trip that things happen if and when they are supposed to.

A good 20 to 30 minutes pass. I run over to the kitchen to try to see the clock, but I cannot see it. It doesn't look like anyone is at breakfast yet, so that's a good sign that it is still early. I look in the room where we met as a group, and no one is in there either. I try to figure out if I need to go knock on Heather Ash's door alone. I go back to the house one last time to wait for Jill. A minute or two later, I hear a voice call my name, "Kristi? Where are you?"

"I'm here," as I walk towards the voice. It is Tamara. She tells me to go join Jill, Heather Ash and Diana in the house in which Heather Ash has been staying. Okay, here we go. As I walk out the door and toward the other house, Sarah comes out of her room and puts on her shoes. She looks at me and asks, "Do you need the crystal?"

I think for a brief moment. "Yes," I reply. Sarah takes it out of her pocket, and I put it in mine. I'm nervous and my heart is pounding, in addition to the vibrating.

I walk into the house. "Welcome!" Heather Ash says to me in a very chipper manner. Obviously *she* got plenty of sleep. "Come sit on the grounding couch…not next to Jill."

So I go in, take off my shoes and head towards a chair, away from Jill. I don't know what Jill has told them, if anything. Diana is next to Jill helping her get grounded. Diana asks Jill how she is doing. She responds that she is feeling a little more grounded. Then Heather Ash says, "And Kristi will be feeling better, too, in a minute." I nod my head in agreement. *Yes, as soon as the ceremony is complete.*

I sit down and am asked to bring in the energy a bit. I try, but everything just feels so huge and expanded. Heather Ash then sits right near me and says, "We need to bring this in," and gets ready to help me do so. Before she can start, I muster up my courage and say, "It's not time yet to bring it in…there are things unfinished." Heather Ash asks me in what regard.

"Regarding the Pyramid of the Sun, the crystal, and the three of us," I start. "The timing of the crystal was off before, when Jill tried to put it in my lap on the pyramid, but now it's ready, all the group's intentions are in the crystal. We need to return to the Pyramid of the Sun, and the crystal will act as a focal point for the energy from the pyramid that then gets dispersed globally. The ceremony that was done before had somewhat of a global effect, but more so a local effect, primarily affecting Teo and this part of the world. With the crystal, the effect will be much stronger and more global," I conclude. The information just spills out. Heather Ash is listening.

Heather Ash asks, "Is this for a later trip to Teo? There are Toltecs coming back in a week." She continues, "We can leave very detailed notes for them."

I waiver momentarily, "It's possible," I say. My gut says no, however. "I keep seeing us."

"Okay," Heather Ash says. "On this trip or a future trip?"

"This one," I reply.

"Is the whole group involved, or just us?" Heather Ash continues, in an attempt to get a clear picture.

"Just you, me and Jill," I clarify.

"Okay, let's do it," she says without hesitation. I think she also understands the time crunch.

"Diana, could you go get the crystal from Sarah?" Heather Ash asks.

"I have it," I say, as I pull it from my pocket and set it on the table.

"Okay!" Heather Ash says, sounding a little surprised, but then again not.

"Inside or outside," she asks.

"Inside is fine," I say.

Jill gets off the couch and joins Heather Ash standing in the room. Heather Ash is holding out her hand for me to join them. I'm halfway up off the chair, but I cannot get all the way off yet. "The room needs to be cleared," I say, recalling that clear message from my dream/vision.

Heather Ash asks me, "Physically, like moving the furniture?"

"No."

"Okay, Diana, clear the space," she instructs. Diana is off to one side of the room, arms out, energetically clearing it.

I now stand up and join the other two. "Diana, to the Pyramid of the Sun," Heather Ash instructs, with the likeness of a Starship captain. Instantly we are energetically transported.

We all hold hands, close our eyes and just breathe. After a few seconds Heather Ash asks, "What are you feeling, Kristi?"

"I need to tell Jill something," I say.

"Okay," she says.

"Jill, the Medicine Woman from last night – you don't need to be her, but feel her energy…her power…and her wisdom." The words are chosen very specifically. I hear the words first, and I feel like I am just allowing them to pass through me to the others. Jill feels into it and understands. A moment later I continue, "She is guiding, directing this ceremony."

I grab the crystal off of the table and let Heather Ash and Jill know we all need to hold it. We take hold of it in the middle of our triangle. I guide us to raise it up above our heads, arms outstretched. I say we need to bring the energy from the bottom of the pyramid up through to the crystal. We close our eyes, breathe and proceed to bring up the energy.

Jill's breathing becomes very intense and heavy. I try to match it. The breathing becomes heavier and heavier. Jill then starts to make this tone, "Aaaaaahhhhhhh…" The tone is long and low. She stops her tone and says a couple words in a language I've never heard, an unknown, primal language. Jill then makes a louder tone, still long, at a slightly higher pitch, "Aaaaaahhhhhhh…" I can feel the energy rising. Somebody is moving her arms, making us all move our arms. I'm shaking, just trying to breathe and bring up energy. I feel Jill move in closer, putting her body directly under the crystal. She continues, "Aaaaaahhhhhhh…" a louder, higher tone. The tones get louder and louder, higher and higher. She has a very powerful voice. The intensity rises more and more. The crystal is vibrating at a higher and higher rate. Jill increases the tone and pitch, higher……higher……..the crystal then energetically EXPLODES!!!

With my eyes still closed, I see this explosion of light and energy spreading out in all directions. At the exact same moment I see the explosion, Jill stops silent, and I quickly say, "It is done." Jill lets go of the crystal and backs away, and I do the same.

As I stand back, still with eyes closed, I see something that looks like a shockwave. It is a healing wave, emanating from this place, from Teo, spreading out in all directions, quickly enveloping the entire globe. The enormity of the situation is taking its toll on my body. I'm shaking down to my very essence, so I sit down on the chair. Diana has a big grin on her face and says, "There are all these light beings dancing around you guys."

"So there's the dancing," I say.

Heather Ash approaches me with the crystal in her hand and asks, "Do you want to hold it to see if it's complete?"

"It's complete," I say without any hesitation, holding my hands back and away.

Jill has reseated herself to get grounded. I tell Heather Ash, as I sit down, "There are a lot of people happy right now." I feel completely in humble service to the entire world.

She smiles at me and says, "You can stay open for a while, you're able to hold it." She says to just let her know when I want to bring it in and she can help if need be.

"It's like I can feel everyone," I say, as I feel humanity – past, present and future. "There is so much gratitude." Again, I am in awe.

As I am about to walk out the door to go to the kitchen to eat breakfast, Heather Ash approaches me with the crystal. I say, "It goes back to Sarah."

"I know. Do you want to give it to her?" she asks.

"No, I can't touch it," I reply.

"I understand," she says.

At the breakfast table, I can only force myself to eat a couple bites of pancakes. I generally LOVE pancakes, but right now the food just sticks in my mouth. Everything tastes really off and, even though my stomach feels hungry, I cannot eat. I also feel hypersensitive to sights, sounds, people, you name it, so I just sit quietly.

Heather Ash sits across from me and Jill is to my left. Jill is talking with Heather Ash, asking if this sort of thing happens frequently. "So we changed the world," Heather Ash says with a shrug. "It's the mind that makes it a big deal. This happens all the time."

%%   %%   %%

Openness and trust. How now do I take these experiences, which have enabled me to see the world through a few less veils, a few less panes of clouded glass, and continue with my day-to-day life? Where do I go from here? What did Diana say in the van on the way back from the hot springs? "Before enlightenment: chop wood, carry water. After enlightenment: chop wood, carry water." That's one option, but I feel there are others. What about teaching, for instance? My answer will come. I must simply listen for it and be ready. Openness and trust.

Just as all our stories, our visions, were part of the same, larger story of Teo, the Teo story is part of an even greater story. This greater story is quite possibly so expansive and full of mystery that we may never be able to see the entire picture. But I am honored, humbled, joyous and filled with love at the opportunity to be a small part of it.

Chapter 24

After the second trip to Teo, everything changes. The first few days after returning, I can hardly speak. I just keep going over all that transpired in the 5-day, life-altering period. I want to make sense of it, but by attempting to do so, I realize I am limiting myself. I opened up and experienced so much more of "reality" while on the trip. I understand that my current life must expand in order to be large enough to encompass my new growth. The other option is to energetically shrink back down to the size of a pea, dismissing everything that happened as "imagination", discounting all I saw, heard and felt. No, I choose growth over shrinkage.

One winter evening I stand in my living room in front of the heater to get warm. I start breathing in a meditative manner, slow and full. After a few minutes of breathing like this, with my eyes closed, I see, with each inhale, the room contract towards me. With each exhale, the room expands. It is like the scene near the end of *The Matrix*, right after Neo leaps into Agent Smith and explodes his code. Neo simply breathes, feeling the wave.

I then sense/see this energy that looks like a huge cobra, almost the size of a person, off to my right. With each breath, the cobra slithers closer to me, then energetically joins with me, entering my body. It then moves up my body. It comes up, up and flares out at my head and shoulder area. It faces out the same direction as I do.

I think to myself, *now what?* It gets communicated to me that I am supposed to see through the cobra's eye, the "third eye." So I begin to see through the eye. For a brief moment I see light, at an angle, converging in the center. It is similar to how the stars look in the process of hitting warp speed on Star Trek. Then I open my eyes and simply see my living room.

Shortly after this, the cobra again makes its appearance, but this time in a dream.

I am in my dad's body. I am going to help him quit smoking. I look in the mirror, open my/Dad's mouth and can see up into my dad's head. There is an image, like a tattoo, on the inside walls of his head. I never knew it was there because I was never before in my dad's body.

The tattoo image within the forehead area looks like a cave painting. There is a snake. Sometimes the snake is a diamondback rattlesnake. Other times it is a cobra. There is also a quartz crystal, lying horizontally. It is pointed at each end. The center of the crystal is wrapped with twine. It looks like an eye and is situated beneath the rattlesnake in the area of the brow. It is the "third eye." Surrounding the snake and crystal, in a half-circle, is something that looks like barbed wire.

When the snake is a cobra, it is in the striking position with head flared. Within the flared part of the snake is an image of the third eye. It represents the same as the crystal accompanied by the rattlesnake.

I think to myself as I see this image in my dad's head, "I didn't know Dad knew anything about the third eye. But then again, I've never been in his body before." I also think about the snakes and how dad had a phobia of snakes when he was alive. He wasn't afraid of anything else, but he was absolutely terrified of snakes, so I know the image is symbolic.

After I see this sight, I proceed to break his habit/addiction to smoking cigarettes. I start coughing intensely. There is something in my throat that needs to come out. It finally comes out, and it is a sun. It is about the size and consistency of an eyeball, but the coloring is like an orange-yellow, fiery sun.

Then I cough some more and some other stuff comes out, stuff from his lungs after decades of smoking. I then lay down and cry for an hour or so, just feeling the pain in my/his body from the craving.

Mom is sitting next to me, patting my back to comfort me. She realizes I am in his body and what I am doing to help him quit his addiction, something she has always wanted him to do. She doesn't know about the image in his head, though, only dad knew. After continuing to cough up more stuff, I wake up.

This dream is the fifth incident involving snakes within a month. First I saw them in Teo in the Women's Temple, then the meditation experience, and three dreams, one of which is above. I know there is some sort of message in the repeated symbolism, but what that is I'm not sure. From my earlier studies in college, I do recall there is a link between snakes and Goddess spirituality.

The connection between the snake and the Goddess is before the writing of the Genesis story in the Bible, which depicts snakes in a negative light, as the Devil. The Genesis story makes sense in this time of transitioning from a Goddess and polytheistic belief system to a supreme male deity and monotheistic system, which is a reflection of the transition to a more patriarchal society.

There had to be a way to encourage those in that time period, but more so future generations, to heed the message of the new, one-male-God belief system rather than the belief system surrounding them. What better way than to write a creation story that tells how listening to the serpent, or following the Goddess, female belief system, leads to the fall of humanity? After all, it is Eve who listened to that wily serpent. Adam then listened to Eve, woman. Doing so resulted in the expulsion of all humankind from the original home of bliss in Eden. Through this story that tells of the beginning of creation, the believers of this one God announce to all that male supremacy is not a new idea. In fact, it was divinely decreed by the male deity at the dawn of human existence. Going against it would be tantamount to disobeying the Creator Himself.

Prior to the writing of the Genesis creation story, serpents were connected with divinity, the Goddess, and generally linked to wisdom and prophetic counsel. Several sculptures unearthed in Sumer, which date from about 4000 B.C.E., portray a female figure with the head of a snake. The Goddess Nidaba, who was worshipped as the first patron deity of writing, was at times depicted as a serpent. The Goddess as Ninlil, who brought the gift of agriculture, and thus civilization, to Her people, had a tail of a serpent. The serpentine Goddess as Nina was an esteemed oracular deity and interpreter of dreams. The association of the serpent with the female deity was found also throughout Babylon, the island of Crete, Sinai and Canaan. One shrine in Sinai had carved into its walls two prayers, both invoking the Goddess as Serpent Lady.

In ancient Egypt, the people worshipped the Cobra Goddess, known as Ua Zit. She is later seen as the *uraeus* cobra worn upon the foreheads of other deities and Egyptian royalty. This headband was constructed so that the snake would emerge from the forehead of the person who wore it as the Eye of Wisdom.

The use of the cobra in the religion of the Goddess in Egypt was so ancient that the picture of a cobra was the hieroglyphic symbol for the word Goddess. From about 3000 B.C.E. onward, the Cobra Goddess was said to have existed when nothing else had yet been created. She then created all that had come into being.

The cobra was known as the Eye, *uzait*, a symbol of mystic insight and wisdom. Later derivations of the Cobra Goddess, such as Hathor and Maat, were also known as "the Eye." This term is always written in feminine form.

There is account after account showing the connection between the Goddess, serpents, and vision or prophesy. I'm not sure what this means for me personally. It does bring up, though, the interesting connection to what transpired in Teo. During the first trip, RMaya felt a "snake-like energy" swirl through her and then received the message about it being time for "the seed to be planted." She then held the feminine energy as a chalice, which was then poured out at the Pyramid of the Sun, the representation of masculine energy, and "fertilized." The two energies joined. Shortly thereafter, I felt strongly that the "seed" would be in the feminine form.

Then during the second trip, there was the birth or rebirth of this feminine energy. As mentioned earlier, I think of this, not in the sense that our society will turn matriarchal, but in the sense of an equal respect of the feminine with the masculine, a beautiful balance and honoring of the two. This also connects with Quetzalcoatl, the part snake, part bird deity and how it is the unification of the divine feminine and the divine masculine, earth and sky. The energy from this rebirth in Teo then spread throughout the globe like a healing shockwave.

※　※　※

Feeling like there could still be missing pieces to the picture, I want to learn more about snakes, beyond their relationship with the Goddess and Quetzalcoatl, and I feel drawn to learn more from Jamie Sams. I wish to learn what they represent from a Native American spirituality perspective. I buy *Medicine Cards*, a book and set of divination cards that Jamie Sams co-authored with David Carson.

The book states that snake medicine is that of transmutation. "Snake medicine people are very rare," it begins. "Their initiation involves experiencing and living through multiple snake bites, which allows them to transmute all poisons, be they mental, physical, spiritual, or emotional....The transmutation of the life-death-rebirth cycle is exemplified by the shedding of Snake's skin. It is the energy of wholeness, cosmic consciousness....It is the knowledge that all things are equal in creation, and that those things which might be experienced as poison can be eaten, ingested, integrated, and transmuted if one has the proper state of mind....Complete understanding and acceptance of the male and female within each organism creates a melding of the two into one, thereby producing divine energy."

I feel a strong connection with and embodiment of snake medicine, but I am unsure how it is fully manifesting in my life. I'll be patient and see what comes.

%% %% %%

Dream

I'm walking into work at the Y. I realize it is in the past. The building is very different from how it is now. Many people do not see me or don't make any indication of seeing me. As I'm walking down the hall, I see my great grandma (my mother's grandmother) and pass by her. At this point, I become lucid in my dream. I turn around after passing her and call, "Granny?"

She turns around and comes to me. "Can I talk with you?" I ask her. I mentally tell myself over and over to stay lucid, stay lucid. We sit face to face. I ask her, "Is there something you want to tell me?" figuring I can take advantage of the dream to see if she has any messages from the "other side."

She pauses and then says, "Remember. Remember who you are." Okay, I feel like I've gotten this message before in my waking state. It may not be a completely new message, but it furthers the message. Stay lucid, stay lucid, I continue to tell myself.

I ask her, "Is there anything else?"

She proceeds to tell me more. "When you remember who you are, you will be moving and living from your heart." I thank her for the information.

Remembering denotes the use of the mind. Yet, through this remembering I will be living from my heart. The prospect fills me with happiness, for I have felt for so long a disconnection between my mind and heart. It seems like I experienced much of my life in my head, feelings cut off and lost in some Bermuda Triangle.

I recall being at Teo, sitting on top of the Pyramid of the Moon. My hope was to one day have my mind and heart in alignment. I feel now that I brought something with me to the Pyramid of the Sun from the Pyramid of the Moon, a connection. I never knew why I wanted so desperately to get to the Pyramid of the Moon. Now I understand. The Moon, the feminine, signifies feeling and intuition. The Sun signifies the masculine, mind and logic. It was another way of linking the two together, bringing both energies in alignment within myself (which also is in line with embodying snake medicine).

Before I go to sleep one night, I repeat to myself, "I am awake in my dreams tonight, and I remember who I am, my essence." Then, for the first time, I ask the spirit guides for help. "If you can help me to remember who I am and please help me overcome my fears surrounding remembering who I am, to help me just literally go with the flow, I'd be very much in gratitude." I then have the following dream:

I am in an unknown house. There are hundreds of huge bugs, of various kinds, crawling on the floor. I jump up on a bed to try to get away from them. They proceed to crawl up after me. In addition to the bugs, there are hundreds of little mice crawling around. The mice seem to have no fur; they are pink.

A very large rat, the size of a shoe (not including the tail) and a large fly-type insect, the same size, seem to be the ones in charge or in control of all the others. The two creatures jump on me. I grab them and throw them off. They keep returning time and time again. I am so scared, and I feel trapped.

I finally realize I have to kill these two main creatures in order for all of them to go away. I have a screwdriver, and I use the handle to pummel the creatures. I corner the fly-type creature and pummel. It keeps moving. I keep pummeling non-stop. I am spilling its guts. I see it has a skeleton of sorts and I know I must crush it. I take the handle of the screwdriver and roll it back and forth over the skeleton until all that remains is a mass of pulp. I have stuff all over my hands from doing this, and it is so disgusting!

I proceed to the rat creature and pummel that to a pulp as well. A moment later I see one open, black, beady eye in the rat mass. "This cannot be!" I say. The rat comes back alive. Then the fly creature comes back alive. "This can't be real!"

I then realize what I have to do. "All right, come and get me!" I say to them. I stand up with both hands raised in the air, the same level as my head. One creature attaches to my left hand, the other to my right hand. I close my eyes and start breathing and meditating. The meditating is difficult, for I feel the two creatures gnawing away at my fingers. I feel the pain. I feel my flesh being eaten off of my body. But I know it isn't real, so none of it matters.

I do not open my eyes. I decide to sit down in order to meditate more easily. I sit cross-legged and breathe. I then let out an "OM". I continue to meditate and OM. I OM louder and more strongly. Suddenly everything disappears, creatures and all, and I wake up.

I will delve more deeply into this dream momentarily, but first I must say how opening up, or seeing, is not *gaining* sight or information that was not previously there. It is merely *recognizing* that it's been there all along. Opening our sight is actually the act of re-seeing. Our minds simply trick us so that we think we no longer see things.

Children see. "What's that?" they ask their parents over and over, taking everything in anew. A young child will have a favorite tree and climb it with joy. He or she will look around and see the faces in the trees or the fairies on the flowers. He or she will gleefully chase butterflies. A child will find magic all around, in everything. Adults tend to lose sight of that.

The trick, I realize, is getting ourselves to see what we once saw, getting past all of the distractions. We must get past all of the things we think are so real. My dream showed that no matter how real the situation seemed, it still wasn't real (or at least it was only real in the sense of being a real dream). I saw the creatures all around. I could feel them crawling on me and even chewing on my hands. I felt intense fear, believing the situation was real. However, it wasn't. Once I meditated and got past all of those distractions and beliefs, I woke up.

Similarly, I know my life purpose is out there. I simply (okay, not always *simply*) must look past the distractions to see it. I just need to recognize it. The greatest distraction is fear.

My biggest fear right now is being "crazy," or at the very least, being perceived as "crazy." I carry sage around my apartment in order to "cleanse" it. I ring my Tibetan singing bowl in order to clear out any heavy energy I feel in myself. I have an altar, which has a Himalayan salt lamp, a wooden Buddha statue I got in Thailand, crystals and feathers. I commune with the trees, do yoga and meditate. I have learned to communicate with spirit guides and power animals. I receive messages in dreams and experience what may be called visions. Yes, it all sounds quite "crazy."

This fear is particularly strong, since I have a "history of mental illness." It can be difficult to shake off that label, even internally, once it has been slapped on. Indeed, there was a time in my life when I perhaps was seen as crazy, being hospitalized and all...or just seen as being in a great deal of pain.

However, people who see me on a day-to-day basis, such as at my work at the Y, would not think me crazy. In this setting I go about my day, responding to emails, answering calls, dealing with software issues, leading workshops and trainings, helping members with their concerns, coordinating special events, engaging in fundraising, etc. It is all a matter of perspective.

Chapter 25

*C*hanging gears just a bit, as I believe it is relevant to my story, I would like to briefly go into the scientific perspective of reality (hang in there, it is all going to come back around). Quantum physics tells us that at the foundation of all we know – matter, force, light – there is energy, quanta. Quanta are not your usual objects. Physicists call them wave-forms. However, I think by giving them this description, it makes us think in terms that they are something, when in fact they are nothing. They are *outside* of space and time. They are not material. In fact, until they are observed, until some conscious being in the form of a quantum physicist tries to study or measure them, they exist only as possibilities, potential.

The ins and outs of quantum mechanics seem to display quite a paradoxical state. However, this paradox is resolved by understanding that *consciousness*, not matter, is the fundamental reality of the universe. There is no split between observer and observed, subject and object, mind and matter. They are two sides to the same coin.

Consciousness *is* creation. Through the very activity of consciousness, the all-possible wave-form that is the quantum materializes; it "collapses" into a particle. From this, our world, our reality surrounding us, comes into being. Consciousness spawns the material universe. It is our common denominator. It is what unifies all of humanity, as well as unifies humanity with everything else – the animals, trees, rocks, stars – everything.

The universe, everything we observe, is a byproduct of an energy sea that exists before anything exists at all. This energy sea is the quantum vacuum, or the realm of unexpressed possibility. This is not just the discovery of quantum physicists. Hindu and Chinese cosmologies have always maintained that the things and beings that exist in the world are a distillation of the basic energy of the cosmos, descending from its original source.

In Indian philosophy, the original source, or "subtle-energy womb", the container, is referred to as Akasha. In several Native American traditions, it is referred to as the Great Mystery. Others refer to it as the Void. It is the pregnant state of being, the unexpressed potential. Whereas, the *expressed* potential is consciousness, the creation.

Altered states of consciousness allow for nonsensory information, or information outside of our usual senses of sight, hearing, taste, touch, and smell, to be received. This can be through meditation, intense prayer, controlled breathing, fasting, and other ways. This has been known for centuries by ancient civilizations. But much of our modern civilization tends to view altered states as pathological, except for dreaming, daydreaming, alcoholic intoxication and sexual orgasm.

Consciousness permeates the universe. Indeed, as mentioned, it is what brings the material universe into being. When we allow ourselves to open to what is beyond simply what our senses take in, we are able to tap into that greater, all-connected consciousness. In tapping into this all-connected consciousness, one can also experience the source of this consciousness. If the Void or unexpressed possibility is the womb, the consciousness/creation is the fetus. We as creation, being the fetus in the womb, in a pure state, without paying any mind to all the static coming in through our senses, would be able to experience the womb itself. It would be impossible *not* to experience the womb, for it is all around us, containing us.

Many people in deeply altered states of consciousness have strikingly similar experiences. They often experience a kind of consciousness that appears to resemble that of the universe itself. This most remarkable of experiences takes place in individuals who are committed to the quest of realizing the ultimate truth of existence. When these seekers of truth come close to attaining their goal, the descriptions of what they regard as the supreme principle of existence are so similar it is uncanny. They describe an unfathomable ocean of consciousness filled with infinite intelligence and creative energy. The ocean of consciousness is at once a cosmic emptiness, a void, and also a fullness. It contains all of existence in potential. It is the ultimate source, the womb, pregnant with all possibility.

The same kind of experience is recounted by many people who practice yoga and other forms of deep meditation. It has been described by people who lived centuries ago and people who live now, by those from cultures around the globe and by those who live next door in our own neighborhood. It is experienced once the gross layers of the mind are stripped away, getting to that core, connected consciousness that links us all.

How many times do we get the sense that someone is watching us and turn to find out there is, even though the person is across the room and has not made a sound? How many times do we just have that "gut feeling" about someone or some situation? How many times have we experienced a "knowing" that a lover, close friend, or child was in trouble, had been in an accident or was sick, before it was validated?

There are invisible, conventionally-unexplainable threads of connectedness. The minds/consciousness of individuals are linked. The threads span and weave through human consciousness and also connect humans with all other life and the environment. Most people, with effort, can become aware of images, intuitions, and feelings that testify that they are in touch with other people and their environment even when they are beyond the reach of physical senses. With effort, people can remember and use these threads of connectedness, much like information gets transmitted through the interconnected network of phone lines. Better yet, like how information is transmitted via the internet through the invisible radio waves in the air around us. (For a more in-depth study of the above information, a good resource is *Science and the Akashic Field* by Ervin Laszlo.)

To put it simply, there is more than meets the eye. We are taught our entire lives that only what we see and hear is "real." As children, we are told to not imagine things. We are told to stop dreaming and be sensible, think logically. As teenagers, we care so much about fitting in with the crowd that all perceived differences are squashed, either by ourselves or by those around us. As a result, in our modern world, we grow up to be commonsense adults for whom everything that does not fit in with the dominant, mainstream world around us is denied and repressed.

Don't believe everything you see and hear. We see only the things we already think we see. We hear only the things we already think we hear. Don't believe everything you think. Our thinking is merely the result of years of family, friends and community teaching us what to think and believe.

Interestingly enough, I just got back from a work conference that mentioned very much the same thing, illustrating how these concepts are being integrated more into the "mainstream". The conference as a whole was about more strongly engaging members of the Board of Directors in a not-for-profit organization. In one of the presentations, there was mention of mental mapping. Basically, a mental map is a deeply held belief that filters our incoming information so that only what we *already* believe is identified as a possible conclusion to a situation. Holding tightly our cup of an existing belief structure, we dive into the pool of all possible data. Our cup scoops up and receives only that which fits with our preexisting belief structure. Once we select our small amount of data, we crawl out of the pool, interpret our data and reach conclusions. We then act based on our conclusions. It is what we refer to when we tell ourselves to "think outside the box," to step outside that preexisting belief structure and soak in the pool for a while to come up with new possibilities.

Humanity as a whole appears to be opening to greater perspectives, greater possibilities. With the help of the recent "discoveries" of quantum physics, there seems to be a melding of spirituality and science. Quantum physics shows there is a universal substance (or non-substance) that ties everything together – quanta. However, this does not actually exist until observed, until consciousness brings it into being. Consciousness is the fundamental reality. This universal consciousness is displayed through all creation. The source of this consciousness, this creation, many call God, Allah, the Creator, Brahman, the Tao, the Supreme Being, the Infinite, the One and so on.

Consciousness, or creation, expressed through humanity seems to be displaying itself at an ever-quickening pace. After thousands of years of human existence, it has been only in the last 100, or even less, 50 years that the creation of ever-more-complex technology has developed at a phenomenal rate.

Are computers and technology connected with our state of consciousness? Is this science, this logic, tied in with us evolving as conscious beings? Observing the things created is often the way we witness human evolution. As we look through the creations of humanity – from the earliest simple tools, to houses and clothing, to the much later harnessing of electricity, to the current computer and digital technology – we see evolution of consciousness. The last century has shown the most growth in technological creation than any time period before, advancing exponentially, as if we are speeding towards and nearing a new state of being.

There are many who speak of an upcoming shift in consciousness, leading to a new understanding of time and space and the nature of existence. The complex and far-reaching calendar of the Mayan and Toltec civilizations show around the year 2012 as ending a more than 5,000 year "Great Cycle," which concludes one age and begins a new. The Hopi, according to their oral prophesies, say we are transitioning from the Fourth World to the Fifth World. Christian belief systems tell of an impending Armageddon, followed by a new world, "God's Kingdom on earth."

The Incans believe there is a cosmic cycle every 1,000 years. Jorge Luis Delgado, whom I had the pleasure to meet and learn from during a recent power journey in Peru (an adventure saved for another time), shares how each cycle is like the cycle of day and night. There are 500 years of nighttime and 500 years of daytime. We are now living in a "New Sunrise", the beginning of a new day. "The sunrise is very special," he says, "because we believe that the 'first light' is the food for the heart. Like all the sunrises everywhere in the world, it brings life-force energy. It is the moment when we awaken. It is the moment when we remember the essence of who we are, the essence of creation."

The current state of the environment and technological advancement, along with several ancient prophesies from a variety of belief systems, all seem to be pointing to an upcoming, inevitable shift.

I believe this shift is already occurring. In this shift I see humanity continuing to recognize, on deeper and deeper levels, the unified nature of science and spirituality, of logic and intuition, and understanding that the essence of all is one. I see a greater recognition of being a global community, and ultimately an acknowledgment and understanding of being part of a larger, universal community.

We have proven ourselves to possess remarkable capacity for intellectualism and logic through technological advancement and other means. There are many "great minds" accomplishing many great things. Couple this with humanity's demonstrated amazing capacity for intuition, non-verbal communication, and connectedness, and what amazing beings we recognize ourselves to be!

The time is past for there to be a perceived division between intuition and logic, between what has been traditionally viewed as feminine and masculine, between what may be referred to as "earth" and "sky" (or "heaven") if we remove the association of gender from it. If you think because you are a man you hold masculine energy, or because you are a woman you hold feminine energy, you are partially correct. Everyone holds both. We are not raised to believe that, however. We are raised having specific rules for boys and a separate set of specific rules for girls. Even in language, males tend to use the term "I think," whereas females tend to use the term "I feel." But this use of language is taught to us as children by the adults around us. We all think and feel. There is no division of sex for thinking and feeling.

But alas this is changing. Consciousness is shifting, evolving. Honoring all aspects *within* ourselves will allow us to honor it *outside* of ourselves. This is more than honoring the masculine and feminine, or logic and intuition, equally. It is an honoring that *all* things are equal and necessary for growth and the evolution of consciousness.

During one meditation experience, the yin yang symbol comes into my consciousness. I see it at first from a frontal view, then I see it lying flat and from a side view. When lying flat, nothingness is beneath it. The symbol is like a wheel at the base of this existence. Shooting upward and outward from the symbol is all the perceived opposites and separateness.

The traditional Chinese yin yang symbol, pictured above, sums up life's seeming polarities – positive/negative, day/night, active/passive, male/female, heaven/earth. Though there is pressure, the light and dark halves of the symbol are not in direct opposition with one another. Instead, they complement and balance each other. There is curvature, even a play, if you will. The two sides seem to forever turn and circle, exchanging places back and forth. In the end, both find themselves encompassed within a whole. Indicative of life, the movement is not toward some fixed point. Rather, it bends back upon itself, time and time again, flowing to the ultimate realization that all is one.

Likewise, we come back around to where this part of my story started. This started with gaining understanding of what is truly real and not getting distracted, as illustrated in my creature dream. As mentioned earlier, most modern people seem to have forgotten the threads of connection we share with one another and our environment, but with effort we can remember and use the connection. In our modern lives, we simply have so much noise around us in our day-to-day functioning that it distracts us from hearing the information, or messages that travel via the cosmic threads. We have work stress, family stress, and financial stress. We have cell phones ringing, computers humming and iPods singing.

It is similar to how we can drown out hearing someone who is just in the next room talking to us while we are watching a football game or our favorite TV show. The person just becomes background noise. At first we may hear the person, hear what he or she is saying. Then, perhaps the game gets really exciting and we just hear noise from the person but not the actual words. Or maybe we don't hear the person at all. Selective hearing, we call it. We get pulled away, distracted. We are so busy watching the TV of this life that we tune out those universal messages. Dare I even say, we tune out hearing God speaking?!

If we were able to cut the ties of all the distractions that pull us off our spiritual path – or path of simply wanting to *know* – we would reach our destination. Imagine you are a fish swimming down a river. There are thousands of fishermen and fisherwomen standing on both shores. You are swimming innocently along the river when all of a sudden a shiny object catches your eye. You swim over to get a closer look. And, oh, there's a delectable, wriggling worm. That looks good. You decide to take the bite. Yank! You get pulled towards shore. You fight and struggle and luckily are able to get free.

You swim down the river some more. "I'm not going to do that again," you tell yourself. But again, something catches your eye. You swim closer. This one looks different. It's like a bright orange marshmallow, and it smells good. But last time was a bad experience, you recall, so you decide to tread cautiously. You take just a little nibble. Nothing happens. You decide it's safe, so you take a big bite. Yank! Now you're getting pulled violently to the other shore. You struggle and struggle and are again able to get away.

So it goes. The fishermen and fisherwomen repeatedly catch us and reel us in. We wriggle and get away and then swim onward. Just as we do, another hook snags us and pulls us close to shore, then another, and another. We may fight off some fisherman for a few minutes, or some for a few years. The difficult part is not getting caught.

However, the more we evade those hooks, the easier it becomes. If we don't get distracted, hooked, and pulled away, we will eventually reach the ocean that we are seeking.

Again, the greatest distraction is fear. Fear will keep us tied up for years, or our entire life. When we fear we cannot do something, we are prevented from even attempting it. Many religions use the highly effective technique of fear. If you do such and such, you will not get into heaven, you will go to hell, you will open yourself to demon possession, or God will disapprove of you in some way. Society uses fear. If you do this and that, you will cause disgrace to your family and to your culture. If you dress, act or talk differently from the majority you will be seen as rebellious or crazy. Fear limits us most, however, through our own internal dialog. We can "what if" ourselves to stagnation, or "I can't do that, what would they think of me?"

My fear of being "crazy" is simply a fear of being different. Many fears, if not all, have their root in difference. This may be something we perceive as different from us, or the fear rests in the unknown, which is merely different from what we know. Different is a matter of perspective, however, just as "crazy" is a matter of perspective. What is real is that essence of sameness, oneness. There is no duality. Experiencing and recognizing this perspective – that is, seeing the yin yang symbol as the whole that it is – will enable us to take that next step to move past letting fear control our lives, and humanity's next leap as conscious beings.

For many centuries there has been a focus on the masculine energy, seeming to originate with the Biblical creation story, which outlines God as male and supreme, as well as the human male being divinely decreed to be over the female. Prior to this story, evidence shows how much of humanity worshipped the Goddess, frequently associated with the serpent. The female God makes sense in ancient times, since the female would likely have been perceived as the creator. It is she who births new life. The serpent, "the eye", was representative of "mystic insight and wisdom." Indeed, the feminine tapped into that which does not strickly rely on physical senses, namely, feeling, intuition, that deep-rooted *knowing*.

The Goddess association with the serpent also harks back to the connection with the earth. The snake's entire body is connected to the earth as it slithers along. The Goddess belief systems also had a strong connection with the earth, often related to the earth's changing seasons and with nature. The singular, male God belief system shifted the focus from earth-centered to sky-centered. The serpent now was the sworn enemy of this male God. Also, the male God was removed from humans, residing somewhere on a throne, far away in heaven.

New growth and life comes from the fertilization, the joining together of these two energies, masculine and feminine, not fearing their seeming differences. Again, snake medicine tells us that it is in the complete understanding and acceptance of the male and female within us that creates a melding of the two into one, which then brings into being divine energy, that of life, creation.

In the Mayan and Toltec civilizations, the completion of the Great Cycle is associated with the return of the deity Quetzalcoatl, the fusion of snake and bird, earth and sky, matter and spirit. Indeed, the combining of the two energies, or more accurately, the recognition and acceptance of the overriding oneness of the energy, leads to new life, creation. Creation, then, leads us back to the Creator.

Chapter 26

*I*t is my birthday. Nicole and I recently broke up again. I am thinking about my life – past, present and future. I'm thinking about unconditional love, but more so, unconditional acceptance. I think how I did not receive this in my past. I think how I also did not provide this in my romantic relationships. I loved the women with whom I have been in relationship, but I did not accept them unconditionally. In the same vein, I feel like I love myself unconditionally, but I have not felt like I accept myself unconditionally.

Today, I give myself unconditional acceptance. I look in the bathroom mirror at my reflection. It is odd how we never truly see our own face. Our entire lives we have seen only a reflection of who we are. The one who *looks* in the mirror is the One Consciousness. The one *in* the mirror is us, all of us. The image I see is a reflection in a single facet of an infinitely-faceted crystal mirror. "You are so beautiful," I tell the reflection in the mirror, that is now crying tears of lightness and joy. I feel an intense amount of love and acceptance as I hold my hand over my heart. Giving this to myself, this can now flow outward, be given to others.

I feel now, for the first time in my life and from my deepest core, that I don't need to be with someone to be happy. I had thought this numerous times before, but now I *feel* it. I make myself happy. I find contentment and enjoyment with myself. I love myself. I finally feel the shift from *needing* to be with someone to simply *desiring* to share with someone. What a free feeling! I know I am whole, I am one. I also know that if and when I am in a relationship again, I will be in it with a person who unconditionally loves *and* accepts me, just as I now do for myself. I deserve that. We all deserve that.

One evening I lie on the couch and meditate. Heather Ash is here in spirit, and she is helping me go down the "rabbit hole." I am reminded again that enlightenment is not all of a sudden like a flash of light. It is a gradual step-by-step process. Going down the rabbit hole is not like dropping a stuffed bunny down a dark well, falling to the bottom in a blink of an eye. No, descending the rabbit hole, for me anyway, is being on an elevator, stopping at each floor. Once I have acclimated to one floor, I am ready to descend to the next one. It is much like a scuba diver descends the sea ever so slowly so as not to get "the bends."

I see the veils pass me by. I see how thought creates our reality. I see how even when quantum physics, or science, comes to a complete understanding of the nature of this reality, it may take humanity as a whole a little while longer to actually comprehend and accept it.

So down the rabbit hole I go with Heather Ash's help. I see the Void that people speak of, the bottom of the rabbit hole. I don't feel I'm actually in it, but I see it. I feel my body breathing and I comprehend how a body breathes without being connected to its consciousness (such is the case with people in comas, people who have had "out-of-body" experiences, even during sleep).

I experience the nature of time in its circular infinity. Time runs in a non-linear way and overlaps. One line runs forward, the other backward. To illustrate, it looks like a flattened "x". The upper left quadrant runs *toward* the center point. The lower right runs *away* from the center point. The upper right runs toward the central point, and the lower left runs away from the center point, just like the "x". The momentum jumps off the track, so to speak, and it flies through the space in between in a semicircle. This works much like gravity works with a motorcycle rider. The momentum carries the motorcycle, in this case, then there is the jumping off point, an exhilarating moment! Then it practically floats in that space between and makes a semicircle, falling to the other side, where momentum resumes and continues it along the infinite loop.

For the visual, add at each side-end of the "x" a dotted semicircular connecting line, creating the infinite loop. It is in the *space between* where the trust in the jumping off occurs. Infinity and timelessness occur simultaneously when one is utterly and completely in the moment.

Fear comes in upon experiencing all of this, and I now feel like I (or my body) could die. I have not lost that fear of death. I think my heart will stop beating and my body will stop breathing after I reach a very deep meditative state. I tell myself that I will be in the deep meditative state and be okay. We surrender our bodies each night as our head hits the pillow. We do not have fear that our last conscious breath will be the last. We have faith that our physical body will continue on without our conscious effort. We surrender willfully! We then go on our merry way, traipsing through the jungles of Africa, flying through the sky, lying on a beach in Hawaii, playing with the dog in the backyard, dream after dream.

I sink back into a more relaxed, less fearful state. I breathe – the inhale creating the momentum of one line of the "x", and the exhale creating the momentum of the other line of the "x." I feel my heartbeat slow. Through my continued yoga practice I am able to control my breathing. I pause at the end of each inhale and at the end of each exhale. My breathing feels like it almost stops. The sound of traffic outside my window stops. The sound of the refrigerator stops. Everything stops.

I am then back at the jumping off point. I am in a state of testing. I am suddenly transported to the Pyramid of Quetzalcoatl, where I am to take that leap of faith, letting go of the fear of the body dying. *Let go of your fear, let go of your fear.* But I am unable to do so. Again the fear comes in. It will have to wait.

The following day, I lay out the Medicine Cards, and I pull Swan. "Surrender to the grace of the rhythm of the universe, and slip from our physical bodies into the Dreamtime....trust in Great Spirit's protection....If you are resisting your self-transformation, relax; it will be easier if you go *with* the flow." Swan says to Dragonfly, "I will be happy to abide by Great Spirit's plan. I won't fight the currents of the black hole. I will surrender to the flow of the spiral and trust what I am shown." After she surrenders, the little "ugly duckling" emerges a beautiful and graceful swan. Eventually I will understand this message – *surrender and trust!* For then, and only then, will I emerge the beautiful swan.

During another time of meditation, I ponder the question, who controls when it's time to wake up? At bedtime our bodies go into a completely different mode, our consciousness an entirely different state. Our bodies simply rest while our minds/souls travel out of body and into dreamland, having countless adventures.

At some point during the night or in the morning, we wake up. Even when there is no outside assistance – like alarm clocks or cats meowing or children crying – we wake up. Who decides when it's time for the dream-world adventure to end and this-reality adventure to resume?

What about waking up in our dreams? What is the purpose of lucid dreaming? Many people experience lucid dreaming on occasion. It is something that can be learned and practiced and become more frequent if one so chooses. But what are we actually doing when we are lucid dreaming? Are we time traveling? Are we entering another dimension? In a way, one could say that, but no.

When we are waking up and becoming aware, lucid in our dreams, we are giving ourselves a clue, revealing a key. The key is to be used to unlock this so-called "waking state" reality and *truly* wake up.

We wake up when we give ourselves a reason to wake up. Like the Buddha, Neo in *The Matrix* wakes up. His reality, though, seems at first not so pleasant, waking up in a tub of pink goo. But it is truth. It is his unquenchable thirst for knowing, his desire for truth, that allows him to experience it. That is his reason. His whole life he felt something was amiss, that there had to be more to his existence. He could feel it, like a "splinter in [his] mind."

Neo wakes up and gets unplugged. The much more difficult process then begins of disconnecting him mentally. "Tank, load the Jump program," Morpheus instructs. The Jump program's purpose is to disconnect the mind from the body, a tool to assist in the mental unplugging. Why does everyone fall the first time? Because it is so hard to flip that switch! After years of believing we are our bodies, our minds become very attached. It is a very strong structure. It is a process to dismantle the structure and fully detach.

"You have to let it all go, Neo – fear, doubt and disbelief. Free your mind," Morpheus says to Neo on the rooftop. Morpheus then leaps with ease to the other rooftop 50 feet away, the movie's version of the Pyramid of Quetzalcoatl. Neo of course falls, and they unplug him from the program.

He has blood in his mouth from the fall. "I thought you said it wasn't real?" he says, feeling the pain in his body.

"Your mind makes it real," Morpheus replies

"If you're killed in the matrix, you die here?" Neo continues with his inquiry, still connecting "you" as body.

The answer is, "The body cannot live without the mind." More accurately stated, the body cannot live without the power source, and we tend to believe the mind is that source.

The refrigerator or the dryer cannot run when it is unplugged from the source of power. Computers are these great and wondrous things, connecting people, countries and realms of imagination. But when it gets disconnected from its power source, it's nothing but a box of parts.

Only Neo, at a later time, walks through a few more doors and is able to wake up to a greater degree and more fully disconnect. His first stage of waking up (the tub of pink goo) is simply his naked rebirth. Everyone else in the movie limits himself or herself by keeping a perception of the mind-body connection, the mind-body illusion. Their statement of "the body cannot live without the mind" illustrates this misperception, because they do not explore it further. Their fear limits them. In actuality, every character in the movie has the potential to be "the One."

At the end of *The Matrix*, the first movie, Neo gets shot and dies while in the matrix. His physical body exhales and expires in the "real world" aboard the hovercraft. He comes back, inhaling once again, exemplifying life anew. What brings him back? What wakes him up once again? His reason this time is that of love. Now he sees even more of the truth of the illusion around him. He sees the matrix scene at its base level – computer code. Through this experience he realizes that he, as a conscious being, is not the same as his body.

We wake up when we give ourselves a reason to do so – whether it is the unquenchable desire to know the truth, whether it is love, or whether it is to find our purpose in life. So who controls when I wake up? I do. *Nosce te ipsum*, know thyself.

I sit on the couch in the most comfortable position I can find. I sit upright, hands relaxed on lap, palms up. I just relax and breathe. My breathing deepens. After a while, it shifts so that my body seems to be breathing on its own.

I trust and let go of fear. A guide approaches me, and together we enter a place of darkness, nothingness. At this point, I become aware I am not in my body and some fear comes up around it. The guide and

I travel back close to my body and see it there, sitting on the couch. It looks very relaxed, appearing as if it is asleep. It's breathing on its own. "See, your body is right there. It's just fine," the guide says to me in a gentle tone. I am okay then to continue my travels. My energetic form travels back to the dark, womb-like space. Within the inner walls of this space, there are flashes of my mind's projections, an uncountable number of them. These flashes are from all my lifetimes in tiny, TV-like form. This physical lifetime is just one of those flashes, my separate self's projection of my separate life. One quick flash – one entire lifetime. I experience seeing my life from a much broader perspective.

Our bodies are equipped like appliances. They come complete with all the necessary parts, wiring and program capabilities. All we need is the power source. It's like our bodies get plugged into the power source as each new lifetime emerges. Oops! Then we get unplugged again – death. Time for a new appliance, perhaps something different.

Once again, it is about perspective. For most of us, our perception throughout much of our lives is that this surrounding us is real, it is truth. Imagine I am a little, white rat. I run around hour after hour. There are walls on all sides of me. Eventually I come up to a contraption. I sniff around, twitch my whiskers, wiggle my tail, and eventually figure out if I hit one of the levers just right, food appears. I gobble it up. This is my life. I do not see my life from the perspective of the human experimenter who is simply putting me in a maze to see how long it takes me to figure out how to dispense the pellet of food.

This example is merely to give an idea of perspective. Both the lab rat's and the experimenter's perspectives are equally "real." I experience the enlightenment or awakening process as a series of changes in perspective. It is experiencing the power source as also real and true. The appliance, the body, is a disposable machine, a disposable toy. It eventually wears out. Enlightenment is following the power cord that runs from the body and seeing how it is plugged into the source.

The difference, though, between the experimenter/lab rat example and the power source/appliance example is that the latter experience reveals our consciousness as *both* within the human and as the power source itself. Our consciousness from the human perspective is referred to as the Little-Self perspective. Consciousness from the power source perspective is the Big-Self perspective. I am borrowing the "Little Self" and "Big Self" terms from Heather Ash and Raven. These words seem to be a good description of the experience.

After the lifting of this particular veil, one may look at this reality and feel life is futile. Truth has been experienced on a much grander scale. This small life may seem insignificant. Who wants to be a rat in a maze upon seeing life from the human experimenter perspective? However, this life is not futile by any means. We live this particular version, this movie flash, this dream, this illusion, just once. Fully experiencing each and every moment is the most joyful way of being when having this Little-Self perspective. Enjoy the dream just as much as the waking state! As Jamie Sams says, it's all about "dancing the dream." Also, once we've seen life without this veil, once we have experienced existence from the Big-Self perspective, we remember where we came from, we remember our essence. We can then choose to experience life from both perspectives.

Chapter 27

There was a time when humanity recognized itself as part of nature, and nature as part of itself. Dreaming and waking were inseparable realities; the natural and the supernatural merged and blended....In the past shamans, priests, and priestesses were the keepers of the sacred knowledge of life.... They helped people remember that all trees are divine and that all animals speak to those who listen.

-- Ted Andrews

Dream

I am in Thailand. There is a couple approximately in their 60's chasing me to do harm.

There is a little black creature, the size of a dime that they throw at me. It lands on my arm. I grab a piece of plastic or the like to scrape it off. My vision is blurry and off. I scrape where it looks like the creature is, but I keep missing it. I figure it is because I don't have my glasses on. I keep trying and eventually scrape it off.

Later the couple has a few more of these creatures and they are on me. They just look like black particles grouped together. I scrape them, but the particles separate so that I am not able to get all of them off. The Thai woman comes at me with a whole container of these creatures to throw on me.

I take off running. Her husband has a bucket full of some other dreadful creatures that he wants to throw on me. I just keep running and try to find a place to hide. At one point I stop running and say, "I want the dream to end now! End the dream!"

I know I am dreaming, but the dream does not end. I figure if I just sit down and meditate I can get the dream to end or shift, but here comes the older couple with their bag of tricks.

I take off running again, not wanting the creatures on me. I come to a stone, circular building, like a castle tower. I run downward, spiraling, and come to a room where there is a blacksmith who makes swords. There are a lot of swords. I figure this could be helpful in my fight against the couple. Then the dream ends.

After awakening from the dream, I feel it is conveying to me my level of awareness in this present dream world. I *know* it is, in a sense, a dream, but I do not yet fully *believe* it. I still look around and let fear and the belief in the scene around me limit me. Since I do not fully believe I am dreaming, I do not yet know how to shape this existence to how I want it. I am in a place of transition.

※　　※　　※

Jill and I stay in contact after Teo, and she invites me to go to a mask-making workshop being conducted by her shaman teacher. I am excited to go. I go to the all-day workshop, inspired by the teachings of the Sisterhood of the Shields, Lynn Andrews' teachers. The creation of the mask is an "act of power" and is designed to help you "discover your sacred self."

After doing a shamanic journey to find our mask of power, we create it in the physical realm. We partner up and, using plaster of Paris, build the mask on our partner's face. After it dries, we peel off our mask and then have the opportunity to paint and decorate it.

I have some difficulty figuring out how I want to decorate it. I look around and see the others in the workshop painting and gluing, being quite creative. I do not associate myself with being an artistic person, not that it is required here, and I have a hard time feeling into what to do. I paint my mask and have a general idea how to decorate it, but I do not finish by the time the workshop ends. Some of the people finish, some do not. I think I am the least finished, but I intend to finish it later at home. It is an enjoyable experience.

Three days later I have a dream. *I am in a room and I have some sort of object. I believe it is my mask of power. I put it on my face, and when I do, something amazing happens. It must be that I come into my power. My body just acts. My feet are placed out wide. My arms are outstretched. The feeling in my body is incredible but indescribable.*

Soon after the mask-making workshop, I start a shamanic apprenticeship with Jill. I feel like I connect deeply with shamanic work. For me, shamanic work is closely tied in with nature, so I also commit to spending as much time as possible with the earth, rekindling that connection I felt as a child. I have a huge amount of love for the outdoors and nature, and I feel like it feeds my soul. It is one of our greatest teachers.

I am reminded of a few lines from singer/songwriter/poet/musician/all-around swell gal, Ani DiFranco:

I walk in stride with people much taller than me
Partly it's the boots, but mostly it's my chi
And I'm becoming transfixed with nature and my part in it,
Which I believe just signifies I'm finally wakin' up.

One morning I go on a hike on a beautiful local trail. Just a few minutes into the hike, I see a large, winged shadow pass before me. I look up but do not see the bird. I do see, though, a beehive. I have my camera with me, and I take several photos of the hive. I then hear a familiar screech. Looking up, I see the magnificent red-tailed hawk, the messenger, gliding on the air currents.

As I continue on, I come across several lizards scampering across the path. One pauses on a log to look at me with its shifty eyes. I hear a woodpecker pounding out a drumbeat on a tree. Then, as I'm rifling through my backpack for some water, a stiff breeze from the north picks up. "What is it?" I internally ask the wind.

"Pay attention," she whispers back to me.

I then hear a "whoosh, whoosh, whoosh" sound. I turn to see two crows flying a few feet behind me. "That's the sound their wings are making!?" I ask myself out loud, incredulously. The sound seems so loud and clear, yet something I have not noticed before.

Further along the trail, I pause to sit on a rock in a dry creek bed. I sit cross-legged, close my eyes and meditate. I open my eyes to see a beautiful butterfly has lit on the rock in front of me.

Nearing the end of the trail, a rock formation catches my attention. I look up at it and see a "face" in the rock. It looks like a mountain lion face. Everything is full of life. *I found my religion*, I tell myself. It is here in nature that I speak to God, or the Divine, or the Source, whichever name it is today. It is here that God speaks to me. I am in awe at all the sights and sounds and messages that Nature displays. Magic happens all the time and is everywhere. All we have to do is pay attention.

On another occasion, at a nearby park, I crawl up into my current favorite tree with notebook in hand, and simply listen. Trees are so amazing, as they hold much of the earth's wisdom. They are like the earth's hands, reaching upward, spreading out, and sharing with us their many offerings.

So in the tree I quietly sit and am held. I feel the delicious familiarity of once again being myself, being "one" with nature. I have questions. I feel surrounded by a loving, white light energy, similar to an angelic presence. I open my notebook and grab my pencil. I take a deep breath and write, "What message do I have to give?" I sit quietly and openly, waiting for the response. I leave my hand relaxed. As the answer comes, I write it down.

"We will speak through you."

I write another question, "What do I then do with that information?" Answer: "Share it."

"For what purpose? In what manner?" I continue.

Again I hear the answer, which I then dictate: "To remember the connection with the Divine, the One, to raise consciousness. People only allow themselves to hear what they are *ready* to hear. Many are now ready to hear. Teach, write, share yourself."

"But why me?" I ask, feeling utterly overwhelmed with such responsibility.

"Because you chose to." I then receive a lot of information about my life. It runs through my mind like viewing archived newspapers on microfiche, quickly spinning the dial, stopping the viewing periodically and abruptly at pertinent slides. I see my life with a new pair of eyes.

Through many experiences in nature and through my shamanic work with Jill, I remember how nature and the animals are so much a part of who I am, a part I must no longer ignore. In working with my power animals, I understand that there is no more hiding myself. I spent most of my life doing that. It is time to be open and share myself with the world. I then commit to create a major change in my work, one that is in complete alignment with who I am. One aspect of that is to spend quality time in nature, learning from Her, and share the magic of nature with others.

Another aspect of that is yoga. After the first trip to Teo, I kept my intention of doing yoga regularly. I bought Shiva Rea yoga DVDs and did yoga in my living room. The more I practiced it, the more I understood it to be one of the most magnificent doorways through which to descend the rabbit hole and discover the truth of ourselves, our essence. Yoga literally means "unite." It is the unification of body and spirit.

Yoga is meditation, involving the use of the body in various postures and the use of the breath to experience the connection to our essence. Like experiencing nature, experiencing yoga heightens awareness. With my Shiva Rea DVD playing in my living room, I feel my feet, with toes spread out flat on the floor, soaking in Earth's marvelous energy. Inhale, as I raise my arms, feeling them float up weightlessly, hands meeting each other, creating a full circle, creating a mandala. Exhale, bringing my hands, palms together, down to my heart, then down to my core, bringing heaven down to meet earth, feeling both held in my body. Inhale, arms float up once again…I repeat these actions for several minutes.

During this particular time of movement meditation, I see how our energy body flows into this physical body at the start of our life. A light infuses into flesh, an incarnation. For a while there is not awareness in the sense we are aware now, of being in physical form. But then, after birth and in the first few years of our lives, we marvel at the wonder of being in fleshly form. Our lives are filled with the new experiences of feeling water, of eating dirt, of putting our hands in the bowl of Malt-O-Meal and spreading it all over our face, of hearing new sounds, music, smells, tastes. All of our sensory experiences are filled with acute awareness. This is our Little-Self perspective experienced in all its joy.

Somewhere along the way, we get desensitized to it all. Oh, it's old news. We know what water feels like on our skin. We don't bother to bring our awareness to it. We stand in the shower each morning thinking about the workday ahead or the errands we need to run. We no longer tune in and marvel at the simple experiences.

Likewise, we tend to take for granted the simple, miraculous experience of breathing, paying no mind how our respiration is the re-spiriting of ourselves. With each breath we have the capability to re-experience our true self. We can take our human form for granted, or not. We can just use it for the machine-like qualities it has. Or, we can use it to remember where we came from, remember our essence. That is what yoga allows. Yoga is a beautiful prayer spoken, not through words, but through our bodies.

Yoga practice also helps align our chakras, which are our personal channel to unplug from this reality matrix and remember our connection with Source. It frees up the flow of divine energy through this chakra system.

Some say all the postures of yoga are intended to lead us to the seated position. It may start out as a cross-legged position, then perhaps half lotus or full lotus. It is in this position that we shift our focus from awareness of our body's movements to complete relaxation and enter the place of stillness, that place between or without thoughts. In this position we are relaxed and in complete alignment, our chakras are in alignment, and there is free flow from Source. Through this we are able to follow the channel, the cord, and experience the joy of life from the Big-Self perspective.

Again, I think to myself, *I found religion!* Yoga is my religion, just as nature is my religion. Nature and yoga are two paths that I walk to experience God. There are of course others. We all have the capacity to "create a religion," one that fits us, one that allows us to find God through our particular way of seeing the world. As we all look through a unique pane of the stained-glass window of this life, we all will see God just a bit differently.

We can think of it as this: the body is a prism, reflecting the pure, white light of the Divine. As the light flows through the prism, it explodes into a spectrum of colors through which we create the hologram of this world. This is similar to how the TV projects the images of live people and places. The TV is simply using light to combine and display colors. The result is creating an image so closely resembling that of the live people and places that we feel we could practically reach out and touch them.

However, our unified essence is that pure, white light. It is not the stained glass window, nor the prism. The window or the prism is the means, the vehicle. We all have the capacity to experience God/Big Self/White Light/Source. And, lucky us, we get to choose *how* to experience that God. Our essence is a constant, but there are an infinite number of ways to express that essence or light. If we all expressed it the same way, life would be a dull, monochrome existence.

%%%   %%%   %%%

Dream

The sun is rising, but in the west. I fly up above my childhood home, above the trees. The sun is creeping up, preparing to emerge over the hill. For a moment, I see my body from an outside perspective. It is just hovering in the sky, arms outstretched.

The sun finally peeks out over the hill. My body is then flooded with the rays of the sun of this new day. My chest expands as I inhale, and I open up fully to the feeling. It is as if I breathe in the sun, becoming filled with light. It is the most amazing feeling. It is better than orgasmic – just pure ecstasy.

※   ※   ※

Several weeks after I started my mask of power, I gather the materials to complete it. I go to an art store and buy some paints and a new brush. I have some materials left over from a beginning art class I took at the Junior College years ago, so I throw those in the mix. I had also brought a few feathers home from the workshop.

I get a paper bag and spread it out to keep from getting paint on the floor. I light some delicious-smelling incense, frankincense and myrrh, put on some "high-vibe" music and have a tasty juice drink nearby. I get situated on the floor and lay all of the colors and materials out before me. All of my 5 senses are getting attention.

I have a vague idea what I want to do regarding the painting of the mask, so I mix some paint. I then pause for a moment, just listening to the music and smelling the sweet scent. I close my eyes and a shape comes into my mind. It is not elaborate, but I know I want to start with it on my mask. I let go of all reservation. I do not allow myself to critique or worry if I'm doing it "right" or if it will turn out the way I intend. I completely surrender to this process of creating.

I pick up the paintbrush and begin, creating a simple shape, then just allowing whatever comes in next to be expressed through the colors and brush, to trust. I pause from time to time to look at the mask taking form. I see the mask continuing to shift and morph. I keep trusting. I do not allow myself to judge my work or even once think, "I'm not an artist; I cannot do this."

After a couple hours, I complete the mask. Various symbols have been painted on it. Feathers are glued on. Bits of pages torn from my journal with words and phrases written on them are also glued onto it. The mask represents various aspects of me and also illustrates the beautiful balance of earth and sky energy. Holding it up in its completion, I feel amazed and empowered. I LOVE it!

I realize it is not the mask itself that gives power. It is the *creation of it*, the letting go, the trusting in self, the beauty in ALL things. I finally understand, through this physical, tangible act, the opening to potential and my next step.

Morpheus says to Neo early in his training, "Stop trying to hit me and *hit* me!"

"I know what you're trying to do," Neo says.

"I'm trying to free your mind, Neo," Morpheus replies, "but I can only show you the door. You're the one that has to walk through it."

There comes a point where we can choose to stop *trying* to do something, and just do it.

Just as in lucid dreaming, where a person can know he or she is dreaming and control the dream, we can "wake up" and control this dream reality. We are the Creator. Quantum physics shows us there is no division between observer and observed, mind and matter. Consciousness creates and simultaneously *is* the creation. The reality around us can be creation where we simply follow along with no choice, like in our dreams where we fully believe we are in a given situation. Or, reality around us can be creation that is created with full awareness, with choice. I have heard this be referred to as *conscious* creation (as opposed to *unconscious* creation). However, so as not to get confused, since creation stems from consciousness (unconscious or otherwise), I will refer to it as creation with awareness.

Much of our lives we are caught in a cycle. The following is an illustration of what I call the "Choice" Response Wheel. Since it is a cycle, there is no start or end point, but we must begin somewhere, so let's start at point "A". A situation presents itself. For example, I would like to ask my boss for a week off of work, but it is very short notice. I will ask or not ask based on past similar experiences and also the expected reaction. If in the past, I have asked at short notice and been denied my time off, I will be less likely to ask now. If, on the other hand, I have always provided plenty of notice for time off, and this is an exception, perhaps my boss will be inclined to approve it.

Let's say the situation is the latter, and I ask my boss for the time off. This action is point "A". My boss decides that it is not enough notice and so declines my request. I am disappointed in my boss' decision. This disappointment is the reaction of my action or "choice". This reaction is point "B."

Now on the wheel, I come back around and am faced with another similar situation. This will be point "C". This point is one of planning. I again want to ask for time off. I will create the situation surrounding asking my boss based on past similar circumstances and my like or dislike of past reactions. I may believe I am living in choice at this moment. I may "choose" to give plenty of notice for my boss. However, I am not truly living in choice. I am basing my "choices" on past reactions, how the lack of notice for time off in my last request resulted in a response I didn't like. Once I make the actual "choice" to ask, I am again at point "A".

"Choice" Response Wheel

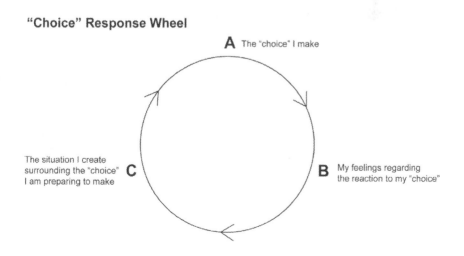

A The "choice" I make

C The situation I create surrounding the "choice" I am preparing to make

B My feelings regarding the reaction to my "choice"

We do this an innumerable amount of times in our lives. It is how we raise our children, and how they then behave. I engage in a certain activity, I get a spanking or some other punishment. I engage in that activity again, either knowing I will again get punished, or perhaps the outcome will be different. We base our choices and behaviors on rewards and punishments. We try to be consistent in our child-rearing habits so as to condition our children to the expected outcomes. During our adult lives, we continue that conditioning.

Rather than basing our "choices" on past consequences and expected outcomes, what if we jumped off the wheel and were able to view the bigger picture? Seeing the wheel from a greater perspective would allow us to see the scene like actors in a play. Watching a play, we may get engrossed in the drama, not knowing what is going to happen next. However, the play has already been written. The actors are merely voicing their well-rehearsed lines, acting out their well-rehearsed roles. The drama is not real; it is just a play.

Again we come to the topic of perspective. Creation with awareness is having true choice, not being controlled by past reactions or expected outcomes, living fully in the present moment. It takes effort to uncover the layers that control our current "choices." We still have our mother's or father's voice ringing in our ears. We have society telling us what is appropriate and what is not.

In some schools of psychology, based on Freud's work, the mind is separated into the conscious and the unconscious. When illustrating this, it is likened to an iceberg, with the relatively tiny, exposed tip being the conscious and all that is submerged under water as the unconscious. Freud believed much of mental illness had its source in the unconscious. Bringing the issues into the conscious realm would enable one to move past being controlled by them and ease the illness.

In using the iceberg analogy for the example of choice, I would say creation with awareness comes from the exposed conscious realm. Much of our perceived "choices" come from the much larger, submerged unconscious realm. We don't realize how much our thoughts and actions are influenced by others and are not done in true choice. There are tools, though, to drain the ocean, so to speak, and bring more or all of our creation into awareness, to make our choices true choices. Though it takes effort, it is within each and every individual's capability.

The place to begin is our words, both the spoken kind and the constant, internal chatter of our minds. All the times we tell ourselves, "I can't," or "that was stupid," we are creating a belief. We *believe* we actually cannot do it, whatever "it" is. We *believe* we did a stupid thing or even that we *are* stupid. This becomes our truth. This becomes our creation with limited options and limited choices.

On the flip side, when we tell ourselves, "I can," or "I am happy," or "I create my reality," we believe that. This becomes our experience of truth. When in this place of truth we have unbounded options and choices.

Our beliefs feed off of our words. There is a circular feeding, though. Our words also are a reflection of our existing conscious and unconscious beliefs. If you absolutely refuse to say, "I am beautiful," it is because you don't believe it. Perhaps you don't believe it because your mother one time said you were ugly and you clung onto her words like a lifeline. As mentioned, the ocean can be drained to expose the unconscious beliefs. Once this occurs, there is freedom. When in freedom, we can create our dream how we choose.

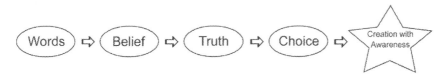

Words ⇨ Belief ⇨ Truth ⇨ Choice ⇨ Creation with Awareness

It may sound overly simplistic, like it couldn't possibly work. Again, if it sounds that way, perhaps it is because you don't yet believe it. There is a transition time between saying your own words of truth and fully believing them. You may say them at first without belief. That's okay. Have patience and say, "I am beautiful" anyway! We are actually saying our truth without even realizing it! Creation with awareness includes seeing the rules of the game and experiencing how we can use them to experience our potential.

Going outside of the realm of words, silencing the internal chatter completely, opens another door of possibility. We equate thoughtlessness as a negative thing. It is this thought-less-ness state that gets us past our illusion. Better yet, the thought-none-ness state.

Thoughts are represented through words. In meditation, one can learn to cease to let words/thoughts arise. What is beneath all of that chatter? What lies in the space between words? A path leading to our essence. This thoughtless state is not itself enlightenment, but a means, a door. To walk through the door is to then experience knowing, truth. This is not something that can be described or explained through words, as it is outside of them. It is in the experience of such a state that one comprehends it. I love words dearly, but they cannot fully convey the darkest depths nor the most brilliant moments of light.

In the speaking of our truth, we open ourselves to our human potential. In the absence of speech and thought, we open ourselves to experiencing a grander truth. Again, it is the case of the Little-Self and Big-Self perspectives and the ability to experience both.

Chapter 28

Spider wove the web that brought humans the first picture of the alphabet. The letters were part of the angles of her web.

Deer asked Spider what she was weaving and why all the lines looked like symbols. Spider replied, "Why Deer, it is time for Earth's children to learn to make records of their progress in their Earth Walk." Deer answered Spider, "But they already have pictures that show through symbols the stories of their experiences." "Yes," Spider said, "But Earth's children are growing more complex, and their future generations will need to know more. The ones to come won't remember how to read the petroglyphs".

So it was that Spider wove the first primordial alphabet.

-- from *Medicine Cards*

Many Native Americans believe Spider is Grandmother, the link to the past and to the future. She is considered the teacher of language and the magic of the written word. Writing is an excellent tool to see where we have been and where we are going. As we write, we weave our next phase of existence. Writing enables us to gain a broader perspective. Through our writings, we can view our personal evolution. On a grander scale, writing documents human evolution.

⁕ ⁕ ⁕

It is in the sharing of great truths that the consciousness of humanity will attain new heights.

-- Jamie Sams & David Carson

⁕ ⁕ ⁕

"Everything begins with choice," Morpheus says.

I was searching for my life purpose as if it were sitting out there in some cosmic bubble. I was waiting for it to float down and burst on my head, spilling its contents over me so that I may finally know what it is I am here to do. What I did not yet recognize is I *create* my purpose. I get to choose. My purpose…(drum roll)…is to help others no longer live under the constraint of fear and judgment and to open to the beauty of their truth, our truth. I do this through my writings, teachings and actions. My purpose is to be a tool, a guide. My purpose is also to love and to live each moment in awe, appreciation and joy, fully experiencing my humanity. I could choose another purpose. I could choose anything, just as you can choose anything. But currently this purpose is what I want for this lifetime. It is where my passion lies.

The end of the book is the most important part – whether it is a suspense novel or a memoir. It is where the whole story comes together, where the last pieces of the puzzle get laid in place so that now the full picture can come into view.

So this part of my story ends where I write this book, where I *share* my story. When I was in the darkest depths of my hell, I read autobiographies and stories of healing from dozens of people. Not only were they completely fascinating to my analytical self – having the opportunity to step into the very minds of others – but they helped me continue on, to have hope. Of course, the story must have a happy ending, for only then could I trust that mine would as well.

The second half of this book took a turn I did not expect when I first began writing. Yes, this story turned into one of finding meaning and awakening, but it still remains a story of healing. For without healing, it would not have been possible for me to find meaning. It was in the Women's Temple at Teotihuacán, where I fully surrendered, giving myself over to the open and loving arms of Mother Earth, that I released the last bit of abuse that remained – that which resided in my body. It was in this place that my body finally spoke and screamed out and stomped and mourned. *That* experience of final releasing freed up the space for me to then more fully experience my spiritual truth. It was the "one last painful push, the last necessary step" in order for me to begin life anew, to be born.

I have not forgotten my rough childhood. I have not forgotten those of you reading this who are currently in pain from being an abuse survivor or otherwise. I have not forgotten my own pain. Being a survivor of abuse is part of who I am in this physical realm, but I have many, *many* other parts. I recall the story of my birth that my grandmother used to tell. I remember my beginnings, as difficult as they were, and I also remember my strength, as I feel she wished to convey to me, as I wish to now convey to you. It is a story for all of us. We are strong. We survive. And we thrive. May this story provide healing through the comfort of shared experience. May it also be one more example of transcendence, providing you hope for the next step of your own journey. Hold onto that hope, for it is truth.

I have not forgotten my beginnings, but I choose to continue to move forward. The writing of this story is an act of creation. I shed my snake skin and emerge anew. I am simultaneously giving birth to myself and being born to live a whole new life.

Creation is bringing potential into being, bringing inspiration into action. Inspiration and action are nothing when they are apart. Inspiration feels like a great and wondrous thing, but if it is not manifested, it is as if it never existed. Likewise, action without inspiration has no purpose. It is only when they are together as one that they are truly something.

In the *Matrix* movies the Oracle is represented by a motherly, black woman. She is the feminine, the intuitive one, the yin. The Architect, on the other hand, is represented as a white man, with white beard, even a very light-colored suit. He is the masculine, logic and reasoning, the yang. In the end they both must work together for existence to live in harmony, for there to be peace.

Neo, at the end of the story, recognizes he is not his body after all. He surrenders willingly at the death of his physical body, knowing full well he will continue. "Will we ever see him again?" the little girl asks the Oracle in the last scene, as they view the beautiful sunrise.

"I suspect so – someday," the Oracle replies.

"Did you always know?" Seraph asks the Oracle, in reference to knowing the outcome of humanity and the prospect of peace.

"Oh, no. No, I didn't," the Oracle says, "but I believed…I believed."

Neo saves humankind. In this we are reminded of other "saviors" – Buddha, Jesus. They are an expression of a state of consciousness, that of an awakened state, knowing who they are, knowing the truth. Their message was that of love, and they embodied this message. Millions of people await the "second-coming of Christ" or "God's Kingdom on earth." Much of humankind is waiting for salvation from above, or simply waiting to experience the bliss of heaven after they die. However, the life and stories of Buddha and Jesus were those of transcendence. They were messages to help us along our way, to enlighten us to our own truth.

As the Hopi say, we are the ones we've been waiting for. It is only ourselves who prevent us from stepping into our power as Creator and bringing heaven to earth. We are consciousness. We are the Creator, the Source. We are God.

The world was not ready to fully accept the message when Jesus was alive 2,000 years ago. But the world is ready now. Consciousness is shifting to one referred to as "Christ Consciousness" or "Cosmic Consciousness." This is simply a state of greater awareness and perspective. This emerging consciousness involves recognizing the union of heaven and earth, the union of the divine masculine and the divine feminine, our Oneness. It involves recognizing ourselves to be connected and as part of a global and even universal community. It is exemplified even through the continually unfolding nature of science and quantum physics.

In this state of existence, as we all share this same planet, we often forget our human connectedness. Throughout my life, I have felt the greatest beauty lies in this connection. It has been in the deepest connections with others that I have experienced the greatest degree of learning, healing and transformation. This connection is a powerful thing, with the ability to transform lives, and ultimately transform human experience.

The biggest and most meaningful thing I learned and experienced while in Teo is how everything has a purpose. Let me repeat that, *everything* has a purpose. The more we pay attention, the more we are able to see it, providing us the opportunity to then live our purpose.

Do we not yearn to understand the nature of our existence? Do we not yearn to understand our purpose, to answer that seemingly-insatiable question, "Why are we here?" The answer is out there. Rather, the answer is in here. It has been inside all along.

When I was young, I was taught to believe in God, and so I did for many years. Many parents teach their children to believe in Santa Claus in much the same way. I only believed in someone else's story of God. Now I truly believe in God, because I know God, I *experience* God. Likewise, we can all experience our essence. It is then we remember. In this remembrance, our yearning is satiated.

Human consciousness evolves, and we are simply evolving. In everything there is constant movement and cycling. In everything there is flow – from life events circling back around, to wave-forms of quantum physics, to breath, to death and rebirth. Change and flow is the nature of existence. There is no stopping this evolution or changing it. It just is.

As individuals, we have the choice to open our hearts to this process. One of my favorite bumper stickers is the one that simply states, "Begin within." We can change our own life and ultimately change the world. Human potential is amazing. Look around and see what we have created and are capable of creating and accomplishing. We have the capacity to create a world that is peaceful, one where there is nourishment for all, one that spreads kindness and love rather than hatred. If we *believe* it to be so, it will be our truth, and we will create it.

Already, our world is filled with the product of inspiration. Someone wanted to have the restaurant down the street and brought it into being. Someone wanted to go to the moon and made it happen. What do we want to imagine and create next?

We don't have to be all the same to accomplish peace. We can believe in different Gods. We can have different languages, skin colors and occupations. We can wear different clothing and raise our children differently. We can be very, very different, honoring and respecting our differences, *and* we can have a common goal. We have the choice to step out of the spiral of fear and judgment and allow ourselves to rise above, gaining a grander perspective, and remember who we are.

My great grandmother came to me in my dream long after her body expired on this earth to share with me a message, "Remember who you are. When you remember who you are, you will be moving and living from your heart."

In that, I find my purpose – sharing my love of Earth and Spirit. "God is love," says 1 John 4:8. When we remember who we are, when we experience our essence, we experience pure love. It is through love that peace – inner and outer – becomes a reality.

The writing of this book is, like making my mask was, an "act of power." It is taking inspiration and putting it into action with complete letting go and trust. My story began, quite naturally, very self-focused and on a personal level but eventually expanded to encompass much more. The view opened up. This story is not just about me. It is about all of us, as we are connected, as we are One. I share my journey with you as a reflection, for we never are able to see the beauty of our own face.

We are on the cusp of a new state of awareness, a new era. Humankind stands on the platform facing the Pyramid of Quetzalcoatl. The situation before us looks to be one of great distance. But we have the choice to trust and make the leap. "Free your mind."

It is our potential as humans to create a world of great beauty – one where seeming differences are honored and respected. Where logic and intuition, science and spirituality, merge in a beautiful dance. Where Quetzalcoatl returns, the union of heaven and earth, spirit and matter, creating new life. A world where we are no longer controlled by fear – within ourselves, between individuals, or between nations. Rather, a world where we live from our hearts.

We are the "children of the sun," according to Incan beliefs and prophecy. We are here at the sunrise, where we breathe in our light, remembering and experiencing the ecstasy, the pure love, of our essence. The sunrise marks the beginning of a new day. It is the time when we first open our eyes, when we *wake up* to experience the truth that we have been asleep and dreaming. When we awaken to our truth, we realize we are free. In freedom, there is choice.

I don't know the future. I didn't come here to tell you how this is going to end. I came here…to tell you how it's going to begin.

Neo, from *The Matrix*